Dog Eldercare: Caring For Your Middle-Aged To Older Dog

Dog Care for the Older Canine

AMY MORFORD

DEDICATION

The joy and excitement of a puppy will eventually lead to the heartache and agony of an aging dog. This book is dedicated to dog lovers who have experienced the loss of a beloved friend and companion, just because time ran out.

TABLE OF CONTENT

PUBLISHER'S NOTES

Dog Eldercare: Caring For Your Middle-Aged To Older Dog
By Amy Morford

Amy Morford
DogTrainingPlace.Net

INTRODUCTION

When Is A Dog Considered "Old"?

The most common (but not the most accurate) way to determine your dog's approximate age is to multiply seven dog years by one human year; however, this method varies greatly with the size and breed of the dog. For example, a larger breed dog may be considered a senior at the younger age of six or seven years. On the other hand, a smaller breed dog may not be considered a senior until the age of 18, or even 20. Generally, middle-aged to senior-aged dogs are about seven years old.

The only way to find out the exact age of your beloved pet is to visit your veterinarian. Scheduling a consultation will also ensure your pet's future health as he or she grows older.

What to Look For and Expect As Your Dog Ages

You may begin to notice that your dog is starting to move around more slowly, that he or she seems to sleep for longer periods of time, and that your dog hesitates when using stairways or jumping into the car with you. There may also be noticeable differences or subtle changes in the ways your dog lays down, and gets up. You may notice decreased physical and/or playtime activities, and excessive sleepiness. Stiffness in the joints is common in older dogs and may indicate arthritis, which can cause even more discomfort during weather changes like colder temperatures, rain, or increased humidity. Lastly, hearing loss, cataracts (the cloudiness or bluish color of the dog's eyes), and the graying of hair on the muzzle, paws, and face may begin to show from anywhere between six to ten years of age.

Follow a Veterinarian-Recommended Strict Diet and Exercise Plan

Plan for your dog's future years by making regular scheduled appointments with the vet, and keep to a strict age-appropriate plan tailored specifically to your pet's special needs. Knowing when your dog enters his senior years helps you to make proper and timely changes to your dog's routine so that he or she will enjoy a healthy, long, and happy life.

Realize That the Aging Process is Stressful for Your Dog, Too

An aging dog can occasionally become confused because he or she does not completely understand what is going on. In fact, barking at inappropriate times and the loss of bladder control–especially during the night–can also indicate that the added stress and confusion may lead to dementia.

Dementia

Dementia can manifest in many ways, due to the variety of breeds of dogs. It's also common for a dog suffering from dementia to become lost in a familiar place. A dog's dementia can also be hard on the family, the ailing dog may alienate him or herself from the rest of family.

Muscle Atrophy

As your aging dog becomes less active, some minor loss of muscle mass in the hind legs can occur with old age. If there is noticeable loss in muscle mass within the area of the stomach and head, this may indicate diseases such as Cushing's disease. The most common form of Cushing's disease is caused by the overproduction of a hormone by the pituitary gland in the brain that in turn controls the amount of cortisol produced by the adrenal glands. Some of the more common signs of Cushing's disease include hair loss, a pot-bellied appearance, increased appetite, and increased drinking and urination, called polydipsia and polyuria (PU/PD). Hair loss caused by Cushing's disease occurs primarily on the body. Less common, more advanced indications of the condition are weakness, panting, and abnormal walking (stiffness when standing or walking with the paws knuckled over).

Another form of atrophy is masticatory myositis, an inflammatory disease that affects the jaws of a dog. The jaw swells up and it can be difficult for a dog to open its mouth. The condition is painful. The chronic form can cause scar formation that keeps the jaw from opening. Bring any noticed muscle loss to your vet's attention as soon as possible.

Arthritis

Arthritis is the inflammation of the joints, and dogs suffer the pain and discomfort of it in almost the same way as humans. Osteoarthritis is caused by aging and deteriorating bone material; known as canine arthritis, it can also be caused by certain infections such as bacterial or septic arthritis. The dog's body begins to attack its own tissues due to an immune deficiency (also referred to as rheumatoid arthritis).

Cancer

Did you know that cancer is a higher leading cause of death in dogs than in humans? Dogs that live in homes with smokers are unfortunately more susceptible to lung, bladder, and breast cancers; veterinarians treat cancers with, chemotherapy, radiation, and surgery. If you smoke, take it outside – just as you would for the people in your home.

Work With Your Veterinarian

Always remember to keep in close communication with your dog's vet so the correct supplements and regimen can continue to help him or her happily along into the golden years.

Supplements that benefit senior pet health and aging:

- ✓ Fatty acids
- ✓ Vitamins
- ✓ Antioxidants
- ✓ Proteins
- ✓ Minerals
- ✓ Calming Herbs
- ✓ Pheromones
- ✓ Whole foods
- ✓ Homeopathic pet medicines
- ✓ Omega 3 fatty acids
- ✓ And other medications to help strengthen the brain and liver

The love, loyalty, and companionship your dog has provided over the years make the extra care your dog needs that much more important, in order to make your dog's last years as enjoyable as the first.

CHAPTER 1: CALCULATING YOUR DOGS AGE

Dogs mature significantly faster than children. They all tend to age at the same rate until about age 5. A dog that is 2 years old is approximately 24 in human years.

After age 5, smaller breeds will age more slowly than medium and larger breeds. Large breed dogs age faster overall. To determine what size category your dog's breed falls in, simply find out their weight. If the dog is over 50 pounds, you have a large breed dog. If the dog is between 21-50 pounds, you have a medium-sized dog. If your dog is 20 pounds or less, you have a small breed.

For large breeds, subtract 5 from the number of years the dog has been alive, multiply the remainder by 6, and add it to 36. For medium breeds, subtract 5 from the number of years the dog has been alive, multiply the remainder by 5, and add it to 36. For small dogs, you subtract 5 from the number of years, multiply the remainder by 4, and add that to 36.

Large breeds can already be considered elderly after the age of 5. If the dog lives to be older than 15, the dog will age approximately 27 human years. Small breeds tend to live a little longer than larger dogs and aren't generally considered elderly until about age 10.

There are two other methods that can be used to calculate a dog's age when you aren't sure when the dog was born:

- Teeth
- Physical signs and behaviors

Teeth are a rough indicator of a dog's approximate age.

In puppies, or dogs that are 1 year old or younger, all permanent teeth will have come in by around 7 months. The teeth will be clean and white. They should have around 28 teeth, whereas adult dogs will have approximately 42 teeth. By age 2 the teeth will appear duller, and the back teeth will have some discoloration or yellowing. By the age of 3 or 4 a dog will have tartar build up and there will be signs of some tooth wear. At about age 5, nearly 80% of dogs will have signs of gum disease.

If the gums appear inflamed, if the tartar buildup is a yellow and brown in color, and the dog has bad breath, it is likely that the dog is anywhere between 5-10 years old. Also check to see if the dog has any missing teeth or teeth that appear to be fractured or extremely worn. This could indicate that the dog is in need of senior level veterinary care.

The last thing you can do to help calculate a dog's age is to look at physical signs and behaviors. When examining the snout, if you notice white hair around the nose and whiskers, the dog may be around 7 years old, or older, especially if there is graying in other areas. This graying can be present on the body, on other areas of the face, and on the head. A dog's skin and eyes are good indicators of age as well. If the coat is a bit greasy to the touch, and there is a lack of skin elasticity, there is a very good chance it is an older dog. An older dog may have eyes that appear cloudy or opaque. Behaviors like lethargy, lack of interest in play, avoiding going up a set of stairs, and stretching more often can also be a sign of an aging dog.

CHAPTER 1.2: LIFE EXPECTANCY BY BREED

Determining the life expectancy of dogs by their breed can be a challenge. Different veterinarians have different schools of thought. Some vets are not familiar with certain types of breeds. And it can be difficult for anyone to estimate the potential life expectancy of a mutt.

Life expectancy for dogs is determined by breed-based criteria. The heart and lung system of a larger dog needs to work harder and as such it deteriorates faster. The life expectancy for a Great Dane is only 5-8 years, while the life expectancy of a Chihuahua is over 15 years.

Life expectancy for breeds is also determined by the unique medical conditions of each breed. Dogs with flat faces, such as pugs, for instance, usually have more medical complications than other dogs, which drags their life expectancy down.

Problems for most dogs tend to occur between 6-7 years of age. Generally, a dog can live up to 15 years, barring a disease or malady that's specific to a particular breed.

A purebred dog's life expectancy generally runs the average length for that breed. Not all purebred dogs are alike, and purebred dogs actually tend to be sicklier than mutts. This is due to a genetic asset called "hybrid vigor" that mutts have and purebred dog's lack.

A careless breeder can keep genetic abnormalities and medical conditions in a dog's line. The owner of a purebred dog should research the lifespan of a dog's parents and siblings.

Mutts tend to live longer, healthier lives because their genetic code is more diverse. When an animal has a diverse genetic code, weak or dangerous genes are weeded out and replaced by stronger genes. Mutts that are a clear cross between two specific breeds, you can expect an average life expectancy between those two breeds. If the dog pulls more towards the larger breed, then the life expectancy may need to be lowered. If the dog pulls more towards the smaller breed, the life expectancy can be adjusted higher.

Owners can request a genetic report for a mutt. These genetic reports will tell the owner what mix of breeds the dog is, but not all genetic reports are accurate because dogs' genetic code contains little differentiation. Dog owners with mutts that simply cannot be identified will want to look to similar breeds for an evaluation. Owners should consider the dog's size, energy level, muscle mass and build. They should also consider any unique breed traits, such as a curly tail, a double coat, a flat face or a furry ridge across the dog's back. These breed traits will point them towards the general breed category of the dog. The owner can then research similar breeds and make a note of the average of the life expectancy of each.

CHAPTER 2: HOW TO HELP YOUR DOG MAINTAIN THE RIGHT WEIGHT

The obesity epidemic is in the news almost daily, but many people don't realize that it is as much a problem for our dogs as it is for people. Dogs are susceptible to most of the obesity-related ailments that also affect humans.

Start Out Right

Managing your dog's weight begins the day that you bring your new puppy home. If you obtained your puppy from a responsible breeder, you will probably come home with precise instructions regarding what to feed your dog and how much. Most breeders will provide you with a supply of food for the first few days, and will welcome your questions and updates.

If your puppy came from another source, your veterinarian should be able to help you develop a feeding plan. Puppies have special needs because they grow rapidly.

How to Tell If Your Dog Is the Right Weight

There are two ways to tell if your dog is the right weight. Dogs' normal weights vary even more widely than those of people. A Chihuahua may be overweight at four pounds, while a Great Dane may be a lean, mean athlete at 140 pounds. Weighing your dog on a regular basis is important, but you should also know what your dog looks like when he is at the right weight. This varies depending on your dog's breed, but, for most dogs, you should be able to easily feel the ribs. Whether you look down on your dog from above or from the side, he should have a "waist."

Weighing Your Dog

Smaller dogs and puppies can be weighed on a regular bathroom scale. First weigh yourself. Then pick up your dog, and step back on the scale. The difference between these two weights is the weight of your dog. Weigh at the same time of day on the same scale. You can keep track of your dog's weight on a wall calendar or something similar. You may want to weigh puppies daily until they get through their growth spurts. Adult dogs should be weighed every couple of weeks. If your dog is too big to pick up, your veterinarian can help. As long as you are at the vet's office, ask the staff to pet your dog and feed him treats. This will help your dog think of the clinic as a friendly place to visit, and your regular veterinary visits will be much less stressful for both of you.

Feeding Your Dog

Feed your dog the best quality food you can afford. Dry or canned is a matter of personal preference. Most dogs do best being fed twice a day. Free feeding, while popular, is not the best way to control your dog's weight or monitor his health. If you free feed and your dog stops eating due to illness, you may not realize it until he is seriously ill. How much to feed your dog depends on breed, age, metabolism, and activity level. Determine how much is right for your dog by carefully tracking his weight. Table scraps (with no bones, spices, sauces, or salt) are okay once in a while in small quantities, but be warned-your dog may develop a taste for scraps and become fussy if he doesn't get them.

What about Exercise?

Exercise is just as important for dogs as it is for people. Like your feeding plan, your exercise plan will be influenced by your dog's breed, age, health, and activity level. A Chihuahua may get all the exercise he needs playing fetch for ten or fifteen minutes in the living room, while a Labrador Retriever, bred for field trials, may need an hour's run alongside a bicycle just to take the edge off. Your veterinarian can help you make sure your exercise plan is right for your dog. Find an activity that you both enjoy and you will both benefit!

If Your Dog is Still Getting Fat

If you have been walking your dog for an hour a day and you have reduced his food until you are counting the kibbles into his bowl, but he is still gaining weight, it's probably time to see your veterinarian. Dogs are susceptible to medical conditions that can cause weight gain. Many of them are genetic. Your veterinarian can help you find out if this is the case with your dog. In the case of genetics, your dog's weight gain is something that can be controlled with medication.

The Bottom Line

Whether you are a dog or a human, maintaining the right weight is an important part of ensuring a long and healthy life. Monitor your dog's weight. Feed the dog a healthy diet in the correct amounts, and follow a good exercise plan, and your dog will be a happy, active companion for a long, long time.

CHAPTER 3: THE IMPORTANCE OF CHECKUPS

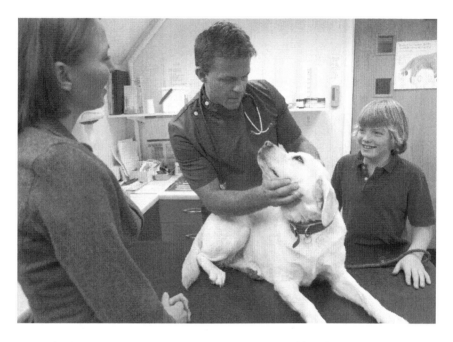

The best way to save money at the vet's office is to take your dog there every year for an annual checkup, whether or not your dog is sick.

Like many human ailments, dog diseases and conditions tend to develop slowly; while they are in their development stages they give few if any overt signs. By the time the symptoms are obvious enough to be worrisome, treatment may come too late.

Do not wait until your dog's yearly exam, especially if you have a puppy; you need to take the pup to a vet shortly after bringing him home for shots and vaccinations. If the pup hasn't been spayed/neutered, discuss this option with your vet.

Your new dog is counting on you to meet all his needs. That's a pretty weighty responsibility, and it can be expensive. The cost will depend on where you live, where you shop and how big your new canine buddy is.

What about pet insurance? It used to be unaffordable for most pet homes, but it has recently become more reasonable. There are numerous companies and lots of options when it comes to coverage and deductibles. A dollar a day plus a deductible could save you thousands in the future.

At home, before your vet visit, practice handling your dog in the same manner as your vet during a checkup so that the experience is not new to your dog. Lift the tail, touch the feet, nails, and the ears.

If you have questions for your vet, write them down so you don't forget.

When you and your dog visit the vet, don't forget to take these items with you:

- ✓ Collar and leash
- ✓ If the dog is small and nervous, a carrier can help
- ✓ A list of any shots already given
- ✓ A sample of a bowel movement
- ✓ A list of what you usually feed

During An Exam

- ✓ The vet will probably start with the dog's nose. Several serious conditions start with a discharge from a dog's nose.
- ✓ Next, the vet will check the eyes. Eye infections start small, but are contagious to everyone else in the home.
- ✓ Next, the vet will look at teeth—they should be nice and white. They may need to be cleared of cavity-causing tartar. Your vet will look for abscesses, any oral tumors could be present, and pale gums that can indicate anemia.
- ✓ Ears, especially on long-eared dogs, can hide bacteria, injuries, and ear mites—all of which can be dealt with.
- ✓ With a stethoscope, your vet will check the lungs for congestion or strange breathing patterns. The heart should be beating 100-130 beats per minute.
- ✓ Your vet check the skin for parasites, fleas and ticks, as well as cuts, scrapes or other injuries.
- ✓ Feeling the abdomen will help detect lumps, distention, infection or indications that something is hurting the dog, and let the vet know that further examination is needed.
- ✓ Finally, the vet will check your dog's spine, tail and paws to see if anything is amiss.

If the vet prescribes any medication, ask them to show you how to administer it.

At the conclusion of the exam, the vet will probably offer your dog a treat and schedule your next routine check-up. Mark your calendar and ask your vet to send a reminder.

CHAPTER 4: BLOOD SCREENING

How often should you bring in your dog for blood screenings? Making sure your dog gets the proper number and type of blood screenings at the appropriate times will help ensure optimal health for your dog.

When Should I Take My Dog for a Blood Screening?

Ask for a blood screen when you are having your dog spayed or neutered. This is a great time to get a baseline of his profile when he is young, healthy, and not suffering from any diseases. An early blood profile will help your veterinarian in the future. He or she will be able to compare the original blood screen with the current blood screen and see changes that can help with future diagnoses.

Some veterinarians recommend a yearly blood screen; a yearly screening can help a veterinarian find subtle signs of disease before they become obvious. The earlier a treatment begins, the better the results. It's a good way to help prevent permanent damage.

You know your pet the best. If you sense your dog is just not himself, and he's been off for few days, it may be a good idea to take your pet to your veterinarian for a checkup. After a thorough physical exam your vet will determine if a blood screen is needed and proceed from there.

Dogs are now living longer than ever before. This is due to better nutrition and better disease control. With increased blood screening common diseases like diabetes, renal disease and hypothyroidism can be diagnosed early, and treatment can help slow down their progression. It's money well spent when you consider how it will improve the quality of life for your dog.

Blood screens are typically needed before surgery or a procedure that requires anesthesia. For instance, if your dog is scheduled for dental work, your vet will need to know how well your dog's liver and kidneys are functioning because a healthy liver and kidneys remove the drugs from your dog's body at a predictable rate. If they are diseased, the correct dosage of anesthesia may become a fatal dose.

Another benefit of a blood screen before a surgery–it may show poorly functioning organs that can make surgery too dangerous to perform.

Take your pet to the vet whenever there seems to be a problem that just will not go away. A blood screen can help to diagnose a problem in its beginning stages, when proper intervention can make all the difference in the world.

CHAPTER 5: DENTAL CARE FOR THE OLDER DOG

Many pet owners are not aware that animals need dental care too, especially dogs that eat a lot of human food. As dogs age, many of them will need regular dental cleanings and dental work. The problems that dogs have are similar to those of humans, except that most dogs' dental problems will be solved by extraction rather than by fillings or root canals.

Dogs do not have as many dental problems as humans because most dental decay in humans is caused by sugar. Dog owners should check their dogs for chipped teeth rather than teeth that have decay.

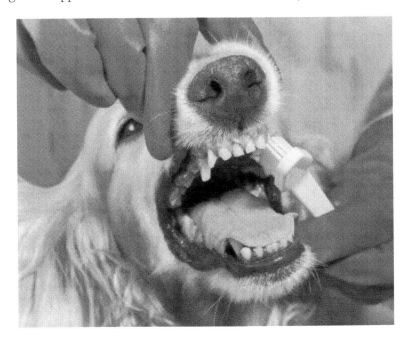

Dogs usually keep their teeth clean by chewing on hard items such as bones, dry dog food, rawhides and other treats. Special treats are available that are designed to clean a dog's teeth. Dogs that eat only wet food will need supplemental treats to make sure that their teeth are appropriately clean. Owners can also mix dry dog food with wet dog food. Dogs that eat a lot of processed food meant for humans may encounter some tooth decay. (There are many reasons that dogs should not eat human food, or only eat human food sparingly.)

Dogs should get regular cleanings at the vet, but pet owners can also clean their dog's teeth using a toothbrush and toothpaste created specifically for dogs. The process of brushing may be difficult at first, but it will become easier as the dog grows accustomed to it. (The toothpaste is usually flavored, which also helps.)

Human toothpaste should never be used on a dog because it is not safe for consumption.

Hard chews such as antlers can damage a dog's teeth. Bones and other traditional dog toys have also been found to be potentially harmful to dogs because they can lacerate the dog's gums and harm the internal organs. Dog chews should be firm but not sharp, and should wear down rather than splinter. Pet owners should also always supervise their pets when they are chewing anything to make sure that they do not choke or injure themselves.

Regardless of how well a pet owner takes care of his or her dog, some tooth injury may occur. A dog owner should be aware of the signs and side effects that point to a tooth injury. A dog with a tooth injury will usually begin losing weight as they avoid food. They may become reclusive, hiding under the bed, and they may also become lethargic and no longer want to play. They may also paw at their mouths or rub their mouths on other things.

A pet owner should examine his or her pet's mouth for any signs of cavities, chips or decay. They can also look at the gums to see if there might be something lodged. If symptoms persist, the dog should be taken to the vet immediately. Emergency vets are usually open 24 hours and other vets will usually take emergency patients first thing in the morning.

The usual course of action when an animal is suffering tooth pain is to extract the teeth. A lost tooth will not affect a dog in the way that a lost tooth affects a human, and the dog will feel immediate relief from the pain. Extraction is usually done under general anesthetic, so the same concerns with other minor surgeries do apply. However, the process is usually very simple and only takes a matter of hours. The dog will then be sent home with some pain relief medication for their gums as well as antibiotics, and the owner will need to make sure that they monitor their dog to make sure that it doesn't develop an infection.

It is very important to get treatment if your dog is in pain. A dog that is in severe pain may simply stop eating until it dies of malnutrition. Even if a dog does continue to eat, a decayed tooth may eventually lead to an abscess in the gums. Once an abscess forms it can be difficult to treat. These abscesses are very painful and can lead to an infection that will spread to the dog's jaw and bones. An infection in a dog's jaw or bones may eventually lead to the infection spreading into the dog's bloodstream, which can lead to death.

Dental problems for dogs are just as serious as those for humans, and treatment is vital for the overall health and well-being of your pet.

CHAPTER 6: TREATING DOG ARTHRITIS

As your canine ages he will be prone to developing arthritis, as part of the normal aging process. Dogs considered overweight are at the highest risk. Heavier, large breed dogs are more susceptible simply because they are heavier. Similar to the human arthritis, canine arthritis is a degenerative disease causing painful stiffness in the muscles and joints. As in humans, pain levels vary and can be excruciating for some.

Younger dogs are not exempt from arthritis. If your dog sustains injuries while still a puppy, it can lead to problems in the joints in the future. Most cases of arthritis in dogs are inherited from their bloodlines. Hip dysplasia and osteochondrosis are two such inherent conditions. Dogs rarely develop arthritis as a result of an immune-related joint disease or infection.

Osteochondrosis (affecting bone and cartilage in the growth centers) is the most common form of arthritis and will affect one in every five dogs. You may notice stiffness during certain times of the day or during cooler weather. Due to its degenerative nature, it will continue to worsen over time.

In order to properly diagnose the issue and see how far it has progressed, you should schedule an appointment with your veterinarian. An x-ray displaying arthritis will show spurs that have formed on the ligaments and uneven bone density. Unfortunately there is no cure for degenerative joint disease, but treatment through a combination of medicine and therapy can help minimize your dog's pain. Treatment will likely address your pet's diet to get them within a healthy weight, and your vet may prescribe medication for pain and joint function.

Chondroprotective agents may also be administered to slow down the degradation of cartilage and repair the joints, slowing down the damage. Included in many therapy regimes is acupuncture; studies have shown that when used in correlation with other treatment, it is a powerful healing aid. Acupuncture can be alternated or added into regular physical therapy sessions and is comforting to dogs. In extremely severe cases, some dogs may lose movement in their joints. To rectify arthritis that is severe, a vet may recommend surgical fusion to relieve pain and possibly restore some movement.

A veterinary physical therapist should be consulted to ensure your dog gets an appropriate amount of exercise. Encouraging a dog to be active keeps him or her strong and promotes joint health and flexibility. Make sure to only perform the recommended amount of therapy – overwork can cause further damage.

If your dog likes to swim, your vet may recommend it. Swimming is beneficial because it doesn't put stress on the joints and still maintains and builds muscle.

Different types of arthritis need different treatments to attain a positive response. Immune-mediated arthritis occurs when a dog's own antibodies turn against its connective tissue, causing either erosion of the surface joints and/or inflammation. An example of erosive arthritis can be seen in rheumatoid arthritis, which typically occurs more often in small breed dogs at around age 4. You may notice your dog waking up stiff-jointed, some slight swelling in the lower leg joints, lameness, or even fever and appetite loss.

Mid to large sized breeds tend to get non-erosive arthritis which shows signs around ages 5-6.

The cause for this form is not known but it presents signs similar to the erosive type. Diagnosis for immune-related arthritis requires an x-ray and lab tests to determine if the arthritis is immune-mediated in nature or if it is infectious. Once a diagnosis has been made, a treatment program of steroids or some other immunosuppressive drug and anti-inflammatory medications may be given. You may cycle through different combinations of medication until you find what works for your pet. Again, weight loss may be encouraged through diet restrictions and physical therapy. Restriction of vigorous exercise is also likely, especially during flare-ups.

Arthritis can also be caused by infection. Protection from infected ticks is essential in order to prevent infectious arthritis. Tick-borne arthritis can include Rickettsial arthritis from a dog contracting Rocky Mountain spotted fever, as well as canine erlichiosis. Lyme disease may lead to spirochetal arthritis. Though rare, a fungal infection can also cause arthritis.

Treatment for infectious arthritis usually includes a treatment of tetracycline. When caught early, you can lower the risk of permanent joint damage.

If you notice your dog waking up stiff or showing pain in its joints, make an appointment with your vet. An x-ray may reveal that your pet has been enduring arthritis. With proper weight management, medication, and therapy, your dog can return to a fairly normal life without pain.

CHAPTER 7: KEEPING FIT – THE RIGHT EXERCISE FOR MIND AND BODY

Staying active for a dog is essentially the same as it is for people (or any other living thing). For dogs, activity is about mental stability as much as physical exercise. There are multiple ways to help your dog stay fit and keep their mind sharp.

Food Puzzle Toys

At pet stores, you'll find puzzles for dogs made from plastic or rubber that give access to treats inside, once the dog figures out the puzzle.

Usually, your canine has to perform an activity to get the reward from the toy in question-for example, one toy may have holes on either end, but the dog can only get to the treat if he shakes the toy, paws at it or chews it a certain way. Your dog figures out the puzzle as he works with the toy. This is a perfect activity for those times when you're away from home.

Scavenger Treat Hunts

One of the best ways to train your dog to hunt is to hide kibble around the yard and help him hunt down the treat. He'll follow the smell around the yard. You can also do this inside the home with treats and food puzzle toys, letting the stay active while also learning how to use their senses better.

Play Games with Your Dog

One favorite for canines is the game of fetch. With a ball, Frisbee or just a stick, you can play with your dog and get him actively running outside and interacting with you.

Bubble Time

Dogs are curious, and they love the unexpected chase. Blowing bubbles is a fun activity that allows your dog to run and jump to snatch those bubbles right from the air.

Socialize with Other Dogs

For puppies or even older dogs with good personalities, it may be fun for them to interact with other dogs. You can organize play groups with neighbors and friends in order to get your dogs socialized and interacting with other people.

Go for Longer Walks

If you find that your dog is staying in too much, it's time to go for a walk. But don't just go around the block. Walk with your dog for at least 20 minutes, and try exploring new habitats like natural areas, hiking trails and shaded streams. Nature sparks imagination for dogs. Your dog will also bond with you as you explore together.

Let Him Chew

Dogs love to chew on things, whether it's a toy or your favorite pair of shoes. However, you don't have to fear for your furniture or shoes if you give him something to chew on that cleans his teeth and tastes better than your socks. Hard rubber toys, pig ears, rawhides, bones and other chew toys are the perfect choices.

A Tug Battle

Get a toy rope or a stretch toy that allows you both to play tug-of-war. As you tug, encourage him to pull back and fight for his toy. Always let your dog win, and refrain from reprimanding your dog during play.

Hide-And-Seek

Dogs are natural hunters, and they have a powerful sense of smell. You can play hide and seek by hiding yourself with a treat and calling out to your dog. While you hide, encourage your dog to find you. Keep moving and calling out to your dog in an encouraging tone. When your dog does find you, offer a treat or a good rub down as a reward.

Chase

Chase toys allow you to pull a toy on a rope, giving your dog something to chase. When your dog catches you or the toy, you should let him tug on it and chew it before going into chase mode again.

Dogs learn new tricks when they're active and expand upon their senses. Keeping your dog's mind and body fit is essential to allow them to grow into happy, healthy adult pups.

CHAPTER 8: WHY A MASSAGE IS IMPORTANT

Dog massage therapy is something pet owners can do at home, and dogs are reaping the benefits.

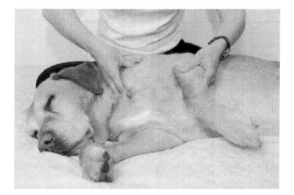

Dogs come in a variety of breeds, sizes, and all come with different traits. Some breeds have inherent health issues common to that breed, while others acquire conditions along the way. For example, some breeds are naturally hyper, which can eventually lead to circulatory problems. Massaging your dog can revive circulation to vital areas of its body.

Stress Reduction - Many dogs are left alone for long hours because their owners have to work; this prolonged absence can produce anxiety and stress. Taking just 30 minutes, 3 to 4 times a week to massage your dog can eliminate this problem.

Immune Support - A dog's immune system is under attack from many different sources. Fatal diseases such as cancer and Addison's disease (a condition that causes low hormone production) weaken a dog's immune function. Arthritis and allergies affect their day-to-day lives. Massaging your dog on a regular basis is a great way to stimulate your dog's immune system to ward off medical problems.

Lower Inflammation - Massage therapy is a blessing to canine friends who suffer from this condition. Inflammation stems from a combination of poor circulation and immune system disorders. Starting a massage routine early in your dog's life can stave off unwanted health issues down the road.

Weight Control - Controlling your dog's weight can go both ways. Hyperactive dogs can form habits that include overeating, and this can really harm your dog in the long run. Anxiety can irritate its metabolism resulting in a lot of food consumption and still being under weight. Stress, anxiety and boredom are all tied together, and they can contribute to different health conditions that negatively impact your dog. An overweight dog can experience joint problems and respiratory stress. You'll be reaping many benefits of a healthier, lighter dog if you practice routine massage.

Reduce Blood Pressure - Like humans, dogs have high blood pressure problems too. Massage therapy helps reduce stress and improves circulation, which can help blood pressure. Massage therapy alone won't solve the problem. Diet and exercise must be part of the routine, but adding in scheduled massage sessions definitely helps the cause.

Growing Pains - The benefits of massage becomes even more evident when pups go through their growing pains. The correlation between bone and muscle growth, especially in large breeds, isn't always in sync in the growing years. If a bone grows faster than the attached muscle, the pain factor for the dog can be extremely high.

Dog owners who have administered massage therapy during this stage of their dog's life have declared excellent results in pain reduction for their pets. Growing pains vary by breed; larger dogs tend to experience them more. No dog owner wants to see his or her pet in pain, and massaging your dog during the growth stage can be practiced as an alternative to expensive pain medication.

Bonding - Massaging your dog can be important for bonding, especially if you are introducing the dog to a new home or you need to build trust. When a dog comes into a new environment, it will understandably be apprehensive. Bonding is a process-sometimes it's instantaneous, and other times it can take weeks to accomplish.

If your dog resists massage, start with petting.

We feed our dogs. We care for our dogs. But many dog owners neglect massaging their dogs. Dog owners who do will tell you their dogs are healthier, happier, and live better lives.

CHAPTER 9: GROOMING YOUR OLDER DOG

Young and old, long or short hair, grooming your dog is a necessity. It will keep them clean and comfortable throughout the year. Grooming is not just about aesthetics. Regular grooming is an essential part of keeping your best friend happy and healthy throughout his life. Older dogs have their own set of special needs and quirks to keep in mind when grooming them.

Grooming covers your pet's hair, nails and teeth and each must be regularly maintained to ensure optimum health. Break your grooming sessions into several smaller jobs, each covering a separate task. All dogs, but larger breeds in particular, are susceptible to maladies such as hip dysplasia and arthritis as they get older. Standing for prolonged periods can cause physical pain and may manifest as anxiety or aggression.

The Tools You Will Need

✓ Brush of your choice
✓ Toothbrush
✓ Nail clippers
✓ Shampoo
✓ Hair trimming scissors
✓ Patience and understanding

Caring For Your Older Dog's Coat

Caring for the coat of your older dog is a more delicate matter than with a younger dog. Especially with long-haired breeds, be mindful of what is going on under the coat. Thinner skin means that bed-sores, rashes, abrasions, cuts and bruises are more likely. Massage your pooch before you begin brushing, looking for areas of raised skin and warm spots. The massage will also sooth and relax your dog, helping ease any anxiety they may feel. Raised skin indicates a potentially tender area that you should take extra care with, and a spot warmer than the rest is a sign of an infected wound. Discover the source, then carefully clean and dress any sores with antibacterial cream.

After the massage, brush your older dog with a soft bristled comb and go slowly. Pulling out hair will be painful and your dog will associate that pain with the grooming session, causing future anxiety. Allow your dog to sit or lay down during the brushing to prevent fatigue and muscle soreness.

Once your dog has been thoroughly brushed and all matted hair has been removed, wash your dog with an approved dog shampoo. Do not use cleansers designed for humans. Keep the water at what you would consider warm-too hot or cold will cause discomfort and exacerbate existing problems. Your goal is to make the brushing and bathing portion of a grooming session as pleasant as possible while still getting the job done. Use this opportunity to look for lumps and bumps in the skin. They can be indicative of minor problems like a rash or more serious issues like tumors.

Trimming Nails

Overgrown nails will limit your older dog's mobility and can cause pain. Puppies tend to keep them short by running and playing, and they require little maintenance. But with age comes less movement, and trimming your dog's nails become a priority. If you have never trimmed your dog's nails, there are a few things you should know.

You will need to find a method with which you are both most comfortable. You can trim with specially designed clippers or with a grinding tool. Many dogs will prefer one over the other. No matter which you choose, remember to make it as calming as you can. If they show signs of anger or anxiety, stop and give them a treat, and start again when your dog has calmed down. Trim to just below the quick—the quick is the blood supply for the nail, and if cut, it will bleed and cause pain.

Tips and Tricks

Start young. If you develop a grooming routine and do the same steps in the same order every time, your dog will be more comfortable with the process.

Get the right tools for the job. Don't use your nail clippers, hair trimmers or shampoo on your dog. Be sure to use specialized products designed just for your dog.

Be patient. As dogs get older, temperaments may change. If you've followed the same process throughout your dog's life and it suddenly bothers him or her, find out why. Pay attention and listen to your dog.

CHAPTER 10: COGNITIVE DETERIORATION

Over time, a dog's awareness, memory and other senses can start to decline. Those who have thoroughly trained their dogs may notice that they are not performing as well as they once did. It may be obvious when your dog doesn't remember all of the things that he or she used to do.

Dogs will likely experience changes in their sleep cycle. They may start to sleep less often and become more restless at night, which can lead to changes in energy levels. They may become more tired and sleep during the day, and they may seem a bit more lethargic. (Signs include staring at things, wandering around, or making more noise.)

When dog owners start to notice these behaviors in their pets, it's time to visit the vet and ask for advice.

As dogs age, they may become more dependent on their owners. They may be more likely to follow their owners around, and become clingier. However, dogs have their own personalities, and some may actually become more detached and may interact less. While many people assume that these are normal signs of aging, it may an indication of specific health problems.

It is important to start to adapt to your dog's reduced energy level. This may include playing with them a little bit less often and somewhat less vigorously. They may also start to become lost in places that they have been many times before. Even a dog that has entered through the same side of a door for years may suddenly start to go to the wrong side. Keep in mind too that they might have more trouble remembering some of the commands that they have been using for their whole lives. The dogs may not be behaving badly; they might just not remember what that command meant. Work with the dog and be patient as time goes on.

Another sign that dogs may be suffering from cognitive deterioration is apathy. A dog that used to be excited to walk around and explore new things may care less about being in new environments. A dog may also start to eat more, and more quickly.

Dogs that are getting older may also start going to the bathroom in the home like they may have when they were puppies. They also may not remember people that they've known for a long time. This can be upsetting, but it can be part of the aging process. If you're prepared, growing older can be less painful for both you and your dog.

The more you can keep your dog engaged, the longer they can maintain good functioning health.

CHAPTER 11: DIETARY CONSIDERATIONS

Your dog has been your best friend for many years. Perhaps you bought him as a pup, and watched him grow into a beautiful adult dog. Or maybe you rescued him from a shelter when he was several years old. Regardless of how long you've had your dog, you love him and want the best for him. He has become an integral part of your family. He is the first one to greet you when you get home, and the last one to kiss you before you go to sleep. What better way to show him that you care than to take great care of him as he ages?

You are the one who feeds your dog and makes sure that he has a diet that will not only fulfill his requirements for health, but will also keep him healthy into his old age. Just as a human's needs change as he or she gets older, your dog's needs also change. His joints are sore, he may limp more than usual, and he cannot run the way he used to. Your dog needs a special diet. Regular dog food will no longer be good enough.

What to Feed Your Dog

Just as a baby's dietary needs differ from those of an adult, so does a senior dog's needs differ from when he was a puppy or even a young adult. You want to provide the right amount of carbohydrates, protein, fat and calories in his food. As a senior dog, more nutrients and vitamins are needed to keep him healthy.

From gourmet organic to vegetarian dog food, there is a perfect meal choice for your older pet. As an older dog, your dog has specific needs that go beyond getting his teeth whiter or taking care of his bad breath. Depending on your dog's size and breed, you will need to adjust how much food you give him and what type of food he needs. Keep in touch with your dog's vet to see if he needs to take extra supplements, and to verify that all his daily dietary needs are being met.

Fat cells increase as dogs get older, so you will need to make sure that your senior dog's food has adequate amount of calories and protein. Limit fat. Over-feeding and giving him more calories than he needs, will cause more problems with his joints and body.

Older dogs also have the tendency to be constipated. Be sure to add fiber to his diet, not too much, but enough to keep him regular. It is also a good idea to add fish oil to help his heart continue to be healthy and strong. Studies have shown that adding a regular amount of fish oil to your older dog's diet helps to prevent not only heart disease, but also kidney disease, certain cancers, and arthritis.

CHAPTER 12: OTHER COMMON DISEASE IN OLDER DOGS

There are over 19 different common diseases that can affect older dogs. Some occur more frequently than others. As heartbreaking as it is to talk about these different conditions, they are part of a normal process that affects all aging dogs.

Heart disease is commonly diagnosed in older dogs. Certain breeds are more prone to getting heart disease than others. Typically, smaller breed dogs are diagnosed with mitral valve disease, while the larger dogs are usually diagnosed with dilated cardiomyopathy. These conditions are usually irreversible and can only be controlled. Medication will help.

Diabetes can occur at any age, but becomes more frequent in older dogs. Typically, a dog will suffer from dramatic weight loss and increased thirst and appetite. Dogs that are overweight run the higher risk of getting diabetes than slimmer and more active dogs. Current treatment plans are effective at reducing the effects of diabetes. Owners can check the dog's glucose levels and provide supplements to help maintain healthy glucose levels, which will aid in controlling the diabetes and further prolong the dog's life.

Kidney disease, though not as common as the other types of disease, is still a disease that affects older dogs. Generally, dogs will have a decreased appetite and increased vomiting, with significant weight loss. Kidney disease can only be diagnosed through blood and urine tests. Even with diagnoses of kidney disease, there are several options available to treat it. Prescription medication, vitamins, and intravenous fluid therapy are ways that kidney disease can be reduced. Kidney problems are difficult to treat in the advanced stages.

Cataracts are associated with aging eyes. Most types of cataracts are usually inherited and can occur anytime; however, there is a higher risk during the dog's mature years. Over a period of time the lens of the eye can become cloudy, which can lead to blurred or reduced vision. Eventually, the cataracts will significantly impair vision and possibly cause blindness. Luckily, there are treatment plans that can reduce the effects of cataracts, if they are treated early enough.

Another type of eye disease common to older dogs is **dry eye or KCS**. When dogs get older, they begin to produce fewer tears, which creates the potential for dirt and other debris to accumulate in the eye. This can lead to infections and potentially cause serious eye damage. There are excellent treatment plans available to help reduce dry eye.

Finally, **bladder stones** are often associated with older dogs. The bladder stones are caused from the buildup of minerals and salts found in the urine tract of a dog. Stones can be a painful experience for a dog (just as in humans). Treatment plans for bladder stones can vary depending on the severity of the stones. Generally, diet and medication can help dissolve or pass the stones through the urinary tract. More serious cases may require surgical removal.

Keep in touch with your vet to keep tabs on your dog's health and to help ensure your canine friend lives the healthiest, best life possible.

MEET THE AUTHOR

Amy and Bruno

Amy Morford has over twenty years of dog training experience with companion dogs, sport dogs and working breeds. Amy's motivation to write about dogs stems from her love for them and their unbiased loyalty and devotion. Amy's goal is to provide helpful, accurate information to assist dog lovers with raising and training a well-mannered, good-tempered, happy, healthy, well-adjusted companion, friend, partner and/or family pet.

Be sure to bookmark and subscribe to DogTrainingPlace.net for articles, tips and tail-wagging fun.

OTHER BOOKS & PRODUCTS BY AMY

DoggyPedia: All You Need To Know About Dogs

Dog Quotes: Proverbs, Quotes & Quips

How To Speak Dog: Dog Training Simplified For Dog Owners

Pet Names and Numerology: Choose the Right Name For Your Pet

Puppy Training: From Day 1 to Adulthood (How to Make Your Puppy Loving and Obedient)

Scared Dog Audio

The German Shepherd Big Book: All About The German Shepherd Breed

Made in the USA
Charleston, SC
19 March 2014

amazon
burning

victoria griffith

ASTOR
+BLUE
EDITIONS

AMAZON BURNING
Astor + Blue Editions
Copyright © 2014 by Victoria Griffith

Astor + Blue Editions
New York, NY 10036
www.astorandblue.com

Publisher's Cataloging-In-Publication Data

GRIFFITH, VICTORIA. AMAZON BURNING—1st ed.

ISBN: 978-1-938231-94-0 (paperback)
ISBN: 978-1-938231-95-7 (epdf)
ISBN: 978-1-938231-93-3 (epub)

1. New Adult—Romance—Fiction 2. Young woman gets swept up in Amazon rainforest conflict—Fiction 3. Murder mystery—Fiction 4. Young adult—Action/Adventure in Brazil—Fiction 5. Coming of Age—Fiction 6. South American Murder and Suspense Story—Fiction 7. Boa Vista and Rio de Janeiro (Brazil) I. Title

Jacket Cover Design: Danielle Fiorello

For my family and friends

PROLOGUE

Amazon

"Don't leave me."

Milton peered out the open window into the darkness. It was impossible to see who or what lurked in the jungle outside. The fear in his young wife's body was palpable as she wound her arms around his neck. For the first time in his life, Milton wished he were under the bright lights of a big city. There, your enemies had to look you in the face. Here, they hid behind the mask of the Amazon. Milton swallowed hard, a frightened child in a man's body, scared to leave the safety of home. If he weren't careful, he would allow his enemies to destroy his soul. He needed to take his life back.

"It's just a game of cards with Ronaldo," he said to his wife, Iara. His voice was soft but steady. "A man can't stay home all the time."

Milton knew what his stalkers wanted. Like jaguars on his tail, watching his every move, they were poised to pounce. They wanted to kill him at a moment when no one else was around to witness the attack, when there was no chance of a stray bullet hitting an unwanted target. They wanted not just a murder, but a clean murder. Milton refused to give them that. He had told his contacts in the press about the death threats. If his enemies killed him now, they would run the risk of being found out. His enemies would wait until the outside world became distracted by other things, Milton told himself.

"We need to go away for a while," Iara urged. "Somewhere safe."

"We'd be playing into their hands," Milton protested. "We'd only come back to the smell of burned trees."

"Let them burn!" Iara pulled her arms from around Milton's neck and stepped back, eyes flashing.

"You don't mean that. This is our home."

"Home? *Mato!*" Iara said, using the derogatory Portuguese term for the wilderness. She waved her hand dismissively. Milton winced at the expression as if his wife had hit him.

"If I don't stand up for this *mato*, in a few years there will be nothing here but mines and cattle ranches. Once the forest is gone, nothing will bring it back. You know that."

Iara lowered her eyes. "Why does it have to be you?"

"People listen to me. They trust me."

"And what is in it for us? There are people out there who want to kill you. And we have nothing. We're just as poor as we ever were, taking our showers outside with the spider monkeys looking down on us. We have to think of our children." She gestured towards the open door of a bedroom, where their toddler twins lay side by side on a mattress on the floor. Young Pedro stirred, and Milton wondered what he was dreaming about. On a rickety table by the side of the bed sat the whistle Milton had made for him out of palm fronds that morning.

"I'm fighting for their future too," Milton said. "For their home."

"*You* are their future!"

"What do you want from me, Iara?" Milton sighed, tired of the argument.

"I want you to stay alive. You could take that job in Brasilia."

"I already told them I didn't want the job. Can you imagine me behind a desk in a city? It would be like a slow death." Iara had never been to the capital city, but Milton had. To him, the sleek concrete buildings there seemed to have been designed by aliens from outer space. He would feel as much at home there as he would on Mars. People in the city lived life differently. No matter how many times Milton took a marble-surrounded bath in a fancy hotel, he would never belong to their world. And neither would Iara, although she didn't seem to realize that. They both belonged here, in the Amazon. It was bad enough that he had been forced to move to the outer edge of Boa Vista so that he could more easily organize his environmental protests. At least the jungle remained close enough that he could feel its rhythms. The forest was his addiction. He couldn't abandon it entirely. "Let's not talk about leaving again, Iara," he said in a conciliatory tone.

A tear ran down Iara's face. "I don't want to lose you," she said.

Milton wiped the moisture from her smooth brown cheek. She had been just sixteen when they had fallen in love and had already been through too much for someone so young. "Nothing will happen to me—not tonight, anyway. I'll climb out the back window and go through the woods. That way, I'll get around anyone who might be watching. Let's turn out the lights and pretend we've gone to bed."

Iara reluctantly went along with the plan, extinguishing first the kitchen, then the bedroom light. Electricity still amazed her. There was none in the deep jungle, where she had grown up. Things had changed after her marriage to Milton. His fame offered glimpses of the world beyond. People from far away sent them gifts. For his birthday this year, Milton had received a package from Rio de Janeiro. Inside were four huge towels in different colors. They were so big and fluffy, Iara at first mistook them for blankets. She liked one in particular. It had a picture of the sun on it, and water. Milton said it was not a river, but the ocean, whose water tasted like salt. Iara had never tasted the ocean. She wanted to. As much as she loved her home, she craved new sights, new experiences. Experiences that didn't come with death threats.

It took a few moments for their eyes to adjust to the dark. Once they did, Milton approached his wife's silhouette. He took her in his arms, rocking her for a few moments as if she were a baby. Then he kissed her on the forehead.

"It will all be okay," he whispered. "You'll see." Before she could protest, he stepped to the bedroom window at the back of the house and swung his leg over the sill. Like most dwellings near the river, their house was built on stilts. Milton kept a firm grip as he lowered himself to the ground. When he was close enough, he let go and dropped down silently, his impact softened by the damp earth of the rainy season.

Iara's good cooking had given him a slight paunch, but Milton remained agile. He slipped as easily as an anaconda into the night. A year earlier, he had cleared a path through the forest to make the walk to Ronaldo's house easier. Now, the vegetation had almost obliterated the trail. In the Amazon, the rapid growth and death of plants was a constant reminder of passing time. Nowhere else on earth generated the same sense of urgency.

As Milton entered the forest, a chorus of insects and frogs sang out its welcome. He kept to the overgrown path, lit only by the glowing eyes of spiders. He didn't need a flashlight. Sometimes he thought he could find his way through the forest even if he were blind. A dog howled in the distance. Milton walked on, listening for the sound of someone on his tail. Nothing. When he saw the lights of Ronaldo's place, his fear ebbed and his pace quickened. As he stepped out of the woods, a whiff of tobacco put him on the alert once more. Some twenty yards away, to his right, he saw the soft glow of a cigarette. The glow fell to the ground and was extinguished.

"Hello?" Milton whispered. No answer. *It must be Rita,* Milton thought. He had caught Ronaldo's eighteen-year-old daughter before, smoking in secret along the path. Well, if she wanted to hide her cigarettes from her father, it was nothing to do with Milton. Moving into the clearing, he picked up a pebble and threw it at the windowpane of Ronaldo's house. His friend would hear it and let him in. The less attention Milton attracted, the safer for everyone.

A door opened, and Ronaldo formed a silhouette against the light in the entryway. Milton smiled. Soon he would be sitting comfortably at a table inside. He wanted to tell Ronaldo about the wildlife smuggling ring he was closing in on. They were a slippery group. His friend might have some ideas about how to root them out of the forest. As Milton stepped toward the house, he heard a soft shuffling from the direction of the cigarette, like someone walking on wet leaves. He glanced in the direction of the sound. Then there was a loud *crack*, and his abdomen and legs went numb. The pain burned into his heart. His hand sought to dam up the warm river that suddenly flowed from his chest, but within seconds, it was covered with blood. Milton willed himself to move, but his body was too heavy, his spirit too light. At the edge of the rain forest, Milton Silva collapsed. A lone potoo bird wailed out the news of his tragic death.

CHAPTER ONE

Sun

EMMA SLIPPED OUT OF the water and wrapped herself in a large, fluffy beach towel with a sun and water design. She was amazed that her father's apartment overlooking the ocean in Rio de Janeiro had its own tiny swimming pool. That was something you didn't see very often in Manhattan. Shaking out her wet hair, Emma stole a glance at the woman sunning nearby in a dental floss bikini.

"It's a shame your skin is so pale," Raquel said as she spread another layer of oil onto her own golden limbs. "How awful to constantly worry about burning."

Raquel had a special talent for wrapping humiliation in a veil of kindness. Determined not to take the bait, Emma shot a feigned smile of appreciation. She resented the fact that her father, Mike, hadn't even mentioned Raquel's existence before she made the trip down to Brazil. Emma hadn't expected her dad to stay single forever after the divorce. But she also hadn't expected him to select a mate closer to Emma's age than his. When she first arrived, Emma had tried, really tried, to get along with her potential stepmother. She stole a glance at Raquel's obviously augmented and deeply bronzed figure. Maybe she shouldn't have mentioned that article about how something like 99.9% of Brazilian women get plastic surgery. The country was full of enhanced lips, breasts, and noses, and she was pretty sure Raquel belonged to that club. *But other than that,* Emma thought, *I've been incredibly open and friendly.*

Emma reached for her iPhone. No messages. *Damn!* Still clutching the phone in the hope that any moment now she would get the text she had been waiting for, she walked to the balcony's railing and looked down. Below her spread Rio's chaotic harbor. The honking horns and shouts from the avenues and streets drifted up. Having grown up in New York City, Emma had always considered herself an urban girl. But she had been unprepared for the tumult of Rio, a town that moved to a frenetic samba beat. The city's extremes of wealth and poverty made New York seem like an egalitarian society. Her eyes took in Rio's mixed messages. The Museum of Tomorrow jutted out into the ocean, like a giant metal shark about to take a plunge. Behind it was the timeless silhouette of Sugar Loaf Mountain. Next door, a luxury high rise reached ambitiously toward the sky, curtains drawn against the fishbowl living. On the nearby hillside stood one of the city's famous *favelas*, a massive slum with thousands of metal and concrete-block houses struggling to stay erect on the precarious red earth that threatened to collapse beneath them at any moment.

When her dad had offered her a summer internship with the *Guardian,* the British newspaper where he worked as Brazilian correspondent, it had seemed like a godsend. Jay Goldberg, Emma's lawyer, had advised her to leave town, at least for a few months. Emma was attracting way too much attention. Newspaper photographers had begun to track her. She had even made the Metropolitan section of the *New York Times* and inspired an op-ed in the *New York Post.* Unfortunately for Emma's career aspirations, the pieces were not *by* her but *about* her. And she couldn't have picked a worse enemy than Tony Horowitz.

Horowitz was a legend in the business, famous for his reporting on the Iraq and Afghanistan wars. A word from him and no news outlet in the country would offer her a job. Sometimes it seemed like Emma's career as a journalist was over even before it started. And she might not even get the chance to finish her degree. New York University, or NYU as everyone called it, was threatening to bar her from completing her last year of journalism school. If Jay failed to get her off the hook, building a career outside the US might be her only hope. Thankfully, her story hadn't crossed the ocean to any overseas outlets, so her reputation at the *Guardian* was still intact. If her dad knew what was at stake, maybe he would take the internship more seriously, give her better assignments. But Emma couldn't bring herself to tell him what had happened.

Emma shifted her gaze to look through the glass doors of the patio. Inside the apartment, her father was huddled over the telephone, his head bowed down as he listened intently. People often talked about how much Emma resembled her dad, with her long, thin figure topped by dark, wavy hair. But the resemblance didn't go beyond the physical, Emma thought. Mike was so emotionally distant that sometimes she had to remind herself that they were related at all. Right now her dad looked even more serious than usual. As Emma watched, he clicked off the telephone with his one good hand and placed it on the countertop. He stood there for a few moments, head down, as if he was trying to absorb some momentous news. Then he walked with an uncharacteristically uncertain step to the terrace.

"Sit down here with me," Raquel purred when Mike pushed open the sliding glass door.

Mike shook his head. Emma's phone emitted a chime, and she glanced down to view the text. *Just mom, checking in.*

"Emma, put that thing down!" Mike said disapprovingly. Emma lowered her hand and turned her attention to her father. "Thank you. I've had some bad news," he said, his voice breaking. "Milton Silva has been killed."

Raquel's expression was a strange mixture of surprise and irritation. *Dad just spoiled her sunny afternoon,* Emma realized. From her father's countenance, she understood that there was more to his announcement than a news bulletin. For Mike Cohen, this was personal. "I'm really sorry, Dad," she said sympathetically. "Was he a friend of yours?"

"I liked to think of him as a friend," Mike said.

"What happened?" Raquel asked.

"Shot last night as he was going to visit Ronaldo for a game of cards."

Raquel grimaced. "Will you have to cover the story?" she asked.

"I'll have to write about the murder, yeah. They've already got the obituary on file. My editors had me do it weeks ago because of the death threats Milton had been getting."

It seemed morbid to write an obituary before a person even died, but Emma understood the need for speed in the world of journalism. The first outlet to get the news out could claim they "broke" the story, that they had the inside scoop. Emma also realized that the murder victim must have been important to warrant an ahead-of-time obit. "He was well-known?" she asked.

"Milton Silva? Greens' best weapon. Hero to anyone wanting to save the Amazon."

Maria, a sweet-faced maid, stepped through the open sliding doors, carrying a tray with three tall cups of watermelon juice. Mike and Raquel shook their heads at the offered refreshment, but Emma had noticed Maria's need for someone to appreciate her efforts. She accepted the drink and murmured an *obrigada*, one of the few words she knew in Portuguese. She took a sip of the sweet juice and watched the maid head back inside the apartment before turning back to her father.

"Judging by the number of forest fires I spotted from the plane on the way down, I'm not sure he was winning his fight," Emma said.

"All politics is local. Ditto for the environment. Protecting one small area can be a monumental achievement. Milton was one of the few people who had the courage to stand up to the ranchers and miners. A lot of people treat the jungle as an easy way to get rich. I don't know who's going to stand up to the filthy exploitation artists now that he's gone."

"Do you think the police will find the killer?" Raquel asked.

"Let's hope Milton's friends in the press give the story enough exposure to put real pressure on them," Mike said. "But let's be realistic. Depending on how fat the murderer's bank account is, they can pay off the cops, who will pretend not to see evidence right in front of their noses." He shook his head vigorously, as if trying to cast off his dark thoughts. "Anyway, have to catch a flight up to Boa Vista later

today. I don't have much time if I want to make it to the funeral."
Mike turned to Emma. "Brazilians bury their dead right away. Not
a good idea to leave bodies hanging around too long in the heat of
the tropics."

In the short time Emma had been here, she had made note of
Raquel's habits. When Raquel got nervous, her eyebrows shot up
quickly—like now. She was clearly digesting the implications of
Mike's statement: namely that this event would make her temporarily responsible for Emma. Raquel definitely wouldn't want that. *Well,
that's something we can agree on,* Emma thought.

"You're not planning to leave Emma here with me, are you?"
Raquel asked. "It's just that I have events to go to every night this
week, and tomorrow is Maria's day off. I'm sure you don't want Emma
to be in the apartment all alone. Might be risky."

The remark was calculated to strike a chord. *Cariocas,* as residents
of Rio called themselves, were obsessed with personal security, and
for good reason. Crime was a part of everyday life here. A few nights
ago, Emma, Raquel, and Mike had gone to dinner at a friend's house.
Emma was shocked to hear that the hostess's apartment complex had
been assaulted by armed intruders earlier that day. The first thing the
criminals did was herd the building's residents into a common room.
They asked each family to hand over their keys and indicate where
the valuables were in their apartment, separating the residents into
a "to-be-robbed" group and an "already-robbed" group. Because of
a bureaucratic error on the part of the thieves, the hostess was mis-
takenly moved to the "already-robbed" section before her apartment
had been touched. At dinner, the guests drank to her good fortune.

Security measures among Rio's elite followed fashion trends all
their own. Since her arrival, Emma had learned that one hundred
thousand dollars could turn a regular car into a bulletproof vehicle,
and that a lot of Brazilians thought it was worth the price. It was
better than spending money on personal bodyguards, who had an
unfortunate tendency to collude with armed attackers. Emma had
discovered that most dogs in Brazil were watchdogs, not pets, and
that *cariocas* like to hang out in shopping malls because they're

safer than the streets. At least they used to be until groups of teenagers from the local *favelas* started to organize massive "walk-throughs" that sent chills up the spines of wealthy shoppers. Kidnapping was one of the most popular ways for criminals to make money. From what Emma could tell, victims were usually released after the family paid a ransom, but sometimes minus a toe, finger, or earlobe. The dangers of the city clearly weighed on Mike as he considered his options.

"Why don't you take Emma along with you, Raquel? She can do some research for that blog piece she's doing on Brazilian society women." Mike had agreed to link Emma's blog to the *Guardian's* web site, but had so far refused to publish anything she wrote under the newspaper's name. Maybe that would change if she could help her father cover the murder of a famous environmentalist.

"I just wouldn't feel comfortable being responsible for Emma," Raquel said. "What if something happens to her?"

"I'm not sure Boa Vista's safer than Rio," Mike said uncertainly.

Emma pressed her advantage. "But would Mom want me to stay here on my own?"

Mike sighed. "Okay, pack your bags," he said to Emma in a re-signed tone. "I'll have Yvonne from the office book us on the next flight. Just bring what you've been wearing here and be ready to leave by five. We might run into some heavy traffic on the way to the airport."

Emma had had enough experience with Rio's epic traffic jams to realize that her father could have dropped the word *might* from the sentence. "Thanks, Dad!" she said. Throwing her towel onto a patio chair, she walked over and gave him a quick hug.

"Hey, if I want to get wet, I'll jump in the pool," Mike protested as Emma's wet hair dampened his shirt. She laughed and stepped away, walked through the sliding doors, and crossed the living room to enter the guest bedroom. The Amazon—it was exotic enough to provide good material for her blog, and maybe even a piece for the newspaper, one with her name on it.

She glanced at her phone. Emma's plan didn't work outside of the US, so Mike had given her a new number to use during her stay. She had made sure Jay had it, and Mary, the NYU alum who said she might have information relevant to Emma's case. She was hoping to hear something—anything from either of them. But no one except her mother had messaged her in the last half hour. Emma would answer her mom later. She would have to rush if she was going to make it to the airport with her dad in a few hours. She put her phone on the nightstand.

Throwing off her bikini, she speed-changed into a T-shirt and jeans. She had just a few days before finished unpacking the contents of the duffel bag she had brought with her from New York. Now she threw it on the bed and began stuffing items of clothing inside. A dress in navy blue was her closest thing to funeral black. The chime of the cell phone announced another incoming message. She grabbed it, glancing down at the screen as she punched a button to view the text. It wasn't from Jay. Or her mom. In fact, she wasn't sure the message was for her at all.

STAY IN RIO U R BEING WATCHED.

CHAPTER TWO

Texting

EMMA READ THE TEXT a second time. The precise intention of the message was difficult to grasp. Was it a threat or a warning? The telephone number of the sender didn't show up on her screen. Despite her shaking hands, she managed to punch out *WHO R U* and press "Send."

She waited. No response. A familiar queasiness formed in the pit of her stomach as she realized the message must be for her father, not her. Emma had worried about Mike her entire childhood. He had never been the kind of journalist who went to the television studio, put on make-up, did his bit, and left the station. Mike was a professional loner, a print journalist who thrived on being in the middle of the action. There was the time he had been on the receiving end of enemy fire in some ongoing Middle Eastern conflict. He spent two weeks in the hospital after that, the doctor removing shrapnel from his body. One month after he checked out, wounds still covered with bandages, Mike was kidnapped in the desert by Taliban sympathizers. Emma and her mother were just reconciling themselves to his probable death when he rang them from the borrowed cell phone of an aid worker. He had escaped, but the torture he suffered during captivity had left him with permanent nerve damage in his left hand.

Soon after Mike's desert mishap, Emma's mom demanded a divorce. She was tired of the stress, tired of a husband who insisted on taking the most dangerous assignments when "in her mind" he should be staying home. Emma's mom had been horrified when her daughter announced that she planned to attend journalism school, and Emma even surprised herself with the decision. But Emma liked to write, and she wanted to make a difference. "It's probably some attempt to work through the pain of the past," said a therapist friend of her mom's, as if Emma's career choice needed to be psycho-analyzed. "Just take a local TV reporter's job when you're through," Emma's mom had advised her. When Emma decided to take the internship, Mike had to promise her mother that he wouldn't allow her to get into any dangerous situations. *But the word "dangerous" is open to interpretation,* Emma thought.

Whoever sent the text didn't know Emma's father very well. Nothing would hold him back if he was after a story, especially if the story had a personal relevance, like the murder of his friend Milton Silva. But the caller had left a message for Mike, and Emma supposed she ought to give it to him. Emma found her dad holed up in his small office, picking out letters on the keyboard with his right hand. Although the door was open, Emma still knocked.

"I'm a little busy, Emma." Her dad hadn't taken his eyes off the screen, and she wondered how he even knew who it was. Raquel and the maid probably knew better than to disturb him while he was writing.

"It's just that someone sent a text on the phone you gave me." Emma tried to keep her voice steady. "It's a little disturbing. I think you should take a look."

"Weird. I thought I'd given everyone my new number when I switched plans," Mike answered, reluctantly dragging his attention away from the computer. "Who was it from?"

"I don't know. Do you want to read the message?"

Mike gave her an irritated look before reaching out his good hand to take the phone Emma offered. He looked down at the screen and frowned. For a few moments he stayed silent. He pressed a button, looking for and not finding the phone number of the sender.

"Sounds melodramatic, don't you think?" he asked, but didn't wait for an answer. "It's written in English, not Portuguese. Probably someone from a competing newspaper who doesn't want me on the story. I wouldn't worry too much about it. Anyway, I'd better get this article off if we're going to get to the airport on time."

He turned his back to her with a sense of finality. Emma stepped reluctantly out of his office. *A competing newspaper*, she repeated to herself. *But what if it wasn't?* It didn't matter what she thought, though. Mike would get on the airplane. Emma couldn't go back to New York, and she couldn't stay here alone with Raquel. She glanced through the glass doors to the patio where her potential stepmother was still roasting in oil. One thing was clear: between the snakes of the jungle and the viper by the pool, she preferred to face the serpents in the Amazon.

CHAPTER THREE

Turbulence

"MIKE! MIKE!"

From the characteristic reluctance to let go of the "k," Emma immediately recognized the testosterone-laden voice as Brazilian. She turned away from her father and Raquel to see one of the most beautiful men she had ever laid eyes on coming through the airport terminal toward them. Tall and bronzed, he wore a closely fitted T-shirt that showed off well-defined muscles beneath. He exuded the magnetic self-confidence of a man who had no doubts about his place in the world. Emma felt a heat in her belly as he drew closer. He was the kind of gorgeous that made her resent her lawyer's orders for a celibate summer. "No boyfriends, no flirtation," Jay had warned. "Remember that everyone has a cell phone these days and can snap a picture. Don't give them any chance to paint you as promiscuous, or it could negatively impact your case against Horowitz."

Emma assumed Mike would be annoyed at being waylaid on the way to the check-in counter. But he showed little emotion other than surprise. "Hey Jimmy!" he called out.

"Who's this?" Jimmy asked as he turned towards Emma, offering her the kind of smile very few people are able to give—a smile that the world could see, but that singled one person out. Emma's chest tightened. He kissed her, Brazilian style, skin grazing both cheeks as she breathed in his fresh body-wash smell.

"Jimmy Feldman!" Raquel put her hand on Jimmy's upper arm as she elbowed Emma out of the way to bestow her own two kisses on him.

"You didn't have to come see us off!" Mike exclaimed. Emma glanced at the large backpack and camera bag Jimmy was carrying. It was clear that Mike hadn't registered the load, or he would have understood that Jimmy was not there for a *bon voyage*.

"I'm coming with you," Jimmy said. "I called the office and Yvonne said she had booked you on this flight."

Mike hesitated, drawing his eyebrows together.

"You don't have to worry about the cost," Jimmy continued. "My father said it was the chance of a lifetime. He's paying for the trip. He said to tell you he's sorry about Milton and that he'll call you when he gets back from South Africa. Unless you've already got a photographer lined up in Boa Vista?"

"Well, no, but-"

"Because I know you won't want images from the freelancers. Every other newspaper will have those."

"I'm not even sure where we're going to stay," Mike hesitated. "Yvonne was still trying to book rooms for us when I talked to her. The Boa Vista hotels are mobbed with journalists and officials traveling there for Milton's funeral."

"Got it covered," Jimmy said.

"How?"

"*Com jeitinho,*" Jimmy responded with a smile that took over his entire face. "Brazilian-style."

"You didn't bribe anyone, did you, Jimmy? It's against newspaper policy."

"Just used my natural charm!" Jimmy responded.

Over the loudspeaker, a woman announced their flight, first in Portuguese, then in English. "We'd better get going, Dad," Emma said.

Mike glanced at the clock before turning to Jimmy. "If anything happens to you up in Boa Vista, the *Guardian* won't be responsible."

Jimmy shrugged and picked up his luggage. It was settled. After checking in at the *TAM* counter, they raced to security. Emma's duffel bag bounced painfully against her hip, but she knew better than to complain. At the conveyer belts, Raquel pulled Mike off to the side and locked him in a passionate embrace. Emma turned away as they kissed.

"C'mon, man," Jimmy called out, extracting a Mac from his backpack and placing it on the belt. "We need to make that flight."

"Hope you don't miss me *too* much, Emma!" Raquel said as Mike disentangled himself.

"Oh, don't worry," Emma responded.

By the time they got to the gate, the flight attendant was pushing the door shut.

"*Espera!*" Mike called, waving their boarding passes. The flight attendant opened the door to let them through, and they ran down the connector and onto the plane.

"My seat's a few rows up," Jimmy said when Mike stopped at rows 11.

"You know, why don't you two sit together here?" Mike suggested. "I've got work to do anyway, so I won't be very good company. And you guys are about the same age, right? Maybe you can talk about, I don't know, Beyoncé or something."

"Or Yo-Yo Ma," Jimmy responded in an amused tone as he exchanged boarding passes with Mike. "Okay. See you in Boa Vista!"

Jimmy allowed Emma to step in first before stashing his backpack under the aisle seat and stowing his camera bag in the overhead bin. Emma pulled her cell phone from her bag. She remembered that she still hadn't responded to her mother's text. Jimmy lowered himself into the seat next to her. Their jean-clad thighs touched, distracting Emma from her task. Her fingers fumbling, she managed to type *off to boa vista with dad* and pressed send. Hopefully, her mom would think Boa Vista was a beach resort. *Senhoras e senhores*, a woman's voice crackled over the PA as Emma stashed the cell phone in her purse and fastened her seatbelt.

The plane was picking up speed, jostling its passengers. Jimmy's leg rubbed against hers, and a warmth spread in the pit of Emma's abdomen. She closed her eyes, imagining what it would be like to feel more than just his leg against her body. By the time the plane leveled out and the noise from the engines diminished, Emma was struggling to hide her heightened state of awareness. *Jay said celibate,* she reminded herself.

"So," she said lightly, "what *do* you think of Beyoncé?"

Jimmy laughed, revealing white, straight teeth that would have been perfect except for one at the top that jutted out slightly. "I saw her in concert once," he said as his leg touched hers.

"Anything to drink?" the flight attendant asked as she leaned towards them, breaking the moment. Emma shook her head. Jimmy ordered a beer. "Well, we might as well get comfortable," said Jimmy, pushing back his seat. "We won't be in Boa Vista for another five hours."

"Three," Emma corrected him. "We get there at one o'clock in the morning."

"With the two-hour time change. Boa Vista is two hours behind Rio." He smiled again at Emma's obvious confusion. "Well we're crossing the whole country, practically. Boa Vista is almost at the border with Venezuela." Emma didn't answer. She hadn't factored in a time change. Jimmy would be right next to her for longer than she had expected, which was fine with her. "Let me help you with the seat," Jimmy said. He leaned across, pressing the button to help her push her seat back. Her breasts tingled as his arm brushed against them. *Pull yourself together, Emma.* "Is it your first time in the Amazon?"

"Well, yeah. I only arrived in Brazil a couple of weeks ago."

"Hope you brought some rain boots with you. Boa Vista is the only Brazilian city that's north of the equator. That means rainy season."

"Sounds lovely. How come you have such an American name? Jimmy doesn't sound very Brazilian."

"My parents are originally from Russia. It's short for Vladimir. The *d* has a *j* sound in Portuguese."

"Your English is excellent."

"Went to the American School in Rio for most of my life. It's full of expats, plus a few locals like me. Our classes were mostly in English. Never could completely get rid of my Brazilian accent, though." Emma remembered a friend of Raquel's complaining about the exorbitant tuition at Rio's American School. If Jimmy went there, he must come from money. There wasn't much in the way of financial aid packages in Brazil. "What about you? Finished college?"

"I've got one more year." *I hope.* "You done with school?"

"Graduated from University of Rio last year."

"Photography?"

Jimmy looked uncomfortable. "No. Medicine."

Emma raised an eyebrow. The Brazilian system, she knew, was different from the American one. There was no such thing as a liberal arts degree. University students studied just one thing, and it would be pretty unusual for someone in the medical program to switch careers after college. "So I guess that's why you're wearing your white coat."

Jimmy shifted in his seat. "I decided I didn't actually want to be a doctor."

"How many years did you study for?"

"Five."

"You put in five years preparing to become a doctor and then decided you really wanted to be a photographer?"

"Yeah, that's about right."

"And your parents were okay with that?"

"My dad told me I had two years to prove that photography was going to be more than just a hobby, or I'd have to put on that white coat after all. But that's not going to happen. I'm going to make it."

"How can you be so sure?" Emma asked. "Sometimes people just aren't lucky in their careers." *Like me,* she thought.

"Yeah. Luck. Well." Jimmy ran a hand through his tousled brown locks. The plane gave a sudden jolt, nearly toppling his can of beer. He caught it just before it fell onto Emma's lap, but a few drops spattered her chest.

"Sorry about that," said Jimmy. His eyes went to the drops of liquid glistening on Emma's skin just above her t-shirt.

"Here, let me take that for you," said the air attendant, leaning over to grab Jimmy's beer can and depositing it in her trash bag.

"I'm going to try to get some sleep," Jimmy murmured. "You should too. You might not find Boa Vista that relaxing."

Emma wanted to ask Jimmy what he meant, but he had already closed his eyes. A lock of sun-streaked brown hair grazed one of his eyebrows, and she felt a sudden longing to push it back. He was close enough that she could feel his deep, even breaths on her cheek.

She struggled to get comfortable. Emma didn't expect to actually get any sleep. For one thing, she was all too aware of Jimmy in apparent dreamland by her side. Eventually, though, her thoughts began to scatter. She didn't know how long she dozed off, but she gradually became aware of a grating, loud snoring that cut through the air. Emma opened her eyes and looked over. The noise was emanating from a short, stout man in the aisle seat across from Jimmy. She hadn't noticed him until now. He wasn't from Rio; she could almost guarantee that. There, the poor looked positively ragged, the wealthy impossibly fashionable and glamorous. This man was from a different place. Around his neck, he wore layers of thick gold chains, one of which supported a golden cross that touched the thickness of his waist. The open buttons of his perfectly ironed white shirt revealed bushy, dark hair underneath. Even seated, she could see that he was short, possibly no more than five feet tall.

"Bet he's a *garimpeiro*," Jimmy whispered in her ear. The intimacy of Jimmy's mouth so near temporarily threw Emma off guard. She hadn't even realized Jimmy was awake.

"What's a garim-?"

"A gold miner. He wears the jewelry to show off his wealth. In the forest around Boa Vista, there's a lot of gold. People go there thinking they'll get rich."

"Looks like he got his wish."

"That gold may be all he has. Tough way to make money. Most *garimpeiros* are ticking time bombs from exposure to mercury and malaria and all sorts of other diseases. Plus they're on the wrong side of the law. Not all of the mining is illegal, but most of it is."

"Why?"

"A lot of land around Boa Vista is protected as an Indian reservation. Milton Silva was fighting to keep it that way."

"Did you know Milton?"

"Met him once last year. A reporter from the *Miami Herald* introduced me. Not a successful meeting from my point of view. Milton wouldn't let me take any pics. Wasn't at all like I expected. Didn't seem to like being the center of attention. Hard to imagine him standing down a bulldozer in the forest."

"Is that what he did?"

Yeah, he and his supporters used to form human rings around an area to prevent the trees from being taken down. Milton said he and his followers were like mosquitoes. One mosquito is just annoying, but a thousand can be a real problem."

"Dad said they may never know who shot Milton."

"Your father could be right. You could make a long list of people who wanted Milton dead. I remember this one rancher I met in Boa Vista—like a cowboy mafioso. He was furious because Milton had reported him to the authorities for using illegal pesticides on his crops. Said he would kill him one day. A lot of government big shots hated Milton for blocking their mining and highway projects. And they're powerful. I mean, they could easily hire a hit man to do it. Being an environmentalist in this part of the world doesn't win you a lot of friends, at least not locally."

The plane lurched suddenly, throwing Emma against Jimmy. She resisted the urge to cling to him, retreating to her own space. The chains around the *garimpeiro's* neck began to rattle noisily, and he woke up with a jolt, looking around with a frightened expression, as if warding off attack. His hand went to the chains around his neck, as if to assure himself that his treasure was still there. He seemed angry that he had allowed himself to fall asleep. He glanced in Emma's direction, and when he caught her looking at him, he stared back with an intensity that disconcerted her. *U R BEING WATCHED.*

"Landing," Jimmy said. Hoping to spot city lights below, Emma looked out the window. Total blackness. The plane jerked down and to the side, dislodging a brown leather briefcase from the seat beneath the *garimpeiro* and out into the aisle. Jimmy reached out to push it over to the miner.

"*Deixa!*" the miner said sharply, brushing his hand away. The *garimpeiro* shoved the case back under the seat in front of him, all the while keeping an eye on Jimmy.

"Over-sensitive, don't you think?" Emma murmured.

"Maybe he's got a pay-off for a hit man in there," Jimmy whispered in her ear.

"You think?"

Jimmy shrugged. "The Amazon is like an onion. The more you peel away the layers, the more it stinks."

CHAPTER FOUR

Bats

THE PLANE'S WHEELS HIT the runway with a jolt, passengers thrown forward as the pilot slammed on the brakes. The cabin erupted in applause as the craft slowed to taxiing speed. Emma breathed a sigh of relief. She couldn't wait to escape the close quarters of the airplane and get away from the tightly-wound *garimpeiro,* who was still eying her and Jimmy warily from the seat across the aisle.

"Let him go first," Emma murmured to Jimmy when the plane drew to a stop and the other passengers stood up to gather their things.

They stepped off the plane into the steamy Amazon night, covering the last fifty feet to the terminal on foot. No jetway here.

"Did you see Braga?" asked Mike, who was waiting for them just inside. "The only guy who would wear an Armani suit in the jungle."

"Who's Braga?" Emma asked.

"The Environment Minister," Jimmy explained. "He had to come to Milton's funeral. It would look bad if he were a no-show."

Outside the terminal stretched a half-empty parking lot, the pavement jet-black from recent rain. Above, a black flock flew with eccentric movements around a tall, illuminated lamppost. Emma realized with revulsion that they were not birds but bats. Unbothered by the swarm of flying rodents, Mike turned to the short line of taxis idling noxious fumes.

"Wait!" Jimmy said, waving at a dark-haired teen walking towards them. "Carlos!" he called above the heads of the crowd. "We don't need a cab, Mike. I asked a friend of mine to pick us up. We need to borrow a car while we're here anyway, and the car rental agency didn't have anything available." Carlos, smooth-skinned and slightly built, approached with a grin. Emma thought he looked part Asian with his almond eyes and coffee skin. He and Jimmy greeted each other with a warm embrace, patting each other on the back for emphasis. "Carlos is the go-to man for journalists in Boa Vista," Jimmy explained to Emma and Mike. "Knows everyone in town worth knowing."

"Now I can add someone to my list," said Carlos flirtatiously as he kissed Emma on both cheeks. Emma warmed to him immediately, in a friends-only way.

"Yeah, well, this is Mike," said Jimmy, grabbing Carlos's shoulder and turning him away from Emma. "With the *Guardian*."

"Thanks, but we can just catch a cab," said Mike, extending his good hand to shake Carlos's.

"You'd be waiting a long time," Carlos said, pointing to a woman getting in the backseat of the last available taxi. The people behind her in line wore anxious expressions, clearly concerned that they might be standing there for a while. "You can drop me off at my place and drive to the hotel yourselves. Where are you staying?"

"The *Itamaraty*," said Jimmy.

As Carlos led them into the parking lot, Emma glanced behind. The words "*Aeroporto Internacional de Boa Vista*" were written in huge neon letters over the entryway of the airport. *The International part is an overstatement,* Emma thought. When they reached Carlos's Fiat, Mike eyed the car suspiciously.

"It runs better than it looks," Carlos said encouragingly. He opened the rusted trunk and reached for Emma's bag.

"I'll get that," Jimmy objected, frowning, as Carlos beat him to it. Emma suddenly felt like a piece of candy two boys were fighting over.

"I can get it myself," she said, removing the luggage from Carlos's hands. Jimmy stepped ahead to open the car door, pushed down a seat, and motioned for Emma to get in the back. Mike sat in front, and Carlos took the wheel.

A professor had told Emma once that taxi drivers are a key source of journalists' "normal guy" interviews in foreign countries. It made sense. They were a captive audience for an interview and often spoke some English. In the absence of a taxi driver, Carlos was the closest thing. So Emma wasn't completely surprised when Mike pulled out a notepad and pen.

"What's the local reaction to Milton's death?" Mike asked Carlos as they pulled away from the terminal.

"Mixed," Carlos said. Emma gazed out at the roadside scenery. She couldn't quite believe she was in the Amazon, a word that conjured all sorts of exotic images that didn't fit with the normalcy of this modern highway. "Even people who weren't exactly what you'd call fans of Milton's aren't happy with the attention his murder is attracting. Foreigners are invading this town like a pack of locusts— sorry, present company excepted. I guess it's not a surprise that some of them got threatening telephone calls." Mike stopped scribbling. *I guess he's reconsidering his theory about the text message being a joke,* Emma thought. Carlos continued. "I ran into a girl from the *Los Angeles Times* and the reporter from the *New York Times*—I knew them from before. They both told me they'd been warned away from Boa Vista."

"What's that all about?" Jimmy asked.

"My guess is the person behind it doesn't want a lot of press coverage. You know, it might rev up the opposition to development plans in the jungle. The question is whether it will work. Everyone's planning to cover the funeral tomorrow, but the *Times* guy, at least, told me he's planning to take the next plane out after that. The situation here is hot."

"You think Souza made the threats?" Mike asked.

"The grease-head cowboy? Maybe. He's been causing trouble, sounding off at anyone who looks slightly foreign, telling them to get out of town. He's promised to build the biggest ranching operation in the region. Says he's not going to let a bunch of tree huggers stop him from making money. But I'm not sure he's behind the text messages."

"Were the texts in English or Portuguese?" Emma asked. She wanted to find out if they were connected to the message she had received.

"English, as far as I know," Carlos answered.

"So that lets Souza off the hook," Jimmy commented.

"He could hire someone to make the calls for him," Carlos said. "It's not that hard."

"Souza's that mafioso cowboy I told you about," Jimmy explained to Emma, pushing close to her in the back seat. "I wouldn't put it past him to do something like that."

"He didn't make his fortune just with soybeans, that's for sure," Carlos said.

"How did he make it?" Emma asked.

"Drug smuggling, kidnapping," Jimmy said.

"Well, I'm not going anywhere 'til I get my story," Mike said firmly as the Fiat pulled up to a small house. Even from the faint glow of the headlights, Emma noted that it could use a fresh coat of paint. In the yard were parked another car and two pick-up trucks.

"I get out here," said Carlos. "Jimmy knows the way to the hotel." The light came on inside the Fiat as Carlos got out. Ducking his head back into the car, he flashed a smile at Emma. "Let me know if you need anything while you're here."

"I've got it covered," responded Jimmy hotly.

"Okay, man," Carlos said, laughing. "See you!"

"We'd better let Emma get in the front," Jimmy said to Mike as he took Carlos's place behind the wheel.

Mike looked surprised at this suggestion. "She's got shorter legs than mine. I think she's fine."

"I can't ride São Paulo style, Mike. I'm from Rio."

To Emma's surprise, Mike conceded.

"In São Paulo, they put men in the front, ladies in the back," Jimmy explained, offering Emma one of his full-face smiles as she switched places with her father. "In Rio, we know better."

"The guys in Rio must have shorter legs," Mike grumbled. "You know where you're going?"

"Yeah," Jimmy said. "The *Itamaraty*'s not exactly five stars, but I think it will be okay."

"Anything works for me. I'm not sure about Emma."

"It will be good for me too," Emma replied. *I'm a journalist. I can put up with some discomfort.*

Traffic was remarkably light, considering how crowded the airport had been. Then red brake lights, and in the headlights of the Fiat, a man dressed in black from head-to-toe, toting an ominous looking rifle with one hand and waving drivers to the side of the road with the other.

"*Puta!*" Jimmy growled. "Police. And I forgot my license."

"You're kidding, right?" Mike vented from the back seat.

"Don't worry. I'll take care of it." Jimmy pulled over to a stop. He turned and winked nonchalantly at Emma before rolling down the window. A second policeman, larger and sporting a bulky bulletproof vest and helmet, approached the Fiat. He raised his visor, revealing hard, dark eyes, and peered inside the car, muttering something in Portuguese. Turning off the engine, Jimmy leaned across Emma to open the glove compartment and pressed a button inside to open the trunk. She was all too aware of his arm across her leg. Jimmy casually rubbed his hand on her knee before straightening up. The officer blinded Emma with his high-intensity flashlight beam before moving to the back of the car. He pulled open the trunk and shone the beam inside.

"There's been a kidnapping, and they're searching all cars coming through this way," Jimmy explained, turning to Emma. Finding nothing of interest in the trunk, the officer slammed it shut and walked around to the side of the car, this time aiming the flashlight at Mike's feet. He bent down, his face close to Jimmy's, and murmured something that sounded like a threat. Jimmy pulled out his wallet. He spoke calmly and politely to the policeman as he extracted a few bills and handed them over. The officer scowled at them as he pocketed the cash. Emma was relieved when he stepped away from the Fiat and waved them on past the other parked cars. Jimmy pulled away slowly.

"I told you bribes are against the newspaper's policy," Mike spoke sharply from the back. "I could lose my job if the *Guardian* found out."

"Well, I didn't have much of a choice this time, did I?"

"Because you didn't have your license," Emma said.

"Not because of that. He didn't even ask to see my license. He just wanted the money. Brazilian policemen will take whatever chance they can to make some extra cash. If I hadn't paid, he might have kept us there for hours. That whole kidnapping thing is just an excuse for a scam. It's okay. He didn't ask for that much."

As if that was the issue, Emma thought.

Within ten minutes, Jimmy pulled into the parking lot of a one-story concrete hotel. A neon sign above the door said *I-mara--*. The lighting behind three of the letters had burned out. Not surprisingly, no one rushed out to fetch their luggage. The three of them unloaded the trunk. Exhausted after her trip, Emma felt the weight of her bag on her shoulder. Inside the lobby, Emma looked around, relieved. It wasn't the Four Seasons, but at least it was clean. Behind a dark wood counter that bore the marks of too many forceful pens sat a morose-looking woman, sound asleep. Her jowls shook as she snored. Mike pressed the bell, and her jowls stilled as her eyes opened wide.

"We're with the *Guardian* party," Mike said.

The receptionist sat unmoved and unmoving. Emma assumed something was wrong, and a moment later she realized what it was. Jimmy pulled a wad of cash out of his pocket and placed it on the counter. Like a mechanical doll jolted into action by a coin, the woman stood up and pocketed the money, suddenly all business. She requested a credit card and passports, entering the information in a clunky desktop computer before placing three large keys on the countertop. Mike picked up the keys and turned to walk away. They were just steps from the counter when they heard the popping.

"Get down!" shouted Mike. It took Emma several seconds to realize that she was hearing the sound of gunfire. The rotund receptionist dropped behind the counter as the glass of the hotel's front door shattered.

Emma was pushed down and flattened on the mildewed brown carpet. A scream pierced the air. Emma felt Mike's weight on top of her. For a horrific moment, she wondered if her father was dead. But then she felt his breath on her temple and realized that he was shielding her from bullet spray. Next to them, Mike's duffel bag jumped as a stray bullet tattooed it with a black hole. Another scream and squealing tires. Emma looked over to see Jimmy, his body sheltered behind the end of counter. He was leaning up on his elbows, incessantly clicking camera in hand as he aimed the lens through the glass doors of the hotel entrance. Mike stood up and ran outside.

"Dad!" Emma yelled, terrified Mike would be caught in the crossfire. Before she could go after him, he returned.

"Everyone okay?" he asked.

Emma nodded. The receptionist timidly poked her head above the counter, muttering a stream of what sounded like prayers in Portuguese as she grabbed the mobile telephone and ducked down again.

"*Puta merda!*" Jimmy swore, standing up and studying his camera. "I didn't get a single good shot."

"Out of the doorway," Mike urged. "They may come back."

"What was that all about?" asked Emma breathlessly as she scurried out of fire range to the far end of the lobby.

"A warning," Mike responded. "That's my guess."

"Yeah. If they were serious, they'd have just come inside and murdered us," Jimmy said.

"That text message wasn't from a competing newspaper, was it?" Emma asked her dad.

Mike looked uneasy. "Maybe not. Obviously, there's someone who doesn't want us here," Mike said. "It's probably the same person who sent texts to the other reporters."

"So what now?" Emma asked.

"The police will be here soon," Jimmy said, nodding toward the counter, where the receptionist was speaking in an urgent tone to someone on the telephone.

"Better get to our rooms," Mike suggested. "The Boa Vista cops are a breed unto themselves." Recalling the black-outfitted, automatic rifle-toting police who had stopped them earlier, Emma grabbed her bag.

They stopped in front of a door with a faded number 15 pasted in gold foil on a wooden door. "This is you, Emma," Mike said, inserting a metal key in the lock and turning it. As the door swung open, a man dressed in a bathrobe hurried down the hallway behind them in the direction of the lobby, rushing to see what the commotion had been about.

"Will you be alright tonight?" Mike asked. Emma forced herself to nod and watched as Jimmy and Mike walked away. She entered Room 15 and closed the door, inserting the key in the lock and turning it from the inside.

Emma took in the jaundiced yellow walls and the mud brown blanket on the bed. A smell of cigarette smoke lingered in the air. She put her nose to the scratchy white sheets, which bore the comforting odor of detergent. The air conditioning had been left on, and the room was cool, at least. From outside in the hallway, Emma could hear footsteps and the sound of people speaking in urgent tones. She presumed that more hotel guests had emerged from their rooms, eager find out what was going on. The sole window in the room was shuttered from within, but Emma noted with satisfaction that if she opened it, it might just be big enough to climb through. If a gunman came this way, at least she'd have an escape route.

CHAPTER FIVE

White Van

"HELLO?" A GROGGY EMMA pushed the talk button of her iPhone as spears of sunlight poked through the slats of the shuttered window. It took a moment to center her mind where her body was—in a hotel room in the Amazon, in the aftermath of a shooting.

"Good morning, Slugger." Jay's Long Island accent sounded out of place in this setting.

"I really hate it when you call me that," Emma said. A slight delay on the telephone made Jay seem especially far away.

"You have to admit the nickname suits you. Just calling with an update. Medical report came in. Wanna hear?"

"Not really."

Jay ignored her. "'Profuse bleeding from the temple just above the eye and severely damaged cornea from repeated trauma with blunt metal object.' That's the bad news. Want the good news?"

"If there is any."

"He's not blind. Or dead. Anyway, I've saved the best for last, which is the motive Horowitz is citing for your complete and utter loss of control."

"Well?"

"He says you offered him sex in return for his raising your grade to an A, and that he declined."

Emma sat bolt upright in bed. *Bastard!* "Jay—you're my lawyer. You can't let him get away with this."

"I'm trying my best."

"Did you get the employment record like I asked you for? We need to check his history. See if there were complaints about him in the past."

"I'm on it. But I have to first establish that it's relevant to the case. Anyway, at this point the chances that NYU will repeal the suspension are less than zero."

"Thanks for the encouraging words."

"Just telling it like it is. I'll call you next week with an update, unless something happens in the meantime. Enjoy your visit with your dad. And remember—no boyfriends. If we're going to have any chance winning this case at all, we'd better make you out to be like a virgin, and I'm not talking Madonna, I'm talking *the* Madonna."

Emma clicked off the phone. She had her doubts about Jay. His specialty was divorce, not disputes between a student and a university administration. Hiring him had been her mom's idea—a connection through the local synagogue. Jewish people trusted other Jewish people, and Emma's mom was no exception. Emma wished she could share her mother's faith in the lawyer, but she had a feeling she might need to take matters into her own hands. *Which reminds me.* Anxious, she checked her text messages. Her pulse beat faster. *Yes!* The one she had been waiting for had finally arrived.

Thx for yr message. Read abt troubles with Horowitz. Thnk I can help. Will be off the grid in Malaysia for a couple of weeks, then back if u want to give me a call. Say hi to Allie—Mary

Emma murmured a silent thanks to Allie, who had passed on Mary's number. A couple of weeks. It would be a long time to wait, but it was much better than nothing.

Will do, Emma texted.

Emma placed her phone back on the nightstand, knocking her birth control pill case onto the carpet. She picked it up and popped one of the tiny tablets in her mouth. After the conversation with the lawyer, it seemed pointless. But she'd been on the pill since she was sixteen—at first to help with her acne and later for its more obvious purpose. Her complexion would probably be fine now, with or without the hormone, but it seemed impractical just to stop taking the medication. She looked at her cell. Seven a.m. Thanks to Jay, she was wide awake. She might as well get dressed. Now was as good a time as any to start building up her international journalism cred. A blog piece on the environmental tensions in Boa Vista might be a good start.

The hotel breakfast room was full when Emma entered, computer bag on her shoulder. Mike was nowhere to be seen, but Jimmy was seated at a table in the corner, staring at the screen of his Mac. As Emma watched, he took a bite out of a crusty white roll that Brazilians referred to as "French" bread.

"Some workers are in the lobby removing the glass with the bullet hole," Emma commented, approaching the table. Jimmy's eyes ate up her closely fitted sundress as she settled into the chair opposite.

"I guess gunshot is not a welcome addition to the décor of the *Itamaraty*," Jimmy commented wryly.

Emma rolled her eyes, took out her computer, and placed it on the table, where it competed for a spot with Jimmy's laptop.

A waiter approached the table. *"Bonita a sua namorada!"* he said, leering at Emma.

"He says my girlfriend is pretty," Jimmy interpreted, grinning.

"Yeah, well maybe you should tell him to mind his own business. *Cafezinho por favor,*" Emma ordered haughtily. The coffee here was a lot stronger than what she was used to at home, but she was acquiring a taste for it. Jimmy offered her some of the food he'd collected from the buffet set up at the end of the breakfast room. Emma accepted a roll and some fruit.

"So," said Jimmy as he leaned back in his chair and chewed on a piece of guava fruit. "Are you scared?"

Emma tucked a tendril of hair behind her ear and looked at him pensively, hypnotized by Jimmy's rhythmic chewing. Her reverie was broken when the waiter breezily placed a cup of coffee next to her laptop. "Well, yeah. It would be kind of stupid if I weren't a little scared. Do you think someone is actually trying to kill us?"

"Possibly," Jimmy said. "But more likely it's just a scare tactic. If they really wanted a dead body, they would have just come inside the hotel. Killing a foreign journalist wouldn't serve their interests, anyway. It would just attract more international attention, which is the last thing these people want. Nothing personal, just business as usual in the Amazon."

"Felt personal last night." She looked around the breakfast area and caught conversational phrases in German and Italian as well as English and Portuguese. "Are all these people here for the funeral?"

"I'd bet on it."

"Journalists?"

"Not all. Those guys over there look like government officials from Brasilia." Jimmy pointed to a somberly-suited group of four men. "Braga's not with them—he must have scored a room at a better hotel. Over there you've got your basic Green Peace kind of crowd." Three bearded men and two stocky women sipped their coffee despondently in another part of the room.

Emma turned on her computer. "I'd better catch up on the news."

"Milton's on the front page of the *New York Times,*" Jimmy said. "Might want to check it out."

Emma logged onto nyt.com. The web page came up. Staring back at her was a photograph of a rough looking middle-aged man with tousled black hair and dark skin.

Environmentalist Murdered in Amazon

Milton Silva, the rubber tapper whose battle to save the Amazon rain forest attracted international admiration, was murdered near his home in Boa Vista yesterday. Hundreds of mourners from all over the world are expected to attend today's funeral.

His death has sent shock waves through the environmental community. Silva was born into a poor family of rubber tappers in the remote jungle. With no local schools in the area, he did not learn to read and write until he was a teenager. "The forest was my teacher," he once said. "And I was an excellent pupil."

Ten years ago, Silva began to organize opposition to the illegal clearing of trees. He and his followers fought against deforestation, on a number of occasions sitting in front of chainsaw crews to prevent them from destroying protected areas. Silva worked to create the national reservation where much of the Yanomami tribe now lives. The Yanomami are considered the most remote native people on the planet, their existence virtually unknown until a generation ago. The indigenous group maintains a simple way of life in the forest, with traditions little changed since the Stone Age.

"The rain forest has lost one of its greatest defenders," said Brazilian Environment Minister José Braga in a statement. "We will not rest until Silva's murderer is brought to justice."

Silva leaves behind a wife, Iara, and two young children.

"Front page," Emma commented. "He must have been a big deal."

"Poster boy of the Amazon's environmental movement. Unfortunately, people have a short attention span." *Maybe that's not so unfortunate,* Emma reflected, thinking of the news stories about her attack on Horowitz. "The news outlets will eventually move on to something else," Jimmy continued.

"And we can go back to Rio."

"Is that what you want? Because of last night?"

"Last night has nothing to do with it," Emma lied. "I just don't see the point of hanging around Boa Vista."

"I thought you wanted to be a journalist?"

He has no right to question my ability, Emma thought, the anger rising up in her. Nothing could make her admit to Jimmy that the shooting had unnerved her. "Like you said, people move on," she said hotly. "There's no point in staying here once people have lost interest in the story."

"Part of our job as journalists is to make sure they stay interested. Why become a reporter at all if you don't want to fight for something? No one would care about the Amazon if it weren't for us journalists."

"I don't need a lecture."

"I'm just saying—"

"Well don't," Emma said, pushing her chair back.

Jimmy knows nothing about me, Emma thought to herself as she stalked back to Room 15. *I'm a writer. My professors liked my work—everyone except Horowitz, that is.* Emma sat on her bed, flipping open her computer and logging onto her blog. A blank computer screen confronted her. She needed to write something. But what? All she had seen of Boa Vista was the inside of a hotel. Readers might get excited about the attack by gunman the evening before, but she had promised Mike she wouldn't write about that.

She needed to get out, generate some original material, even if it was just local flavor. But how? Feeling deflated, she acknowledged that Jimmy had a point. She could function as a reporter in New York, but it was very different in a foreign country like Brazil, where she didn't speak the language and didn't know her way around. If she were with a big organization like CNN, she might be able to hire interpreters and drivers to help her. But obviously she couldn't do that on her own. A knock came at the door. Emma opened it.

"Sorry," Jimmy said abruptly.

Emma shrugged her shoulders. She didn't want Jimmy to see that his words had affected her. "No biggie. I'm used to being verbally abused over breakfast."

Jimmy laughed. "I've come with a peace offering. Mike's working on an article this morning on local reaction to the killing, and I wondered if you wanted to come along with me on a reporting gig."

"Where to?"

"Ronaldo's place."

"Who's Ronaldo?"

"Milton was shot just outside his house. I hear he's really upset about his friend's death. I don't blame him. Anyway, I wanted to check up on his daughter, Rita. I met her in January. She's our age. I spoke with her on the phone and she sounded kind of emotional. It would be good to see her. And I can get a few shots of the murder site while we're there."

Emma smiled wryly. "So basically you're pretending to pay her a friendly visit so that you can get some exclusive pics for publication."

"Friendship and work don't necessarily have to be separate," Jimmy responded. "If you're going to make it as a photographer these days, you've got to take your chances where you can get them."

That goes for writers too, Emma thought. Maybe this was her chance to pull together some original material. A blog piece on the scene of the murder could attract attention, maybe even make it in some form into the *Guardian* itself.

"How will we get to Ronaldo's?"

"By car."

"What about the driver's license issue?"

"My mom's sending it up by courier. Should be here tomorrow."

"Let me know when it gets here. In the meantime, I'm driving."

"Okay, okay," Jimmy said, pulling a set of keys out of his pocket and dangling it in front of her. He laughed as Emma snatched them away. "I'll go get my camera equipment. Meet me in the lobby in ten minutes?"

A short time later, Emma took her seat behind the steering wheel of Carlos's Fiat, with Jimmy in the passenger seat. Emma eyed the stick shift warily. She had limited experience with a standard shift, and she had a couple of embarrassing moments stalling the car and grinding the gears before she got the hang of it.

"Make sure we're not being followed," Jimmy said as she backed up and made her way out of the hotel parking lot.

"Who would be following us?"

"I don't know," Jimmy said. "But even in the best of times, they don't like foreigners in Boa Vista."

"A bad case of xenophobia?"

"Foreigners in Boa Vista fall into two main categories—journalists and ecologists. No one from here sees any difference between the two. When I was here in January, people kept tabs on me all the time."

"But *you're* not foreign."

"Guilty by association."

"So are you telling me it's risky just to leave the hotel?"

Jimmy didn't answer. Emma's hands gripped the steering wheel as she turned onto a busy road. Her eyes shifted frenetically back and forth between the rearview mirror and the road.

"Turn left here," Jimmy instructed her. "Now right. "

Emma did as he said, trying to keep an eye on the cars in back of her as well as the ones ahead. As she made the turns, the mix of vehicles behind them changed. But one stayed constant.

"You know," said Emma tentatively, "I don't have a lot of experience when it comes to having someone on my tail, but to me that muddy white van looks suspicious." Jimmy pivoted in his seat for a better look.

"I'm watching it," said Jimmy.

Traffic thinned as they left the center of the city behind. The scenery outside shifted first to fields, then to forest. Traffic was getting lighter, but still the cruddy white van continued to follow, and now there were no cars between them. Jimmy swore.

"What do they want?" Emma asked.

"I'm not eager to find out. Take the next right. Let's see if we can shake them."

Emma looked in the mirror. The van was near enough now that Emma could spot its driver: a heavy-set man with a thick black beard. He hunched over the steering wheel, staring in their direction with unflinching intensity. Emma steered the Fiat to the right. The white van came after them.

"Gun it," said Jimmy.

Emma pressed the accelerator to the floor. The needle on the speedometer bobbled to the right. They were going one hundred kilometers an hour, about sixty miles per hour, way too fast for the narrowing stretch. There were no other vehicles on the road now—just the Fiat and the white van. But instead of falling behind, the white van moved closer. The Fiat's wheels screeched as Emma hugged a bend in the road.

"I can't seem to shake him!"

"Move faster!" Jimmy urged.

"I can't," Emma protested. "The car won't go any faster." The Fiat was bouncing alarmingly over the rutted road. Emma struggled to keep her hands on the shaking steering wheel.

"He's closing in on us."

"I can't keep this up!" Emma shouted at Jimmy. "I'm losing control! We're going to crash!"

"If the car doesn't fall apart first," Jimmy added. "Look—up ahead is a gas station. Pull in there!"

The gas station drew closer. At the last moment, she turned. The Fiat screeched and tilted precariously as one of the tires rode up on the curb. Emma drew to a stop between the gas pumps and the rickety service shed. The white van shot past the station, and Emma expelled a sigh of relief.

"Maybe they weren't following us after all," she said hopefully.

"Or they didn't want to kill us in front of a witness," Jimmy said as a young boy emerged from the shack.

"Next time, you drive," said Emma. "With or without a license."

Jimmy asked the boy to fill the tank with ethanol, the alcohol fuel that many Brazilian cars ran on. The youth sprayed blue cleaner on the windshield before carefully squeegeeing the liquid away. Jimmy pulled out some cash, and a few minutes later, they exited the station. A short time later, the pavement gave way to red dirt. There was no one behind them this time, and Emma relaxed. Outside her window, the scenery was becoming more like the Amazon she had imagined, lush and green.

"Why does Ronaldo live all the way out here?" she asked.

"He's a botany professor. Likes easy access to the jungle. His house is near Milton's."

"Can we be sure there's not another gunman on our tail? An ambush ahead?"

"Emma," Jimmy said, placing his hand on her knee and offering her one of his all-encompassing smiles. The heat emanated up Emma's leg, and she suddenly had trouble concentrating on the road. "You're safe with me."

CHAPTER SIX

Sticks

A PETITE, GRAY-HAIRED MAID answered the door of Ronaldo's bungalow and ushered them inside.

"*Esperem aqui,*" she said as she showed them into the living room, a comfortable space with unexpectedly modern upholstered chairs and sofas. Framed artwork on the walls revealed the sophisticated taste of their host. Emma was surprised by the coolness. "I thought Ronaldo was concerned about the environment," she whispered to Jimmy. "How come he's got the air conditioning turned up?"

"He's got delicate scientific equipment here," Jimmy explained under his breath. After a few minutes, Ronaldo entered the room to greet them. He offered Jimmy a weak smile and a half-embrace.

"*Senta, senta!*" he said, waving them to the couch as he settled into an armchair. Ronaldo was attractive in a middle-aged, professorial way, with cropped brown hair and crooked gold-framed glasses. His pants and shirt were clean but had clearly seen better years. He exchanged pleasantries in broken English with Emma before he and Jimmy lapsed into Portuguese. Emma couldn't follow the conversation, but she noticed that Ronaldo wasn't really focusing on what Jimmy had to say. He seemed distracted, and Emma got the impression that he would have preferred to be left alone. Once or twice, Jimmy asked him a question and in return received a blank stare. He had to repeat himself to elicit a response. *No wonder Ronaldo's unfocused*, Emma thought. *His best friend was killed right in front of his eyes.* She felt guilty for coming over. It was obvious that Ronaldo didn't want them there. He was just too polite to send them away. The maid shuffled back in with a tray of hot drinks. Emma accepted a cup, grateful for the distraction from the awkward one-sided conversation. It looked like some kind of herbal concoction.

"*Unha de gato,*" Ronaldo said as she picked it up. "How do you say—cat's nails."

"I think it translates as cat's claw," Jimmy explained. "It's supposed to cure everything from arthritis to indigestion."

"I'm sure I have something that needs improving," Emma said, raising the cup to her lips. The beverage was sickly sweet, but for the sake of politeness she resisted the urge to spit the liquid back into the cup. Ronaldo drank his down in a few gulps.

The conversation quickly reverted to Portuguese, and Emma's attention wandered. She looked out the window. *It would be strange to live in a place like this,* she thought, *at the edge of the rain forest.* Emma was accustomed to the comfortable familiarity of the small apartment she shared with her mom in New York's Upper West Side, surrounded by kosher delis and grocery stores. Manhattan had a constant buzz. This place was deceptive. For the moment, all was quiet, but Emma sensed a restless undercurrent. Just as Jimmy seemed to run out of things to say, a young woman came into the room. All heads turned in her direction, and Ronaldo's face visibly brightened.

"Ah, Rita," Ronaldo said. "Emma, is my daughter, Rita."

Rita smiled, revealing two rows of flawless teeth. Anywhere in the world, Rita's looks would have attracted attention. In the Amazon, where most people are darker, her blond beauty was particularly striking. Jimmy stood up to give her the customary kiss on each cheek. Emma felt surprised to feel something akin to jealousy stir inside her. *I have no right to feel like that just because he flirted with me,* Emma thought. *For all I know they could be boyfriend and girlfriend. Maybe that's why he wanted to come here.* Emma stood up and hesitated before Rita kissed her too.

Into the room bounded a small monkey, which jumped onto Rita's shoulder, clinging to her hair. Their hostess laughed. "Meet Charlotte," she said. "My pet spider monkey. She was orphaned after some poachers killed her mother. Milton Silva found her and gave her to me to take care of. When I first got her, I had to bottle-feed her."

"I'm sorry about Milton," Jimmy said. "It must be terrible for you."

Rita nodded, tilting her head slightly to the side as if lost in thought. After a momentary pause, she turned back to her guests. "What are you doing in Boa Vista?" she asked.

"I'm interning as a photographer with a journalist at the *Guardian*, Emma's father actually. Came to cover the funeral."

"Always working."

"For the right causes. Listen, would you mind if I took some photos of the yard? The paper might be interested."

Rita pursed her lips. "I thought you'd come as a friend," she pouted.

"We want to make sure Milton's death gets plenty of publicity," said Jimmy. "That will help keep the police honest."

"Yes, yes, of course," Ronaldo responded. "Go ahead."

Rita sighed, scratching Charlotte's head. "It's just that we need some more private time. With all those journalists around, it feels like a circus."

"Milton would want the journalists to be here," Ronaldo said.

"I guess you're right," said Rita ruefully.

Jimmy cleared his throat. "I'll go out back, if that's okay? Is that where he got shot?"

Ronaldo nodded.

"I'll come out in a little while," Emma said. She couldn't shake the feeling that they had barged in where they weren't wanted. Jimmy raised an eyebrow in her direction. She ignored him, and he shrugged, heading outside with his camera. Rita cast a worried look at Ronaldo, who had sat down again and was slumping forlornly in the armchair.

"Would you like to see my father's laboratory, Emma?" she asked. "I think he needs to rest." Emma accepted gratefully. "We'll be back in a little while, Dad," Rita murmured. Ronaldo just nodded his head distractedly. "It's just through here," Rita continued, leading Emma down the hall. The monkey rode on its owner's shoulder, nibbling on a blond lock as it stared at Emma with huge brown eyes.

"Your English is excellent," Emma commented.

"My mother was from London, and she usually spoke to me in English." Emma thought the past tense was a linguistic error until Rita continued: "She died a couple of years ago."

"Oh, I'm sorry." It was bad enough, Emma thought, to have one parent living in a foreign country. She couldn't imagine how painful it would be to lose a mother.

"One day she went into the jungle to do some research and never came back. We searched for her for months before giving up. My father took it worse than anyone. He can't seem to get over it. All he wants to do these days is work on his projects. And now, with Milton's death, I'm really worried about him." They turned into a room off the corridor. "Well, here it is, the center of my father's life."

It was one of the oddest rooms Emma had ever seen. In the middle sat a table with one powerful-looking microscope in its center, a few smaller ones to the side. Around the room were strewn leaves, nuts, and other plant clippings. The shelves were piled with research volumes and wooden books that resembled larger versions of the ones Emma had used to press flowers as a little girl. On the wall was a picture of a younger Ronaldo climbing a gigantic tree, his foot resting on what looked like metal rungs inserted into the trunk.

"Here in the Amazon, a botanist has to climb," Rita explained when she saw Emma examining the photo. "On the ground, the trees look pretty much the same. It's at the upper level that you can see their fruits and leaves and figure out what species they are. My father has identified four new species." The last remark was made with pride.

Emma nodded, genuinely impressed. On the windowsill, several huge five-sided red fruits—or were they vegetables?—sat ripening. Rita took one, grabbed a knife from the dish rack of a nearby sink, and cut a slice. She offered it to Emma.

"Try it. It's a relative of the tomato."

After the experience with the tea, Emma was reluctant, but she didn't want to be impolite. She put the slice in her mouth and was surprised by its pleasant taste. The juice from the fruit ran down her hand. Rita offered her a paper towel.

"It's really good," Emma said. "It does kind of taste tomato-y, but sweeter."

"My father's specialty is identifying edible plants. Here, have another piece." As Rita held out the fruit, Charlotte scampered down her arm and snatched it away. Rita laughed. "That wasn't for you, naughty girl!" As if aware she had done something wrong, Charlotte climbed to the top shelf. Safely out of reach, she surveyed them from her perch as she devoured the red morsel.

Emma walked to the window and looked outside. The entire Amazon forest lay ahead of her. Yet from here, it just seemed like a bunch of tall trees, nothing special. As she watched, she noticed something moving. She thought it might be Jimmy, but she looked closer and was startled to see a short man with a bowl-like haircut step gingerly out of the forest and into the clearing. He was naked except for a red loincloth. He carried a large bow, and around his arms were feathered bands.

"Samuel Yanomami," Rita said, following Emma's gaze. She pronounced it EE-a-no-MA-mee. "I wonder what he's doing here. Samuel is a leader of the Yanomami tribe. One of the few that can speak Portuguese, although I find him almost impossible to understand. I've never seen him this close to the city. Must have something to do with Milton's death. Let's find out what he wants. You stay here, Charlotte!" The monkey stayed put, more out of concern for the red fruit than in obedience to its owner, Emma thought.

As Emma and Rita headed out the side door, Jimmy approached the man and exchanged some words with him in Portuguese. Ronaldo, probably alerted to the Yanomami's presence by the maid, joined them, adjusting his glasses behind his ears with his left hand as he waved to the visitor with his right. Samuel Yanomami grunted, shifting his weight from one leg to the next. Then, out of the blue, he let out a whistle that sounded just like a bird song. Immediately, about twenty other men, women, and children emerged from the jungle. Emma was amazed. *Where did they all come from?* she wondered. She would never have guessed anyone else was out there.

It felt as if they had suddenly landed in a scene from *National Geographic*. The women had short sticks protruding from their nose and lips. Their bodies were painted with brownish-red squiggles and lines. A few of the women had rounded bellies, whether from pregnancy or malnutrition, Emma couldn't tell. The children were naked, but the older Yanomami wore red loincloths. One woman had on a Harvard University T-shirt.

"I'm pretty sure she didn't go to Harvard," Emma commented.

Rita laughed. "It was probably a gift from a researcher. My father sometimes gives them things like that too, in exchange for information on plants. They like Western clothing. They think it's beautiful."

As Jimmy took shots of the group, Ronaldo's maid emerged from the house with a bowl of oranges and a large foil bag of potato chips. One of the Yanomami men reached into the bag of oranges, pulled one out and bit into the skin. He screwed up his lips in disgust at the bitter taste of the peel, but he continued to chomp on the orange anyway. After some difficulty with the wrapping, a young woman managed to open the bag of potato chips. She stuffed a few in her mouth as others crowded in for their share.

"They must be hungry," said Rita. "They don't usually like salty things. There's no salt in the forest. I guess they must have got tired of their insect sandwiches during the hike."

"Insect sandwiches?"

"It's like their take-out. When they're traveling they put slugs or caterpillars in leaves and eat them like a squirmy sushi roll." Emma couldn't help grimacing, and Rita shrugged. "They think a lot of our food is gross." Rita and Emma moved within earshot of Ronaldo, who was conversing stiltedly with Samuel Yanomami. "He says they walked for two days," Rita translated. "They want to go to Milton's funeral. They're asking how to get to the church."

"But didn't Milton only get killed two days ago? How would they find out that quickly?"

Rita shrugged. "Who knows? Yanomami aren't the best counters. In their language, there are only words for one, two, and more than two. Maybe they got mixed up. Anyway, their coming to the funeral is a sign of how much they respected Milton. They've probably never been to a Christian funeral before, and they're bound to find the whole thing disgusting. They'll be really upset when they find out that his body hasn't been cremated. And they'll expect to see Iara eat her husband's ashes."

"Seriously?"

"That's what they do with their own dead. They burn the body and the relatives eat the ashes."

"And they'll think a Christian funeral is disgusting?"

While the Yanomami men gathered around Ronaldo and Jimmy, the women and a few children approached Rita and Emma. A few of them smiled shyly. One acted out an elaborate pantomime, mimicking a gun shot to the chest and someone falling to the ground. They all ran their fingers down their face from their eyes to indicate tears. Emma, too, ran her own fingers down her cheeks.

Emma noticed that Rita's attention had been distracted by something Samuel Yanomami was saying. The group's leader, who had not himself accepted any of the food, was gesturing toward the forest. From the belt below his belly he took out the stub of a cigarette.

"What's he saying?" Emma asked Rita, who suddenly looked very pale.

"He's asking why there's a big pile of cigarette stubs out there," Rita replied softly.

Ronaldo glared at Rita but said nothing. Jimmy and Ronaldo started to follow Samuel Yanomami toward the forest with the rest of the men right behind.

"Let's go with them!" Emma suggested to Rita.

Rita shook her head. "No thanks. I'll stay here." Emma wondered if Yanomami protocol prohibited the women from joining the men. *I'll risk it,* she thought, hurrying after the group. They didn't have far to walk. Samuel Yanomami led them to an area just inside the forest. He pointed to a pile of a hundred or more cigarette butts.

"Someone must have been watching this house for some time to have smoked all of these," said Jimmy. "But why would anyone watch your house, Ronaldo?"

Ronaldo frowned. When he spoke, his voice shook a little. "My work makes me not a lot more popular than Milton."

"Maybe," answered Jimmy. He began taking shots of the cigarettes from different angles. Emma picked up an empty carton that had been thrown on the ground.

"Derby," she said, reading the label on the box. "A clue?"

"Half the city smokes Derby," Jimmy said. "It's the most popular brand in Brazil."

"Did the police search this area?" Jimmy asked Ronaldo.

Ronaldo shook his head. "You know police don't care. They are paid by Souza and others. They search nothing here."

"Then someone besides the police will have to figure this thing out," said Jimmy.

CHAPTER SEVEN

Rain

THE SKIES OPENED AS they exited the church, rain soaking the unprepared mourners as they struggled to open their umbrellas. The elegantly suited Environment Minister, Braga, who had given a speech at the funeral, sprinted toward a chauffeur-driven black car. An assistant trailed him, trying to keep an umbrella over the head of his boss. Iara alone was unperturbed by the downpour. Milton's widow walked with a determined air, head held high as the water trickled down her face. Ronaldo, visibly overwhelmed by grief, placed a protective arm around Rita, shielding her. The rain was as relentless as it was sudden, creating huge puddles where minutes before had been dry red earth. Most of the crowd fled, leaving a diminished group to follow the coffin down the road to the cemetery.

"Braga could have had the decency to come to the actual burial," Mike whispered to Jimmy as they trudged down the road.

"Give him a break, Mike," Jimmy said. "He probably didn't want to ruin that nice suit he was wearing."

"The hug he gave Iara at the service was pretty fake," Mike insisted. "Do you think he really cares that she was left on her own with two babies to support? He should have given Milton police protection years ago."

Jimmy turned to Emma and gave a wry smile. "Your father is always thinking the worst of people. I keep telling him that not all Brazilian officials are corrupt. Most, maybe, but not all."

"You're saying that because Braga's a friend of your family," Mike protested.

"I went to school with his son," Jimmy acknowledged. "But I'm not defending him because of that. I just think he's a decent guy."

The rain soaked through Emma's blue dress, and her shoes sank into the red mud. Jimmy had offered her his umbrella, but Mike thought it was more important to protect the camera equipment, and so he held it instead over Jimmy, who was taking pictures of the procession. Emma wiped a wet strand of hair from her face to see where they were going. The group of Yanomami followed at a slight distance from the others. Ronaldo had given them a ride to the funeral in his van. It was amazing how tightly they had managed to pack themselves in. The graveyard, which they entered through large iron gates, looked different from the ones Emma was used to at home. A high wall surrounded it, as if to shield the rest of the world from the sorrow within. A single sprig of damp, white flowers lay on the coffin, a gesture from a young girl. They were the only flowers at the burial, and no one had the heart to take them away. Milton had left instructions with Iara that there were to be no bouquets at his funeral since they might be taken from his beloved forest.

The Yanomami held back. Rita was right—they seemed to find this part of the ceremony especially alien. The sad group stopped at a brick crypt built above the ground, and Milton's casket was carefully placed inside. A couple of workers cemented the closing before laying white tiles on top. The rain kept up through the burial, ceasing only after the workers had placed the last tile on the crypt. Emma looked back at the Yanomami. Standing beyond the tribe near the iron entrance was another figure. He was wearing a black rain poncho and a cowboy hat. He was young and handsome, with dark hair and chiseled features. Emma was certain he had not been at the funeral, yet he stared intently at the mourners surrounding the crypt.

As Emma watched, he took a pack of cigarettes out of a pocket beneath his poncho, placing one in his mouth and holding a lighter flame to the end. Emma was about to turn away when she saw the stranger tip his hat. Emma followed his gaze to see who he was acknowledging. Ronaldo, arm still around his daughter, stared back, his face suddenly transformed. He was no longer the vague, mild-mannered professor Emma had spoken with earlier in the day. And the emotion registered behind his gold-framed glasses was not difficult to discern. It was raw hatred.

CHAPTER EIGHT

Antarctica

EMMA WAS HOT AND tired by the time she peeled off her clothes and stepped under the stream of lukewarm water that ran from the showerhead in the *Itamaraty's* exuberantly tiled bathroom. There were no temperature controls, something Emma was having a hard time getting used to. It had been a long, frustrating day. Mike had barely looked at the notes she drafted for him to use as background material, including descriptions of the murder site. Yet Emma was determined not to let her work go to waste. If Mike didn't want it, she'd fold it into a blog piece about her encounter with the Yanomami.

Turning off the shower, Emma wrapped herself in a towel and entered the bedroom. It was so humid! She flicked on the air conditioner. Nothing happened. She tried again, but still nothing. An involuntary sigh escaped her. *It's hard enough to work with the air conditioning, never mind without it.* She'd have to ask the hotel staff to take a look. Emma threw on a pair of shorts and a loose T-shirt, grabbed the key, and made her way to the hotel lobby.

"My air conditioning seems to be broken," she said to a man behind the counter. A blank stare. For a moment, Emma wondered if he was waiting for a bribe. Then she realized that he just didn't understand English.

"*Esta quebrado o ar-condicionado da moça,*" said a voice. Emma turned to see Jimmy standing behind her.

"*Ah,*" the hotel worker said, smiling and adding a few phrases in Portuguese.

"They're sending someone to take a look," Jimmy translated. Emma felt a little embarrassed to have him come to her linguistic rescue, especially after his comments over breakfast. He was wearing a close-fitting white T-shirt that showed off his tan. She wished she had thrown on something more flattering. "They won't get around to it for a while," Jimmy continued after Emma thanked the hotelier. "Why don't you come to my room? I turned on the air conditioning when I got back, so it should be cool by now. You can help me pick out photos for Mike."

"Actually, I was hoping you could spare a few of the Yanomami for my blog," Emma ventured.

"If they're up to your standards," Jimmy flashed her one of those smiles that singled her out as the only person in the universe. He grabbed Emma's hand and led her down the corridor of the hotel. *Our hands fit together perfectly*, Emma thought. She was sorry when Jimmy released her to unlock his door and fantasized for a moment that they were going to do something in his bedroom besides look at photographs. She imagined running her tongue over his teeth and exploring the moistness beneath. *Celibate*, she repeated to herself... but in the privacy of Jimmy's room, who would know?

Jimmy closed the door behind them, and Emma breathed in the room's fresh body wash smell. An open laptop rested on the bed. Jimmy sat down next to it and turned it on. Lounging on the bed like that, a hand straying up to scratch his muscular torso, he looked like the subject of a *GQ* spread. Emma had a hard time tearing her eyes away.

"Take a look," said Jimmy, turning the screen toward her. Emma lowered herself onto the bed next to him, the heat from his body flowing into hers as their elbows and legs brushed. With difficulty, Emma shifted her focus to the photographs. Jimmy had taken dozens of shots since their arrival in Boa Vista. Emma was surprised to see that there were a few of images of herself in the mix, pictures Jimmy had taken when she wasn't paying attention to the camera. Jimmy

caught her in shifting moods: in one, she looked slightly goofy, her
elbows raised and her eyes widened in surprise. In another, Emma
wore a serious expression, her eyebrows were drawn together as she
pushed a tendril of hair behind her ears. "You didn't exactly catch me
in model poses," Emma said wryly.

"Models are boring," Jimmy said. "Believe me. I know some. Though
you could probably do that if you wanted. Or get a job as a TV anchor. They always want pretty girls to announce the news."

"I'm a reporter," Emma said. "I don't want to just read the news
in front of a camera. I *can* actually write, you know."

"Okay, okay," Jimmy held up his hand, grinning. "Didn't mean to
set you off." He took the computer from Emma and clicked ahead to
the funeral procession. "What about these?" he asked, handing the
laptop back to her. The photographs were black-and-whites, which
suited the somber mood of the burial. Emma realized, as soon as she
saw them, that Jimmy had real talent. Through unusual camera angles
and unexpected compositions, Jimmy's images had turned the sad
event into a larger-than-life tragedy. Iara had been promoted to saint-
hood through the eyes of Jimmy's camera. In one the grieving widow
stood statuesque, rain streaming down her face, her large eyes turned
longingly toward the crypt. The Yanomami in the background were
a reminder of the jungle, of everything Milton had been fighting for.

"This one is great," Emma said sincerely. She identified a few of
her favorites before moving to the ones taken at Ronaldo's house that
morning. There were shots of Samuel Yanomami and the others. Rita,
Emma noted wryly, *did* look like a *Vogue* model, her blond hair especially striking in the context of the Amazonian setting. "I'll take these
two of the Yanomami for my blog, if that's okay with you."

"We haven't talked about a price," Jimmy said in a teasing tone.
"Some kind of barter arrangement."

Emma felt the blood rush to her groin. He grinned at her before
turning his attention back to the screen.

"I don't know what to do with the pictures of the cigarette stubs,"
Jimmy continued. "They're really important, but they seem a little
boring on their own."

"Blow them up," Emma suggested. "More artsy that way."

"Worth a try." Jimmy took the computer from her and zoomed in. "How's this?" It was now possible to see the finest detail in the shot. Emma studied one of the photos carefully.

"Well, we know one thing," Emma said.

"What?" Jimmy asked.

"It was a man smoking these cigarettes outside of Ronaldo's house."

"How do you know that?"

"No lipstick."

"Couldn't it have been a woman who doesn't wear make-up?"

"Yanomami women don't smoke Derbys, do they?"

"Not likely."

"So it was probably a man."

"Detective Emma!" Jimmy said playfully.

Emma was about to move onto the next image when something in the corner of the shot caught her eye. "Can you enlarge some of the others?" Emma she asked. Jimmy did so, and Emma inspected the sequence carefully, moving the cursor around to zoom in on a specific area. "There!"

Jimmy looked at the image intently before his eyes registered surprise. "*Puta!*" he said. "I was so focused on the cigarette stubs that I must have missed that."

"It looks like a piece of broken glass," Emma said. "And if you get in even closer—like this—look, you can even make out the first letters on the label—"

"It's a bottle of Antarctica beer. Now we know that whoever killed Milton probably liked Antarctica."

"And was a man who smoked Derby."

"Yeah. Which narrows the field down to—I don't know, maybe a few thousand people in Boa Vista. At least I'm off the hook. I don't smoke, though I like Antarctica. But then, I could always have had an accomplice."

"Well it's something, anyway," Emma said defensively.

Jimmy's expression changed suddenly. "Hey," he said softly. "Don't get offended. I'm impressed, really." He took her chin in his hand and looked penetratingly into her eyes. Emma felt drawn toward his strength. She wanted him. She wanted him to kiss her. Yet as his lips moved toward hers, her mind flashed back to another moment, the last time someone had done that. Suddenly, she was in Professor Horowitz's office, reliving the moment when he was leaning toward her, his lips closing in on hers. Her heart started beating wildly, and she was overcome with dizziness. Then her entire body went stone cold and she pushed back, abruptly standing up from the bed. Jimmy reached out to pull her back onto the mattress, but she retreated.

Outside in the corridor, Emma leaned against the yellowed wall, emotionally spent. Beads of sweat collected on her forehead. *Why didn't you just go for it?* she asked herself. *It can't be because of your promise to Jay. No one was there to snap photos of you in a compromising situation. Just because of Professor Horowitz, you're never going to have sex again?* Well, not with Jimmy, anyway. She had seen the mixture of surprise and frustration in his eyes when she stepped out of the room. And with all her heart she wished she could relive that one moment, when he had taken her chin in his hand and it seemed like anything was possible.

CHAPTER NINE

Smugglers

JIMMY STUDIED THE DERELICT appearance of Carlos's abode as he turned off the engine. Most of the people he knew back in Rio could buy this place for less than they spent on a single party. But Carlos wasn't like his other friends. His American father had been a Catholic missionary who originally came to the Amazon to convert the Yanomami to Christianity. Instead of growing the church ranks, he fell in love with an Yanomami woman, Carlos's mother, an emotional accident that turned his life inside out. He abandoned his religious crusade, left the priesthood, got married, and became an anthropologist. As a result, Carlos had grown up with one foot in the jungle, the other in town. During the school year, the family had lived in Boa Vista. Holidays they spent with his mother's tribe in the forest.

"Brought you some beer," said Jimmy, brandishing two large bottles of Antarctica. They stepped into the house, Carlos leaving the front door open for cross-ventilation. The smell of citronella candles permeated the two-room shack, the only thing staving off a full-scale mosquito invasion. Jimmy knew the citronella was mostly for his benefit. Carlos seemed immune to the insects. Inside, Jimmy examined the walls, which Carlos had plastered with detailed maps. "You've been working hard," he said.

"Making progress." Carlos was obsessed with mapping the landscape around Boa Vista, in particular the area where his mother's tribe lived.

"This is the land mass in rainy season." Carlos indicated a line on one of the maps. "And this is the same mass in the dry months."

"You could make a fortune if you sold these to Google."

"Like we need to make it easier for Westerners to navigate the jungle."

"What are they for, then?"

Carlos hesitated, as if unsure of how much he wanted to share. "See this bend in the river here?" He pointed to a spot on the map. "It's where I was born. This area over here is where my mother and father first met. His heart melted when she emerged from the river stark naked after a bath."

"You still miss them, don't you?" Jimmy asked.

"No closure," Carlos said, his voice getting hoarse. "Tough." Carlos's parents had been murdered a few years earlier under suspicious circumstances. He thought it was retaliation for their work to carve out a larger Yanomami territory north of the city. The area was teeming with illegal gold miners who didn't want to come under the microscope of the feds. No one was ever brought to trial for their killing. As one of the few people in the world who spoke fluent English, Portuguese, and Yanomami, Carlos managed to get by, barely, on his own by providing logistical support to visiting journalists. Fixing up old cars provided him with a little extra income.

"Do you still get back to see your tribe?" Jimmy asked.

"I'll go at the end of the year. They're building a new *shabono* right now. Had to move when Souza burned down the forest near their old village."

"Tough. How about that beer?" Jimmy asked. Carlos opened a bottle and split its contents evenly between two glasses, which Jimmy recognized as emptied-out containers from Brazilian cream cheese.

"She's gorgeous," said Carlos, handing a glass to his friend.

"Who?"

"You know who I'm talking about."

"She's not my type."

"Yeah, right."

"Even if she were, I don't want to get involved with anyone right now. I need to focus on my photography."

"So maybe I should give her a call. See if she wants to go out."

"If you do, I'll break every bone in your body."

Carlos laughed and held up his hands in surrender.

"You think Souza killed Milton?" asked Jimmy, changing the subject.

"He tops most people's list of suspects, I guess. It wasn't exactly a secret that Souza was sending Milton death threats. He was bent out of shape when Milton reported him to the feds for the illegal pesticides. I'm not sure, though. I mean, after the murder, he went kind of quiet. Why brag for months about how he was going to kill Milton, and then all of a sudden, when Milton's dead, disappear from the radar?"

"Maybe because the Environment Minister and a whole bunch of journalists showed up in town. He probably didn't know it would be that big of a deal to the outside world. The local police may be on his side, but his bribes probably aren't big enough to sway the guys in Brasilia."

"Could be. But I think it's someone else. Things got really hot here after you left in January. Rita told me her dad was really worried about Milton the last few weeks."

"Wasn't Ronaldo always worried about Milton?"

"He was more worried than usual. A few months ago, Sam Yanomami's ten-year-old son got caught in the snare of poacher's trap. Almost lost his leg. Wildlife smuggling's big money these days. Can be more profitable than drugs. A hundred thousand dollars for a parrot."

"Hard to believe there's that much money in pets."

"It's not just pets. There's also big demand for dead body parts. Some people think if they swallow a jaguar penis, they'll start looking like Superman and be able to have sex twenty times a day. People say we Indians are superstitious, but man, we're not that crazy."

"What's it got to do with Milton?"

"Rita used to hear Ronaldo and Milton talk over card games. For months, they had been discussing a wildlife smuggling ring that was causing a lot of trouble for the Yanomami. Right before the murder, Milton bragged that he was about to bust it open."

"So you think it was smugglers?"

"Could be. Problem is, there are just too many people who had reason to kill Milton."

"What happened to the smugglers?"

"Still out there. My tribe tells me they move camp every few weeks to avoid detection."

"No idea who's involved?"

"Rita said one name came up a lot in connection with the smuggling operation. Amoeba."

"Amoeba? What kind of name is that?"

"There's only one guy with that name, as far as I know. He's a pilot. Pilots are essential to any smuggling operation. They need someone to fly the animals out of the jungle, whether they're dead or alive."

"Transporting a jaguar could make for a pretty dangerous plane ride. Why not just stick to drugs?"

"The feds have cracked down on the drug trade lately, so people are looking for alternative sources of income. Anyway, it's just what I heard. People in Boa Vista like to talk. And what they say is as reliable as a white guy's promise to an Yanomami Indian."

CHAPTER TEN

Goal

"*Goooool!*" screamed the sports announcer on the large-screen television, stretching out the word until he ran out of breath. Three minutes to go in the soccer game and Brazil had sneaked the ball over the Argentinian goalie's head and into the net. Communal rays of joy emanated from the screen into Ronaldo's living room, causing everyone to jump up and down, shouting. Even Emma, who just days earlier couldn't have cared less who won the match, was caught up in the moment. Rita's pet monkey raced along the back of the sofa, screeching. Carlos lifted Emma up and swung her around. Emma glanced in Jimmy's direction, hoping his friend's attention to her might spark a reaction. But Jimmy was too busy embracing Rita in a celebratory hug that, in Emma's opinion, lasted a few seconds too long.

Except for the Yanomami photos Jimmy had emailed Emma, without comment, for her blog entry, they hadn't communicated since viewing the pictures in his hotel room the day before. They had arrived at Ronaldo's in separate vehicles. Mike and Emma came in the Fiat. Jimmy got a lift to the party with Carlos, who was now driving a Ford Escort even more run-down than his other car.

"*Gol! Gol!*" chanted Iara's toddlers. The score was four-two. Argentina would need a miracle just to tie the game. After a brief celebration on the field, the players resumed their positions and the guests fell silent, anxiously watching the television clock mark the final minutes, then seconds of the game. To everyone's relief, miracles were in short supply, and the game finished in triumph. The Argentinian players publicly pouted while the Brazilians danced on the field.

Elated, Carlos pulled the tab off a can of Brahma beer and topped off Ronaldo's glass. A smiling Rita, Charlotte perched on her shoulder, brewed a fresh batch of *caipirinhas*, a potent cocktail made of vodka, limes, and sugar. Emma and Iara were the only two adults present who hadn't indulged, Emma because she didn't like the sweet-and-sour taste and Iara because she didn't touch alcohol. "Probably saw too many lives destroyed by drinking," Mike had explained on the way over. "Alcoholism is always a risk for indigenous people. No genetic resistance to the stuff, and Iara is part Indian."

Everyone Emma knew in Boa Vista was at the party. Getting them together for the match had been Rita's idea. She thought it would provide a distraction from Milton's death, and at least temporarily, it had accomplished that. The Brazilian victory lifted even Ronaldo's spirits. Game over, conversation flowed at a higher decibel level until Ronaldo broke in with an announcement.

"*Iara quer falar umas palavras*—Iara wants to say something," Ronaldo translated for Emma's sake. All eyes turned to the attractive young widow, who took the place of honor in front of the now dark television. Iara began to speak, softly at first, then warming to her subject, her voice rising and falling with an appealing cadence. In the space of a few minutes, the feeling in her voice ran the emotional gamut from hesitant to rousing. The guests gave Iara their full attention as they hung on her every word. Even Emma, who couldn't understand much of the speech, could see that Iara held her small audience in the palm of her hand. Astonished by Iara's charisma, Emma felt as if she were in the presence of a great politician delivering a speech. When Milton's widow finished speaking, the room burst into spontaneous applause.

"She wants us to keep Milton's memory alive, make sure the world doesn't forget him," said a voice in Emma's ear as everyone clapped. Her heart raced as she felt Jimmy's breath on her cheek.

"I thought you weren't talking to me," Emma said.

"Because you bolted? I'm not that desperate." Jimmy sipped his beer. He had shed his customary T-shirt in favor of a short-sleeve button-down, and he looked elegantly handsome in the spiffed up garb. "It's too bad you're not sticking around Boa Vista. I thought we made a good team. We'd be doing Iara a big favor if we could point the finger at who killed her husband. And between the two of us, we might be able to do it. Rooting out Milton's murderer wouldn't hurt our careers, either. Front page for sure, plus television interviews."

He was painting an appealing, if unrealistic picture, and Emma wasn't in the mood to burst his bubble. "I'm sticking around for a few more weeks at least," she said. "What were you planning to do?"

Jimmy frowned. "Mike told me you were flying out tomorrow."

"Dad's decided to stay in Boa Vista a while longer to research a book on Milton. Aren't you doing the pics?"

"I know Mike's staying, but he said *you* were heading back to New York."

"You heard wrong." Emma tried to ignore the worm of doubt wriggling in her stomach.

Jimmy shrugged. "I'm going to take Iara and her boys back home," he said. "Everyone's nervous about them getting back in the dark by themselves. I'll catch a ride back to the *Itamaraty* with Carlos." Around them, the party was breaking up and guests were saying their good-byes. "Ask Mike about it," Jimmy said in a low voice as he turned away.

Emma thanked Rita and Ronaldo for their hospitality, trying to mask her eagerness to talk to her father. She had to find out if there was any truth to what Jimmy had said.

"Say goodbye, Charlotte," Rita said to her pet. The monkey obediently held up a hand in farewell.

"That monkey will be *really* useful when you teach it to mix *caipirinhas*," Mike said.

"Come on, Dad," said Emma, pulling on her father's arm. Together, father and daughter stepped into the Amazon night as a chorus of frogs belted out a song. Even the jungle, it seemed, was celebrating Brazil's soccer win.

"Great party!" Mike said. He swayed to the right and almost toppled over before catching his balance.

"Looks like you've been a little too enthusiastic about the *caipirinhas*," Emma said. "I think you'd better give me the car keys." She expected him to challenge her, but to her surprise, he reached into his pocket and threw her the keys without protest. Mike slumped into the passenger seat of the Fiat as Emma turned on the ignition and engaged the gears.

"Let me know when we're back at the hotel," Mike yawned as he closed his eyes.

"Oh no," said Emma, pressing her dad's shoulder in an effort to get him to sit up. "You're not going to sleep until you tell me what's going on," Emma said.

"With what?" Mike slurred.

"Are you planning to put me on the plane to New York City tomorrow or aren't you?"

Mike stirred uncomfortably. "Who told you?"

"Jimmy."

"Master of discretion."

"Maybe he thought I should know which country I'm going to be in day after tomorrow. How could you do something like that? Without even telling me?"

"I thought you'd be mad at me, so it was better to let you know at the last minute. Less trouble that way."

"For you anyway!" Emma's voice rose. "Of course I'm mad. You promised me this internship!"

"Plans change."

"I've been doing some good work. My blog post on the Yanomami got dozens of comments. I bet you didn't even read it."

"Read it. Fluff. Loincloths and insect sandwiches. You didn't say a word about what's really happening to the indigenous tribes here, how the miners are poisoning their water supplies with mercury and making them sick with malaria and other diseases that were completely unknown to them before Westerners showed up. That's the story that needs to get out. Not what you wrote." Mike's words stung.

"Whatever you say, I'm not going back to New York!" Emma snapped. "Not yet! I can't go back there right now."

"Because of what happened with Tony?"

Emma drew in her breath. "You knew?"

"I read the papers. I'm a journalist for God's sake. Why do you think I invited you down?"

Emma shifted to a higher gear and pressed her foot on the accelerator. "You haven't heard my side of the story."

"Spare me the details. I can imagine. I worked the Metro desk with Tony years ago on the *New York Times*. I know what he's like."

"So why send me back?"

"I don't have much choice. You're racking up quite a hotel bill, in case you haven't noticed. The *Itamaraty* isn't *that* cheap, and the *Guardian's* refusing to foot the bill. Raquel doesn't want you in Rio either."

"Isn't Jimmy staying?"

"His dad is paying his hotel bill. Anyway, his photos are actually useful."

"So put me to work! I can help with the research."

"You don't even speak Portuguese!"

"I'm learning. I can already understand a little. You—" In the rearview mirror, Emma glimpsed the bright lights of a vehicle slamming toward them. She put her foot on the gas, but the lights were approaching at an alarming speed. The road was too narrow to allow her to pull to the side. Her heart in her throat, she floored it, trying to avoid a rear end collision. The pick-up truck behind stayed on her tail.

Whooping shouts filled the air, the sound of a group with too much drink and testosterone in them. Emma spotted the outlines of a dozen or so men in the rear of the truck as they egged the driver on. They were going much too fast, and it was all Emma could do to keep the car on the path. Although the road was straight, ruts and potholes threw the Fiat about as if they were on an amusement park ride. Emma struggled to keep control of the car. No matter how hard she pressed on the accelerator, the truck pursued them.

When the pick-up bumped against the rear of the Fiat, fear coursed through her. The truck's blinding high beams flashed in warning, telling her to get out of the way. But there was nowhere to go. Emma knew it was a matter of time before the truck ran them through. She glanced at her father, who was as white as paper. Emma focused on keeping as close to the edge of the road as possible without colliding into the trees. And still the truck bore down.

The Fiat shook violently, throwing Emma's hands off the steering wheel. The driver behind them leaned on his horn as Emma tried to regain control. The pick-up truck bumped them from behind once again. Emma fought the instinct to slam on the brakes. If she did, the truck would decapitate the Fiat, slicing its occupants in two. Just as Emma thought she would break under the pressure, the road abruptly widened. Emma took advantage of the extra girth to swerve to the right. To her relief, the truck sped past them on the left, the men in the back making obscene gestures as they passed.

Emma slowed to a crawl, her hands trembling. She glanced sideways at her dad in the passenger seat. He was sitting upright, more alert than his drunken state warranted. "Shit!" he swore.

"You never answered my question," Emma said.

"What question?"

"Can I stay?"

"Okay, yes—you convinced me just now that you're up to more than I gave you credit for," said Mike. "I'll cancel your flight tomorrow."

"And include me in your research?"

"Yeah, sure. Maybe you inherited more of my journalistic balls than I thought."

CHAPTER ELEVEN

Cell Phone

EMMA TURNED THE AIR conditioner on full blast and flung herself on the bed, her emotions bouncing hysterically between relief and anger. *I don't have to go back to New York, not yet,* she thought. New York—it was galling to think that her home had become a place that she had to avoid. It was all Horowitz's fault.

Her mind returned to the moment, almost a year ago, when she heard that she had been accepted to the seminar course taught by the famous Tony Horowitz. Every student at NYU was dying to take a course with one of the biggest legends in the business. Horowitz was known for being in the right place at the right time. He had snagged an interview with Saddam Hussein right before the bombs began to fall on Baghdad and published an account of the drunken weekend he had spent with Boris Yeltsin. At first, Emma was thrilled to be taking a course with a star professor. The readings and classroom discussions were stimulating. Emma worked hard on her first paper, in the style of a magazine feature. Her subject was homeless kids being forced to spend the holidays in a New York City shelter. It was well-trodden journalistic territory, but Emma had added a fresh angle. She wrote what she thought was a heart-wrenching piece about a little girl whose one Christmas present, a Barbie doll, was stolen from her bed in the middle of the night. Emma had expected an A, a B-plus at worst, and was horrified to see her work returned a week later with a C-minus at the top and a hand-scrawled note—*See me in my office.*

Emma was a volatile cocktail of anger, humiliation, and nervousness when she arrived at Horowitz's office. Prepared to argue her case for a higher grade, she had made an extra effort with her appearance, selecting a herringbone pencil skirt, a sweater, and knee high boots in an attempt to look as professional as possible. Horowitz greeted her with a smile and politely offered to take her coat as he shut the door behind her.

"Sit down, sit down," Horowitz urged. Emma sank into an armchair across from his desk. "So we're here to talk about your work."

"There weren't any actual comments on my paper. I was hoping you could just go through it with me and tell me what the issues are."

"Could I see it again?"

Emma rummaged in her bag and pulled it out.

"I remember now," Tony said, glancing down at the first page. "You write okay. What you need is a better nose." *Nose,* in journalist lingo, meant the first few sentences. "Not newsy enough."

"But—it wasn't a news piece," Emma objected, striving to maintain a polite tone. "It was a feature, so I thought I'd start with an anecdote. That's how Professor Leal taught us to do it. And actually, she thought I was pretty good at it." At that moment, Emma's iPhone rang out a tune. Embarrassed by the interruption, she reached inside her purse and pulled it out, silencing the device. "Sorry," she muttered.

"If you need to take a call—"

"No. Nothing important."

"So back to your paper." Horowitz leaned back in his chair and looked across his oak desk at her, a superior expression on his face. He had the confidence of someone used to being in the limelight. So what if he was now well past middle age, thickening around the middle, and fighting a receding hairline. Horowitz was a power broker, and he knew it. "It's simple," he said. "Some people have a talent for the news business. Others don't. You may fall into that latter category."

Emma felt the anger rise up like bile inside her. It was one thing to criticize her paper; it was another to tell her that she had no talent. *How dare he?* She struggled to keep her voice under control. "I'd really appreciate it if you'd just take me through the points, one by one."

Horowitz laughed, leaned forward, and stood up. He walked around the desk and looked down at Emma, seated in the chair in front of him. His tone changed suddenly. "You know," he said huskily, "there is another way. An easier way. If you have other talents, you could make up for a weak writing style."

Emma was growing uneasy. "What do you mean?"

Horowitz reached out, put his hand under her chin, and lifted it up. "The only Jewish thing about your looks is your hair," he said, studying her. Then he leaned down. Emma didn't realize his intentions until his tongue was fully inside her mouth. He tasted of mouthwash that couldn't quite overcome the sourness of his stale breath. Her stomach did a turn as she struggled to push him away. He straightened up, and Emma expected him to back off. Instead, his hands encircled her head and pulled it towards his crotch. Her nose and mouth were shoved against a hard lump that she realized with a sense of revulsion was Horowitz's penis. Emma tried to stand up, but as she stumbled out of the chair, Horowitz shoved her down to the floor. The breath was knocked out of her as her back hit the thinly carpeted floor. Horowitz's weight was fully on top of her, one hand pinning her down as the other searched wildly for the bottom edge of her skirt. He found it and pushed his hand up hard into her crotch. Emma fought to get her bearings. Her left arm was held in his vice-like grip. Her right hand still gripped the phone she had silenced moments before. Horowitz's fingers discovered the upper lining of her tights, and he tugged at them, determined to lay claim to what was beneath. *This is it,* Emma thought. *I'm going to be raped right here.*

She acted out of pure instinct, overcome by anger, hatred, and fear. Something snapped inside her, and she panicked. Emma raised her iPhone slammed it on Horowitz's temple with all her might. His weight lifted off her, but fear still flooded her body. Emma stood up, pounding unrelentingly at the monster before her. Horowitz screamed as he backed away, but Emma kept at him, hitting his head with the sharp metal edge of her phone over and over. Emma didn't see the door opening behind her, didn't notice Horowitz's assistant entering the room and calling out for help. It took three people to pull her off. By that time Horowitz's face was a bloody mess and Emma's life had changed forever.

CHAPTER TWELVE

Amoeba

"Eight hundred dollars. That's my price." Amoeba—Emma still had
a hard time believing someone would actually call himself that, but
there it was—leaned back in the white plastic chair.

"Too much," said Mike. They were seated at an outdoor snack bar by
the Rio Branco, the White River. Rivers in Brazil were often named for
their color, which they acquired from the sediments they carried—a
piece of information Emma had picked up in her research. The Rio
Branco had a milky appearance. The river was crowded with motor-
boats and sailboats. A lazy Saturday afternoon, and a good portion of
the city was here. That wasn't surprising. People in Boa Vista wanted
to have fun, like everyone else in the world, and there wasn't a lot to
do around town.

Emma sipped her *Guaraná* and picked up a french fry. In Brazil,
Guaraná was more popular than Coke or Pepsi. Emma thought it was
an appropriate drink for the rainforest, since the guarana berry that
flavored the beverage came from the Amazon. According to folklore,
it gave the person who consumed it a sense of well-being. *There might
be something to it,* Emma thought. *Ronaldo could make a lot of money if
he discovered a plant like this.* Whether from the guarana or her state
of mind, Emma was feeling good. Mike had promised to give her a
chance, and so far, he had been true to his word. Emma was helping
to gather information for Mike's book and had even been recognized
in print as a contributor to a *Guardian* piece on how Boa Vista had
resumed its usual routine after Milton's murder. And it looked like

they might finally get out to the real jungle. The *Guardian* wanted a story on how the Yanomami's lives were being impacted by the environmental changes around Boa Vista. But getting out to Indian territory was a challenge. Amoeba was one of the few pilots in town willing to hire himself out, for a price. The only thing that bothered Emma about the meeting was Jimmy's reaction to it. He had seemed surprised, and none too pleased, at the mention of Amoeba's name. Emma meant to ask him about it later if she got a chance. Out of habit, Emma checked her cell phone while Mike haggled over the price. No reception.

"For eight hundred, I'm doing you a favor," Amoeba repeated. *His nickname couldn't be more appropriate,* Emma thought. The pilot had a disturbingly changeable appearance, as if you couldn't count on his facial parts being in the same place if you looked away for a moment. He smoked incessantly and had a nervous way of tapping his cigarette on the ashtray every few seconds. His chosen brand was Derby, Emma noted, a detail that probably meant very little. Jimmy's estimate, that half the city smoked the brand, turned out to be only a slight exaggeration. Emma had noticed dozens of people smoking Derby.

"Come on, Amoeba," Mike said cajolingly to the pilot. "I know you think we Americans are rich, but I just don't have that kind of money."

"I don't need the business. Other people will pay much more," Amoeba said in his squeaky voice, the end of his mouth twitching as if it wasn't sure exactly where it belonged on the pilot's face. Emma didn't doubt that Amoeba could get more money elsewhere. Her research on private pilots in the Amazon had not painted an appetizing picture. Most of them were hired to transport drugs out of the country and could name their price for services.

"Five hundred," Mike offered.

Amoeba tapped his cigarette and stayed silent for a minute, considering. *In the States,* Emma thought, *you'd have to pay someone to get in a plane with that guy at the controls.* But as Mike had told her, there weren't a lot of private pilots around Boa Vista willing to work for foreign journalists, who were seen as the enemy to development.

Amoeba's own country of origin was a mystery. Emma's best guess was that he was from Holland or Belgium. In any case, his English was excellent.

"Six hundred." Amoeba stubbed out his cigarette in a sign that this was his final offer. "You're robbing me, you American bastard!"

"Okay, six hundred," Mike agreed with a sigh. "Tomorrow morning at the airfield? Seven o'clock?"

Amoeba nodded and stood up. Now that the negotiation was concluded, he didn't seem inclined to stick around to socialize.

"Just wait until I try to put this on my expense report at the *Guardian*," Mike muttered as Amoeba slithered away. "And I won't even get a receipt!"

Emma didn't answer. She was watching the entrance of the cafe. "Isn't that Braga?" she asked. The Environment Minister's out of place elegance, which she had seen in full display at Milton's funeral, was hard to miss. He was the only person in the crowd in a suit and tie.

Mike turned around, his eyes following Emma's gaze. "Yeah, you're right. I wonder what he's still doing in town. If I'd known he was still here, I'd have asked for an interview. Got a lot to answer for, as far as I'm concerned. Between the poachers and miners, it's like an ecological free-for-all around here." Mike turned his attention back to his beer. But Emma's gaze lingered on Braga. Amoeba passed him on his way out. They almost imperceptibly exchanged glances and nodded.

"Looks like Braga and Amoeba know each other," Emma commented.

"Unlikely," said Mike, as he scribbled some numbers on a napkin. "Braga's a top government official. He's got all the military planes he wants at his disposal. Doesn't need a private pilot."

"*Journalistas e estrangeiros não são bemvindos aqui.*" The harsh words cut through the thick air. Emma looked up to see a man towering over their table and glaring at Mike. His eyes were filled with anger as he spat the words. Just short of middle age, he had a long, curling mustache and a cowboy hat. He was extremely thin, and his face was lined. He looked like a comic strip version of a Wild West cowboy. In New York, Emma might have laughed him off as crazy, but here the man's threats felt menacing.

"Souza," Mike said. *So this is Souza,* Emma thought as her gaze dropped from the man's face to the gun secured in a belt around his waist. The comparison with a Wild West cowboy suddenly seemed a little too fitting.

"Dad," Emma began. "Maybe we should go." The customers at the table next to them were hurriedly getting up to leave. But Mike stayed seated, staring defiantly at Souza. His silence seemed more insulting than any response would have been. At least, that was how the cowboy interpreted it. His hand moved toward the gun. Emma inhaled sharply. *I could turn over the table,* she thought quickly. *That might distract him for a few seconds.*

A shout came from a nearby table, and the cowboy looked away. She heard the name "Braga." Emma turned and observed the Environment Minister lingering outside of the café's entrance, observing the incident. He was staring at the cowboy in the way a teacher would look at a student misbehaving in class. The cowboy frowned as if weighing his options. He started to turn away, and Emma breathed out in relief. Then, a split second later, he pulled out his gun, aiming it at Mike. Emma heard a familiar crack split the air. The bottom fell out of her heart, and she looked toward Mike, expecting to see her father collapsed and bleeding. But he sat calmly in his chair. Behind him, a palm tree was now dimpled with a bullet hole. Having let out his frustration, Souza put the gun back in his holster and stepped towards the exit.

Mike shouted after him, "*Como 'ce matou o Milton, Souza?*"

Souza turned and looked Mike in the eyes. His hand rested on the holster. Emma sucked in her breath again. Then, unexpectedly, Souza smiled. "*O unico problema com Milton é que ele viveu tanto tempo,*" he responded. All eyes upon him, he headed to a pick-up truck parked by the bar. He got in, slammed the door shut, and peeled off, disappearing in a cloud of red dust.

"That was Souza?" Emma asked in a shaky voice.

Mike nodded. "Said we foreigners should mind our own business and get out of town. Someone pointed out that it probably wasn't a good time to attack a foreign journalist with a government minister present. I asked him how he killed Milton."

"And what did he say?"

Mike looked down into his beer. "He said the only problem with Milton Silva was that he lived so long."

CHAPTER THIRTEEN

Parachute

EMMA HUGGED HER KNEES to her chest and peered out the small oval window of the airplane. Somehow, this was not what she had expected from the six hundred dollar flight her father had negotiated with Amoeba. There were no safety belts or even seats, except for the pilot's. Emma crouched in the back with Mike and Jimmy. It felt like they were in the trunk of a station wagon, except it was a lot darker. This was a cargo plane, Amoeba reminded Jimmy when he questioned the seating arrangements, built to carry stuff, not people.

The plane was at the back end of a dirt runway, nowhere near Boa Vista's International Airport. Eight fifteen in the morning and they were poised for takeoff. The weather outside was warm, but not yet hot. Still, it was stuffy in the cargo area. A bead of sweat trickled down Emma's forehead as she fought off a growing sense of claustrophobia. In front, Amoeba, sporting a pair of Dolce & Gabbana designer sunglasses, was madly flicking switches. Unperturbed by the "No Smoking" sign partially peeling off the control panel, he clenched a lit cigarette between his teeth. At last, the engine sputtered to a start, and a few seconds later, the propellers on the side of the craft began to spin. Emma braced herself for movement, but the airplane stood still. Instead, a loud choking sound was followed by an ominous silence. The engine had stopped. The propellers slowed down. Mike looked uneasy, but said nothing. From the front, Amoeba let out a storm of oaths. The pilot opened the plane door and jumped down, tossing the stub of his cigarette onto the ground.

"José!" he called to a short, grease-spattered man standing by a hut just off the runway. José sauntered over. The two men exchanged information, and the mechanic opened up a front section of the plane and began tinkering with the engine.

"Well, this is confidence-inspiring!" Emma remarked.

Mike scribbled notes while Jimmy unscrewed the lens of his camera, fishing in his bag for a replacement. He was uncharacteristically nervous and hadn't been acting like himself all morning. He seemed preoccupied, fidgety. Outside, the sun shone brilliantly. Emma had grown used to the predictable pattern of weather here. In the morning, the skies were usually clear. A few hours later, some puffy clouds started to pop up. By afternoon, they had gained a stacked appearance. Eventually, they turned gray and the downpours would begin. The rain never lasted long, though, before the skies cleared again, the steam rising from the newly dampened red earth.

After a few minutes, the mechanic closed the lid. "That didn't take long," Emma said. "Good sign or bad?"

"I'm not sure anything's a good sign with Amoeba at the controls," Jimmy answered.

"It's not like we had our choice of airlines," Mike said. "No Expedia for this trip."

Amoeba climbed back into the pilot seat and began flipping switches again. The propellers started spinning once more. This time, the airplane lurched forward and lumbered down the bumpy runway, quickly gaining momentum. They were going fast, but not fast enough for takeoff. *We're going to crash into the trees!* Emma thought. At the last moment, though, the craft lifted, straining to climb higher. Emma jumped as she heard a loud scratching noise under the floor. She realized the airplane belly had scraped the tops of the trees near the runway.

Despite the rough takeoff, they were on their way. Emma peered out the window again. The scrubby landscape below gave way to increasingly dense tree cover. The trees were close, too close for comfort. She was relieved when the plane lifted higher. The engine was too loud for casual conversation. The craft tilted wildly, throwing Emma into the hard metal of the side of the cargo section. She tried to convince herself that this was just a normal, average trip out to the rainforest. There must be hundreds of flights like this every day, she told herself, or dozens anyway. Jimmy screwed a new lens on his camera.

Then, suddenly, the noise from the engine ceased. Emma breathed a sigh of relief at the renewed quiet. *The airplane must be running better now,* she thought. She was unprepared for what happened next. Amoeba clapped his open right hand down onto his left fist a few times. Emma recognized the Brazilian gesture, and the implication was not comforting: something had gone terribly wrong. Somehow, the pilot's silence was more disturbing than the earlier string of curses. One look at the frightened expressions on Jimmy's and Mike's faces told her that they were in trouble.

"The engine stopped," Jimmy said thinly. Amoeba began frantically flipping switches. "*Puta!*" he swore, grabbing the stick control and pushing it hard. The plane swerved sharply to the left. "We'll have to head back to the air field."

"Without an engine?" Emma asked, her voice rising nervously.

"We'll make it," Mike said. But from his demeanor, it was clear he was not convinced. Emma looked out the window. They were slowly but surely losing altitude, getting closer to the tops of the trees below. Ahead lay the desolate landscape they had flown over minutes before.

Amoeba reached toward a metal box next to the pilot's seat and flipped it open, pulling out something that resembled a backpack. With horror, Emma realized that it was a parachute. Amoeba was going to bail.

CHAPTER FOURTEEN

Feather

"PUT THAT PARACHUTE ON and I'll blow your brains out." Jimmy pressed the metal edge of his camera lens to the pilot's neck. Amoeba obviously believed it was a gun, because he dropped the parachute on the floor of the plane and held his hands up, staring straight ahead. "Take this thing in for a landing," Jimmy ordered. "Now!"

"I can't make it to the runway!" Amoeba protested. "We'll all die!"

"Then you'll die with us," Jimmy said. "Pilot this fucking thing!"

"I have to pitch the nose up to stop the propellers," Amoeba said. "It's creating too much drag."

"Do it!"

The plane's nose turned up and the propellers on either side stopped spinning. Still, the aircraft continued to lose altitude. For what seemed like an eternity, they floated quietly through the air. Mike reached out and put his arm around Emma, hugging her close, his bad hand draped on her shoulder.

"We'll make it," he said, trying to convince them both. It was deathly still. *Strange that disaster can be preceded by moments of complete calm*, Emma thought. Jimmy kept the camera lens trained on Amoeba's neck. With no chance of escape, the pilot was doing his best to steer them in for a landing. Emma tried to prepare herself mentally for a crash. *I should say something—tell Dad I love him*, Emma thought. *Aren't people supposed to say stuff like that when they're facing death?* But somehow, she couldn't string the words together. The plane tilted, giving Emma full view of the ground, which was even closer than she had feared. She shut her eyes to block the vision as the plane continued to descend.

They hit the ground with an impact that shot up Emma's spine. She continued to hug her knees, bracing for an encounter with a tree. Miraculously, the crash didn't happen. Instead, the plane screeched to a halt, sending their bags to the far end of the craft and forcing the passengers to steady themselves with their hands to keep from toppling over.

Amoeba turned around. "Fuck you, man!" he screamed, shoving Jimmy's camera out of the way as he realized he'd been tricked.

Mike lifted the door of the aircraft, grabbed his bag, and jumped out. Jimmy and Emma followed as Amoeba lashed them with curses. Emma was a tumult of nerves as she followed Jimmy off the airfield. Mike stayed behind, yelling at Amoeba in Portuguese.

"Thank you," Emma said in a small voice as they reached the bench by the shack that constituted the airport's so-called terminal. Jimmy threw his bag on top of it and turned to face her. Then, unexpectedly, he took her in his arms and pulled her towards his chest. Emma breathed in his body wash smell and felt his hot skin beneath his thin T-shirt. She felt safe in Jimmy's arms. She wanted to stay in that position, but Jimmy grabbed her shoulders and pushed her back.

"I said you'd be safe with me," he said fiercely.

"I was."

"I should never have even let you get on that plane."

"Well we're here, right? We're okay."

Jimmy ran his hand through his hair. "If Amoeba hadn't believed that the camera lens was a gun—"

"But he did."

Emma glanced over Jimmy's shoulder toward the plane. Her father was still shouting at Amoeba, who turned pointedly away. José, the mechanic, approached them. Mike placed his hand on the pilot's shoulder, pulling him around to face him. He would have pounded Amoeba with his one good fist, Emma was sure, if José hadn't at that moment stepped in front of the pilot and shoved Mike away.

"Mike wants his money back," Jimmy said, "but our friend Amoeba refuses to give a refund."

"Leave it to Mike to think about money when we could easily have all died in an airplane accident. "

"If it *was* an accident."

"What do you mean?" Emma asked sharply.

"Carlos told me Amoeba is not the most kosher operator in Boa Vista. I mentioned it to Mike, but he had already paid him the money and refused to listen." Emma looked toward the pilot, for the first time wondering whether the engine failure had been on purpose. She was relieved when, with one last parting verbal shot at Amoeba, Mike turned and walked away from the plane.

———

Emma rolled down the passenger seat window of the old Fiat, impatient for motion and a breeze that would provide some relief from the extreme heat. She wanted to get away from the airfield as quickly as possible. Jimmy reached over to deposit his camera case at Emma's feet, his hand brushing against her knee. Emma was helpless to control the hyperawareness of his presence next to her. She wished he would hold her once again, that she could feel the comfort of his arms around her.

Putting a hand in the pocket of his shorts, Jimmy pulled out a small, bright blue feather and studied it for a moment.

"What's that?" Emma asked.

"Found it in the cargo section."

"It's pretty," Emma said. "Nice souvenir from a near-miss plane crash."

"The question is—what was it doing there?" Jimmy stuffed the feather back in his pocket and started the car. "A feather like this doesn't just float inside a plane. Listen, there's something I have to tell you. It has to do with Milton's murder. According to Rita, Milton was closing in on a wildlife smuggling ring right before he got killed. And Amoeba's name came up as a suspected member of the group."

"If you believe every rumor you hear about people in the Amazon, you'd never trust anyone," said Mike from the back seat.

"Carlos said certain kinds of parrots can get a hundred thousand bucks on the black market," Jimmy continued as he steered the car onto the road.

Emma frowned, staring distractedly at a scratch on the dashboard. "Even if Amoeba *was* involved in some smuggling operation, why would he want to kill us?"

"He may have heard we're looking into Milton's murder," Jimmy said. "Maybe Milton's killing was connected to the smuggling ring. And maybe Amoeba is part of the ring. He wants us out of the way."

"That's a lot of speculation," Mike said. "If Amoeba wanted us killed, he wouldn't crash his plane to do it. Those things cost a fortune. Cheaper to hire a hit man. The feather probably fell off some souvenir he was transporting." The Fiat covered the remaining distance to the *Itamaraty* in silence. Jimmy parked the car and they all got out. "I guess I should say thank you, Jimmy," Mike said awkwardly. Gratitude was clearly not something he was used to expressing. "Quick thinking on your part. Anyway, I'd better get some work done. Somehow I have to justify a six hundred dollar flight that never got off the ground." Mike strode away from them towards the hotel.

"We should show the feather to Carlos," said Jimmy, as he walked with Emma toward the lobby of the hotel. "He might know something about it."

Emma stopped and studied Jimmy's determined expression. "You're serious about this, aren't you?"

"Dead serious."

"Then go ahead and ask Carlos," said Emma. "But don't get too excited. Remember, it's just a feather. Maybe Amoeba flew someone's pet parrot to the vet."

"Wildlife smuggling is big money," Jimmy pressed his case. "A jaguar could fetch twenty thousand dollars."

"A parrot's worth more than a jaguar?"

"It's not the easiest thing in the world to catch a rare parrot."

"Wouldn't it be a little nerve-wracking to fly a plane with a bunch of wild animals in cages in the cargo section?" she asked.

Jimmy shrugged. "Something tells me there's not much that could make Amoeba more jittery than he already is."

CHAPTER FIFTEEN

Banana

"So we're on the same page," Emma said, turning in the passenger seat to face Jimmy. "We don't say anything else to Mike unless we have something solid to go on, right?"

It was late afternoon, and the heat of the day was dissipating. Vehicles in various states of repair reflected the rays of the mercifully weakening sun in the yard behind Carlos's house. A red pick-up truck sat under the lone tree.

"You know," Jimmy said, "I can do this on my own. You don't have to get involved."

"I *want* to get involved. This is what it's all about for me as a journalist. Getting the bad guys, making a difference. Otherwise what's the point? I'd have been better off going to business school."

"This stuff could get serious really quickly, that's all. I want you to know what you're getting involved with."

"You don't have to spell it out for me," Emma said. She didn't tell him her real concern—that his theory about the feather being connected to Milton's murder seemed flimsy. Still, the wildlife smuggling lead was intriguing by itself. Cracking something like that wouldn't get them on CNN, but it could make a large feature story in the *Guardian*. And there was another reason for going along with Jimmy—namely that she would get to spend more time with him.

Jimmy's eyebrows pulled together as he looked hard into Emma's eyes. It was as if he was trying to figure something out. A lock of his hair brushed his forehead, and Emma was overcome by the urge to push it out of the way. She forced Jay's warnings of compromising photographs out of her mind as she leaned toward Jimmy. Her hand tenderly lifted the strand back into place, fingers lingering on the silky softness of his temple. They were so close. Desire coursed through her. She desperately needed to feel his skin against hers. And then, his hands on her shoulders, Jimmy pushed her away. He got out of the car; she felt as if she had been abandoned. She watched, hypnotized by his movements, as he walked around to open the door on her side of the Fiat. He stretched out his open hand in invitation. *I get it,* Emma thought. *Just friends.* She put her palm in his, and he pulled her out of the car.

She immediately felt the tension in Jimmy's body as he reached behind her to shut the door of the Fiat. And then, it was as if something inside him snapped. He pushed toward her, his mouth drawn to hers. Waves of longing broke over Emma. She opened herself completely to Jimmy as his tongue sought her own. Emma's back was against the Fiat, and he was pressing against her. His body was as hard as his mouth was soft. She wanted him to cover every inch of her skin. Emma felt dizzy, but this time there was no flashback, simply raw desire.

And then something was on her shoulder, nails biting into her skin. Emma broke away. Out of the corner of her eye, she saw Rita, standing by the side of Carlos's house, and she realized that the thing on her shoulder was Charlotte.

"Sweet shot!" said Rita, looking down at her cell phone. "Straight to Instagram!" Emma realized that Rita had taken a picture of them with her cell phone, and the panic rose up in her as Jay's warnings flooded back.

"You need to ask me before you take a photo," Emma said, stepping towards Rita. "You have to delete that."

Rita, taken aback at the vehemence of Emma's reaction, instinctively pulled her hand away. In a split second, Charlotte had grabbed the phone out of Rita's elevated grasp and jumped to the roof of Carlos's shack. Emma lunged for the monkey, who screeched as though overcome with laughter. As Emma strained for the phone,

Charlotte moved just out of reach, looking down from her perch and chirruping happily.

"She thinks it's a game," Rita said.

"Well, it's not!" said Emma.

"I understand," Rita responded, annoyed. "I just thought it was a fun pic, but whatever you say. Charlotte, come!" But Charlotte was amusing herself too much to consider obeying her owner. The monkey jumped up and down, screeching. After a few minutes, during which Rita and Emma pleaded in vain for her to come down, Charlotte sat in the middle of the roof, examining the cell phone in her hands and pressing the screen with her tiny monkey fingers, obviously imitating an action she had seen Rita perform many times. *The photo's probably on Instagram by now,* Emma thought.

"Charlotte!" Everyone turned to see Carlos, who had emerged from his house holding a peeled banana in his hand. He walked toward Rita's pet, holding out the fruit. "You know you want it," he said to the spider monkey. "So come get it."

Charlotte hesitated only a moment before ditching the cell phone and jumping to Carlos's shoulder. He rewarded the animal with the banana as Rita scrambled for the phone, which tumbled to the ground.

Rita pressed some buttons and held out the screen to Emma. "A picture of you with Charlotte on your shoulder," she said. "I don't see the problem, but I'll delete it if you want." Emma was mortified. Jimmy did not even appear in the image that she had just made such a fuss over.

"No, it's fine," Emma said. "I just—"

"Gone!" Rita said, pressing a button. She put the cell phone in the pocket of her flowered skirt and pulled out a set of keys. "Wish I could stay for another beer, Carlos, but I need to get back home. Dad just sent me a text wondering where I've got to. I'll let you know how the truck runs!" Rita jingled her keys at Charlotte, who, having devoured the banana, scampered happily to her owner's shoulder. With a toss of her golden hair, Rita climbed into the driver's seat of the red pick-up. She beeped her horn lightly and waved before backing away.

Emma turned to see Carlos and Jimmy staring at her. *I must have looked like a crazy person,* she realized. She couldn't believe that she had once again blown her chance with Jimmy. She wanted to explain. But obviously this was not the moment to tell them how she had beaten up her famous professor and now had to avoid publicity.

"Let's get inside," Carlos suggested, opening the door.

Flies buzzed around two near-empty glasses of beer and a half-eaten plate of rice and beans on the kitchen table.

"You and Rita getting closer?" Jimmy asked, gesturing toward the remains of their shared meal.

"I wish. No, she just got her driver's license," said Carlos. "I sold her the red truck. Didn't make much of a profit on it, but whatever." He stepped toward the rust-tinged refrigerator, plastered with magnets holding up various bits of paper—telephone numbers, newspaper articles, and photos. Opening the door, Carlos removed the last remaining item, a large glass bottle of Antarctica, then grabbed two more glasses from the shelf and set them on the table. Tearing off the cap with a bottle opener, he carefully divided the yellow liquid between three small glass cups. Carlos waved his guests into the two plastic patio chairs while he remained standing. Emma sipped the beer, ice-cold and refreshing, the way Brazilians liked it. She needed the drink. The incident with Jimmy and Charlotte had left her a bundle of nerves. Jimmy took a plastic storage bag out of the pocket of his shorts and from it extracted the blue feather, laying it on the table. Carlos picked the feather up and twirled it between his fingertips.

"Where'd you get this?" he asked.

"The cargo section of Amoeba's plane."

"Oh yeah, weren't you going out to the jungle today?"

"We never made it," Jimmy said. "Engine trouble."

"To say the least," Emma added.

"Not surprising," Carlos said. "Given Amoeba's reputation."

"Do you have any idea what kind of bird that feather came from?" Jimmy asked.

"Could be a Hyacinth Macaw. It's got that intense blue color you get with that bird. I don't know for certain."

"But it's possible," said Jimmy.

"It's possible."

"How much could you get for a Hyacinth Macaw on the black market?"

"I don't know, a couple hundred thousand, probably. Maybe more. Why? Are you guys working on a story?"

"We're going to try to crack the wildlife smuggling operation you told me about," said Jimmy. "And maybe find out who murdered Milton Silva at the same time."

Carlos drew in his breath and put the feather down. "Are you serious? You could be getting in some serious shit, man."

"You know everyone," Emma pressed him. "How can we find out more?"

Carlos shook his head and held up his hands. "It's not worth it. Listen, why don't you guys do a piece on Yanomami shamans or something? I can put you in touch with my tribe. Would make a great photo spread."

"You *knew* Milton, didn't you?" Jimmy said.

"He was like a father to me after my own dad died," said Carlos in a quiet voice.

"Don't we owe it to him to follow up on something like this?" Jimmy asked.

For several minutes, Carlos appeared mired in his own thoughts. Then he stepped toward the refrigerator, lifting the magnet of a Brazilian flag to let a scrap of paper fall into his hand. "Do you remember that guy from the LA Times, Jimmy? He was here when you were in January. Called a couple of weeks ago. Said he was putting together an investigative piece on wildlife contraband. He had come across some operation in California that sold illegal pets. Pretended to be a buyer. They gave him a contact number for a source. He gave it to me—asked me to check it out."

"Did you?" Jimmy asked.

"For the money he was offering, it wasn't worth it," Carlos said. "But I kept the number." He solemnly handed the scrap of paper to Jimmy. "He said I should ask for *Papagaio*. That's their password. But if I were you, I'd take it easy. And maybe you should download my mapping app to your cell. That way if you get out of your league, at least I'll know where you are."

CHAPTER SIXTEEN

Malaria

THE ADOLESCENT GIRL STARED up at the ceiling with blank eyes, convulsed with shivers despite the heat pervading the makeshift hospital at the edge of Boa Vista. Her small, frail body was hooked up to an intravenous feed precariously connected to her violently shaking arm.

"She arrived yesterday," said Dr. Herzog, a tall German woman with cropped silver-studded hair and a severe jaw. The doctor tenderly threw an extra blanket over the shivering girl. "An advanced case. Her father carried her two days through the jungle to get her to us. I hope it's not too late."

"What's her name?" Emma asked, scribbling notes in her pad.

"Yanomami names are secret. We call her Beatriz." *Beatriz Yanomami*, Emma wrote. For lack of a better solution, Westerners had given the entire tribe of thirty-five thousand people the same surname.

Jimmy stopped taking photos for a moment to lay his hand on Beatriz's forehead. "Classic malarial symptoms," he observed. "Severe chills. In a few hours, her fever could spike out of control."

"That's when air conditioning would come in handy," said Dr. Herzog. "Or at least a bigger freezer for our ice packs."

Jimmy raised his camera and stepped back for a better angle. The visit to the hospital had been Emma's idea. An editor at the *Observer*, the Sunday sister publication to the *Guardian*, had tentatively agreed to run a piece she proposed on the Yanomami health crisis. Ever helpful, Carlos had put her in touch with Dr. Herzog. Jimmy had reluctantly agreed to do the photos. "I don't like hospitals," he had said to Emma.

"Malaria has become a bigger problem with the increased presence of gold miners in the area," said Dr. Herzog, sighing. "New malaria strains, and the Yanomami never had much genetic resistance. There was no malaria here until the Europeans arrived. Mimi!" she called to a passing nurse. "We need a refill on the intravenous!" Dr. Herzog led them away from the overpowering smell of antiseptic to another room. "Through here are our recovering patients. They will be released shortly." They entered a space packed with thirty or more patients, mostly children. The walls had just been painted white, but the fresh color was unable to camouflage the cracking plaster. In one corner, a bare-breasted, pre-pubescent girl swayed in a hammock and offered them a weak smile.

"Amelia," said Dr. Herzog. "She's still more lethargic than we'd like to see, but we'll be sending her back to her tribe tomorrow. I wish we could keep her longer, but our resources are so limited. We have to make room for new patients."

"How will she get back to her family?" Emma asked.

"On foot."

"How far does she have to go?"

"About three days. We'll send some food with her. Hopefully she'll have enough stamina to make it back."

A cluster of small children was grouped on a bench at the far end of the room, a few placing black beads on a string, others observing a giant black and purple beetle crawling along the rutted concrete floor. One boy poked at the insect with a stick, causing it to rise up on its hind legs in fighting position. They seemed tired and bored, longing to be anywhere but here. Jimmy approached the group and playfully stuck out his tongue to break the ice. One girl laughed, but the others paid no attention. Raising the stakes, Jimmy began to jump up and down like a monkey, screeching and showing his teeth. The Yanomami children giggled hysterically at his antics, a few imitating Jimmy's moves. Jimmy's camera clicked away. He then turned the small screen toward the group, showing them digital images of themselves. Enchanted, they begged him to take more.

"This one here—Silvio—was suffering from mercury poisoning," said the doctor, running her hand along the cheek of the smallest boy, who was laughing uncontrollably.

"Hence the hair loss," Jimmy said, lowering his camera and throwing the youth a sympathetic look.

"Yes. Another health problem the Yanomami didn't know before the Westerners arrived."

"And this little one?" Emma asked, roughing up the hair of a skinny boy of about eight whose leg was wrapped in bandages.

"That one we can't blame on the miners," said Dr. Herzog. "An arrow wound to the leg. Likely during an attack from one Yanomami village on a rival group."

"'The Fierce People,'" Emma said. "Isn't that what they're called?"

"That's controversial," said Jimmy. "The anthropologist who came up with that label was translating the Yanomami's name for themselves. Some people think they called themselves that for marketing purposes—you know, 'We're fierce, so stay away from us.'"

As Dr. Herzog told Emma about the clinic's financial troubles, Jimmy stepped toward a little boy sitting stone still on the floor. He reached out, cupping the boy's chin in his hand and lifting it up.

"Dr. Herzog," Jimmy said, his brow furrowing. "I think you need to take another look at this case."

"What is it?"

"Looks like jaundice to me."

The doctor squatted in front of the boy, one hand reaching to stretch out his eyelid for a closer examination. "You're right," she said. "Yellowing of the sclera. I hadn't noticed it earlier. Mimi!" The long-suffering Mimi—a stout, dark-haired woman with a round face and narrow eyes—stepped into the room. "This boy needs to be placed on intravenous immediately!" Mimi nodded, gently lifting the boy in her arms and carrying him back to the critical care room. Dr. Herzog turned to Jimmy. "Thank you. I hadn't caught it when I examined him earlier today. Sometimes I feel there are too many patients for me to look after properly. Hopefully Emma's article will help us attract funding."

"This girl here seems to need some cheering up," Emma said, stopping in front of a pre-adolescent girl sitting by herself in the only plastic chair available. The girl stared down at her hands as she rubbed her bare foot listlessly back and forth on the concrete floor.

"Soraia is angry with us," said the doctor. "When we evacuated her a week ago, we were planning to go back for her younger sister, who had also started to show signs of the disease. Our plane broke down, and we haven't been able to get back to the tribe. I'm worried about the situation there. If the FUNAI plane isn't fixed soon, I don't know what we'll do."

Soraia turned her gaze toward the visitors. In the Yanomami girl's eyes, Emma recognized an infinite sadness. Dr. Herzog pulled a banana out of the pocket of her scrubs and held it out, but Soraia shook her head and looked down once more at the floor.

"Can't someone else fetch her sister?" Emma asked.

Dr. Herzog shook her head. "We don't have the money to book private transportation," she said. "We just have to pray that the FUNAI plane will be fixed soon. Otherwise, we'll have to look for alternative care arrangements for Soraia as well. We can't keep her here with us if she's no longer ill."

"Where will she go?" Emma asked.

"A friend of mine, a local priest, runs an orphanage in town," said Dr. Herzog. "He might be able to take her for a while, though I'd hate to resort to that. Yanomami don't usually do well in those situations. It's so foreign to them. But if there's no other choice…"

They said their goodbyes, Emma promising to get Dr. Herzog a copy of her article after it was published. "Thank you for showing us around," she said, pressing the physician's hand.

"It's important to get word out about our work," said Dr. Herzog. "We rely on funding from people all around the world." She turned and shook hands with Jimmy next. "You should think about becoming a doctor yourself, you know. You're a natural."

Jimmy and Emma walked somberly to the Fiat. "It's hard to see all that suffering and not be affected by it," said Emma. "I feel so horrible for that girl, Soraia. Imagine being in a strange place, far away from your family, and not knowing if they are alright or when you might get back to see them."

"I don't know what anyone can do about it," said Jimmy. "The private pilots in town are not likely to offer her a lift for free." He opened the car door and rolled down the window as the heat rushed out. "A kid like Soraia takes up valuable cargo space, which they'd rather fill with drugs or other illegal goods."

"I wish we could do something. I mean, besides just writing an article. Did you get good pics?"

"I'm sure there are a few you can use."

"Thanks for helping me out. I know you didn't want to come."

"No problem." Jimmy shrugged.

"I don't understand why you said you hate hospitals, though. Dr. Herzog was right when she called you a natural. You were great with those patients!"

Jimmy turned to Emma with an irritated look. "Believe me, medicine is not my niche," he said as he nudged the Fiat into traffic.

"But you even diagnosed that little boy in there," Emma insisted. "If it hadn't been for you, he wouldn't have gotten the care he needed. Doesn't that make you feel good?"

"I'm not a doctor!" Jimmy snapped. He lifted his hands off the steering wheel and slammed them back down.

"But—"

"Listen, I'm a photographer. And I don't want to talk about this any more."

"I just don't understand."

"You don't need to understand. You just have to let it go."

CHAPTER SEVENTEEN

Soraia

"HI SLUGGER!"

"It's Emma, Jay. Just Emma."

"Okay, Emma," Jay said. "I'm calling with the latest update. I've suggested community service as punishment, but NYU's not buying into it."

"I love it when you wake me up with good news," Emma said, glancing at the digital clock on the nightstand. It was almost eleven. She hadn't planned to sleep in, but she had been up late working on the article for the *Observer*. "So that's it. I'm not going back to NYU."

"Nothing's final. I wouldn't give up hope just yet. I would just be prepared for bad news."

"Hope for the best. Expect the worst."

"Exactly."

"Easier said than done," Emma sighed. "Listen, have you done the leg work on those ex-students of his? Remember I sent you a list of names to contact."

Jay hesitated. "I've started on that. I'm expecting a call today from that woman—what's her name, Mary?"

"Really, Mary?"

"I think that's her name."

"Mary's off the grid in Malaysia, Jay."

"How do you know?"

"She texted me last week. You didn't call her did you? Or any of the other women whose names I gave you?"

"I haven't gotten around to it yet."

"Well, *do* it, goddamn it! What the hell are we paying you for?"

Emma clicked off the phone, fuming at Jay. If he wasn't going to do his job, she'd need to find another lawyer, although how she was supposed to do that from Boa Vista was beyond her. Emma climbed out of bed and grabbed her laptop, flipping it open and logging onto her email. She scrolled down the list of useless coupons and advertisements, pausing on a message from her mom, who was demanding to know more about safety issues in Boa Vista. *I'll answer that one later,* Emma thought. And then, she saw the reply she'd been waiting for. She remembered that the UK was several hours ahead of Boa Vista. The editors must have had a chance to look at her piece. Her heart pounding, she opened the email.

It took a moment for her to register the fact that she was not reading another rejection. They actually liked her story and expected to publish it sometime in the next few weeks. Emma couldn't believe it. For the first time in her life, she would have her own piece in a major newspaper. She would even get paid as a freelancer for her work, money she could use to foot her hotel bill at the *Itamaraty*. And yet, it didn't feel like a complete victory. Emma scanned the suggested layout of the article. A photograph of Soraia was to accompany the story, her big eyes staring out at a world that refused to help her. Something stirred inside Emma. She would finally get her byline out there, and maybe the story would inspire donors to give money to the Yanomami clinic. But what would Soraia get? For her, it might be too late.

"I got it!" Mike beamed when he ran into Emma in the lobby. "I finally got Braga to agree to an interview. I'm going to meet him early this afternoon at the federal offices downtown."

"Will the offices be open on Sunday?"

"They'll open up for the Environment Minister. He's agreed to talk about the miners' situation. Even if he doesn't say anything important, I can show that I've covered all the bases, got everyone's point of view."

"Do you need Jimmy for a pic?"

"No. The paper's got plenty of stock photos of Braga. But tell him I'd like a ride to the *Praça Cívica* around two."

"You can tell him yourself," Emma said as Jimmy, effortlessly gorgeous in a pair of khaki shorts and a close-fitting T-shirt, strode into the lobby. Since the moment he had kissed her outside Carlos's house, Emma found herself more drawn to him than ever. But Jimmy now seemed determined to keep their relationship platonic, which Emma couldn't blame him for after her semi-nuts behavior.

"They accepted the piece," Emma said to Jimmy as Mike walked away, having arranged for Jimmy to give him a ride. "They're running it with your pic of Soraia. Thanks for doing it. They'll send you a payment. Wish it could be more."

"Glad it was useful," Jimmy said. "Listen, I'm on my way to a pool party. Wanna come?"

"Would be nice to cool down," said Emma, lifting a sweaty lock from her forehead. "But I'm not in the mood for a party."

"Hard to get Soraia Yanomami off your mind?"

Emma nodded.

"Believe it or not, attending this party might be the best thing you can do for her."

"Will they be giving away airplanes for party favors?"

Jimmy grinned. "Next best thing."

"You're up to something. Okay, ready in five."

CHAPTER EIGHTEEN

Samba

EMMA'S CHEST THROBBED AS the samba band pumped out its urgent, circular one-two-three-four rhythm. A group of young dancers in dental-floss bikinis and abbreviated swim trunks swayed their hips erotically to the insistent beat. Emma envied their ease of movement. She pulled herself out of the pool and grabbed a fluffy white towel from a passing maid, shaking out her long, wavy hair. It was early afternoon, probably still a few hours from any downpour, and the guests had thrown themselves entirely into the task of having a good time. As she watched, a boy picked up one of the dancers and walked with her to the edge of the pool as she let out fake screams of terror. Laughing, he unceremoniously dumped her in the water, then jumped in after her. Emma grabbed an ice-cold beer from a passing silver tray.

The size of the house, the number of servants, and the quantity of food and alcohol were effective advertisements of their host's wealth. The owner of the house, Julio Santos, headed up the only legal mining corporation in the area. According to Jimmy, it was an accepted fact that Julio lined the pockets of politicians in Boa Vista and Brasilia to maintain his profitable stranglehold on gold and diamond extraction in the region. He tolerated the presence of small-time wildcat miners as a convenient scapegoat for environmental critics. A smooth operator, Jimmy said. Emma temporarily suspended ethical judgment.

"Emma!" Jimmy called out from behind her. Emma turned and did a double take, almost dropping her glass of beer. Approaching her, Jimmy at his side, was the man from the cemetery, the one Ronaldo had regarded with such hostility. "I want you to meet the person who invited us here, Fernando Santos," said Jimmy as Fernando kissed Emma on each cheek. Out of the corner of her eye, Emma monitored Jimmy for signs of jealousy. Nothing. Unfortunately. Especially since Fernando was the type most guys would probably see as a rival. Of medium height, he was dressed in a perfectly pressed white shirt and dark blue shorts that set off his handsome dark features. His body was compactly muscular, and his features had movie-star regularity. Every inch of his appearance, including his nails, had been buffed to perfection. He was standing so close that Emma could smell his aftershave. She lifted her head flirtatiously but got nothing more than a polite smile in return. Fernando was clearly not up for grabs.

"Fernando's a cousin of a friend of mine from the American School in Rio," Jimmy explained. "He's just got his pilot's license and said he'd be happy to help us take Soraia back to her tribe."

"When you want!" Fernando responded affably.

"Really? That's amazing!" Emma said.

"No problem," said Fernando. "Are you American? I love America. I spent almost one year as an exchange student in the US with the Rotary Club. In Ohio."

"Ohio must have been pretty different from Boa Vista."

"Yes. The American kids don't believe I'm from the Amazon. They think I should be carrying a knife and wearing feathers or something." Fernando was so amicable that Emma was mystified by Ronaldo's negative reaction to him.

"'Nando!" A pretty girl approached with a case of cigarettes, holding it out. No thanks, I quit," Fernando said. That must have been recent, Emma thought. She had seen him smoking at the funeral. Fernando politely introduced the girl to Emma and Jimmy, and Emma promptly forgot her name.

"Could you take us Tuesday, seven a.m.?" Emma asked.

"I'll send Jimmy a text where to meet me," Fernando confirmed.

"Fernando!" a young woman, full breasts poking up just above the water line, beckoned from the edge of the pool. *"Vem nadar!"*

"Excuse me," Fernando said. "I need a swim. Have some barbecue!" The smell of freshly roasted meat wafted through the air from the outdoor oven at the other side of the pool. Fernando nodded to Emma politely before shedding his shirt and shorts to reveal a perfectly sculpted torso and legs. He folded his clothes carefully and placed them on a patio chair. Then he stepped onto the diving board and performed a perfect jack-knife dive into the water.

"That was impressive," Emma whispered to Jimmy.

"That dive? It was okay."

"No, your managing to get us a lift in Fernando's plane. How did you do it?"

"Easy. Doing a favor like that for a sick Yanomami girl and getting a write-up for it in the press will do wonders for the image of his dad's company. Fernando will probably see a big fat increase in his allowance this month."

"Isn't it a little slimy of us to give them that publicity?"

"You want to help Soraia, don't you? If you're going to make it as a journalist, you'll have to accept that not everything is black and white. Especially in a place like Boa Vista." Jimmy glanced at his cell phone. "That barbeque smells tempting, but I've got to give Mike a lift to the *Praça Cívica.*

"I'll come along," said Emma. "The gold traders have stalls near there, right? I'm considering a piece about *garimpeiros.*" Emma threw her dress over the still-damp bikini and waved at Fernando.

"See you Tuesday!" he called out as they walked away from the pool.

"Does Ronaldo know Fernando?" Emma asked Jimmy when they were out of earshot.

"I'm not sure. Probably. Boa Vista's a small city. Why?"

"I got the impression that they don't like each other."

"Have you seen them together?" Jimmy was curious.

"He was at the cemetery during Milton's funeral, but he sort of held back. It seemed like Ronaldo was furious with him for being there. The look he gave him was pure hatred."

Jimmy frowned. "I don't know what to tell you. There was bad blood between Julio Santos and Milton Silva. But Santos is not like Souza. He's not violent. He gets his way with bribes and charm. From his point of view, diamonds and gold in the forest around here were put there for a reason, and that reason is to make the Santos family rich."

"So Ronaldo might be mad at Fernando because his dad's company is ruining the environment?"

"Probably."

"I'm not sure. It seemed more personal than that."

"Believe me, in the Amazon, the environment is personal. Personal enough for murder."

CHAPTER NINETEEN

Fire

THE GOVERNMENT BUILDING AT the *Praça Cívica* looked like a lot of other architecture in Boa Vista: a strip mall-like box desperately dressed up with a few fake columns in a futile attempt to make it look important. Emma opened the door to let Mike out of the back seat. They had been riding Rio style, as Jimmy called it.

"See you back at the hotel!" Mike called. As Emma waved good-bye, someone coming down the steps of the government building attracted her attention—a short man wearing dozens of gold chains and carrying a beat-up briefcase.

"Jimmy," Emma said as she got back in the passenger seat. "Isn't that the *garimpeiro* from the plane? What's he doing here?"

"Paying taxes?"

"On Sunday?"

The *garimpeiro* walked in front of the Fiat to a Ford Escort, the lone car parked directly across from the staircase.

"As far as I know, Braga's the only one in the office today," Emma said. "You have to admit it's strange."

Jimmy gave her a sideways glance. "You know I was only kidding about that payment for a hit man, don't you?"

"Let's follow him."

"Why?"

"Humor me. I'm putting together a piece on *garimpeiros*. I want to find out why a *garimpeiro* would be visiting government offices on the weekend."

Jimmy sighed, maneuvering the car toward the road after the Ford Escort. Despite his initial reluctance to tail the miner, it soon became apparent that Jimmy had a talent for discreet vehicular stalking. Jimmy took care to leave one or two vehicles between the Fiat and the Ford. They didn't go far before the *garimpeiro* parked his car again.

"The gold market," Jimmy said. "Makes sense. Isn't this where you wanted to come anyway?" They were parked in front of a colonial building, arched columns framing a walkway lined with shops and stalls. As they watched, the *garimpeiro* approached one of the open stalls. The man behind the counter rose from his stool and shook hands with the miner, placing a hand on the *garimpeiro's* upper arm in a gesture of familiarity.

"He's a regular," said Emma.

"How can you be sure?"

"From the way the owner treats him. Give me your camera!" By looking through Jimmy's camera on zoom, Emma was able to get a better view of the *garimpeiro's* transaction. "He's opening the suitcase and taking something out—a wad of money."

"*Reais?*"

"Dollars. A cosmopolitan *garimpeiro*. It would be a good way to launder money," Emma said excitedly. "The money would become untraceable. Think about it. The *garimpeiro* leaves a federal office building carrying a suitcase full of money. Braga's pay-off for the murder of Milton Silva?"

"Leave Braga out of it for the time being," Jimmy said testily.

"Sorry. I forgot you went to school with Braga's son."

"One of the few kids I knew who never even cheated on an exam. I always got the impression his parents were kind of uptight—not the type to accept bribes. Anyway, what would Braga have to gain from a dead Milton Silva?"

"Didn't Milton make him look bad by exposing all the ecological problems around Boa Vista? And his work as an activist might have made it harder for Braga to cash in, if he was accepting bribes from ranchers and miners to look the other way."

"What's the *garimpeiro* doing now?"

"The shop owner is handing him a few small bars of gold, which he's putting back in the briefcase."

"Nothing illegal about buying gold. Especially in Boa Vista."

"Here he comes!" Emma hastily handed the camera back to Jimmy and pretended to admire the streetscape as the *garimpeiro* walked back to his car. She wasn't sure whether he would recognize them from the airplane, but she wasn't taking chances. Fortunately, he didn't even look in their direction as he got behind the steering wheel. "Let's follow him, Jimmy."

"And you thought my theory about the wildlife smugglers was flimsy." But he obligingly turned the key in the ignition. It was mid-afternoon and traffic was light. Within fifteen minutes, they had crossed the city. Following the Ford Escort onto a nearly deserted, newly paved road heading out of town, Jimmy had a harder time keeping a low profile. But the *garimpeiro* showed no sign that he knew he was being shadowed, keeping a steady pace at just over the speed limit. Twenty minutes later, they turned onto a dirt road. Jimmy and Emma instinctively rolled up their windows to prevent dust from flying inside. By this time of day the ground had usually dried out and formed choke-worthy clouds when passed over by tires. Emma had already had more than her share of clothing permanently stained by the red clay dust of the Amazon. Without the ventilation it quickly grew stuffy inside the car.

"This is near Ronaldo's and Milton's," Jimmy said. "Wonder why he's going so far from town."

Emma recognized the area. They were driving slowly now, the only two cars on the road. Jimmy tried as best as he could to distance himself from the Ford without losing sight of the *garimpeiro's* car. Every time they cleared a bend, they could just spot the tail of the Escort up ahead. Then, all of a sudden, the road curved dramatically. Coming around the turn, they could no longer see their quarry.

"Where'd he go?" Jimmy asked.

Emma frowned. "We must have lost him." Then, something caught her eye. "No! Look!"

They were passing a tiny thatched bar, perched at the edge of the Rio Branco. Emma had seen many places like it around Boa Vista, so insignificant that you could go by one without even noticing. Emma pointed to the Escort parked just outside the precarious structure, which had the appearance of having been there far longer than its construction quality merited. Three horses were tethered to a stake outside. Their presence gave the bar the uncanny appearance of an Old West saloon. A chorus of raucous voices rang out from the bar. Although Emma couldn't see anyone behind the closed doors, it was clear that the place was far from empty.

"I'm not sure about this, Emma," Jimmy said as he pulled the Fiat to a stop and turned off the engine. "Could be a rough crowd."

"Well we're here now," said Emma. "Let's take a look." Together, they walked to the bar's entrance through the cloud of dust they had stirred up. On the threshold of the saloon, Emma hesitated. She didn't know what was behind the thin plywood door. But she couldn't turn back now. Summoning her courage, she pushed it open. A haze of smoke greeted them, this time not from dust, but from cigarettes. Despite the noise level, Emma wasn't quite prepared for the number of customers inside. It didn't seem possible, given that there were just a few cars and horses outside, that the bar would be so packed.

"How did all these people get here?" she whispered to Jimmy.

"Boat and foot," Jimmy responded. "The bigger mystery is why they all want to come to *this* place." The bar didn't improve on closer inspection. Inside was dark and gloomy. Along one wall was a long Formica-topped bar, behind which stood an unsmiling middle-aged woman whose lined face suggested she'd already seen more than she should have in life. She was serving customers drinks as quickly as she could pour them. There were just two other women in the place, outfitted in maximum makeup and minimal clothing. The one in the corner was removing a needle from her arm. Emma's stomach turned. She was still wearing her bikini with a sundress thrown over it and wished she had donned something more modest. The bar's male clientele, a mix of jungle cowboys with wide-brim hats and pointed boots, and miners with their trademark open shirts with gold chains, leered at her as she walked by. The *garimpeiro* they had been following sat on a wooden stool at the counter, his back turned, legs protecting the briefcase on the floor at his feet.

Jimmy put his right arm around Emma's waist like a man staking claim to his woman, and in this crowd, Emma was grateful. She tried not to think about how natural his hand felt at the curve just above her hips. Together they edged toward the counter, taking care to leave a few customers between themselves and the *garimpeiro*.

"*Cachaça*," Jimmy ordered the strong Brazilian alcohol made from sugar cane. "*Duas*. This is a hard liquor kind of place," he whispered in Emma's ear. "We want to blend in." His right arm still around Emma's waist, Jimmy dug a few loose bills out of his left pocket and laid them on the counter of the bar as the woman poured the pungent, clear liquid into two unappetizingly smudged glasses. Jimmy and Emma grabbed their drinks and retreated from the bar toward a small wooden table and bench in the corner.

In the back section of the saloon stood a billiard table around which had gathered a small but raucous group of men. Emma grabbed Jimmy's arm and nodded in the direction of the players. She recognized the man now taking a shot. It was Souza. Swaying on his feet, his cue performing its own *samba*, Souza scraped the peeling green carpet surface of the pool table. The white ball careened into a green one, which plunged down the hole. Souza let out a shout of victory.

"I'm afraid Souza will recognize me," Emma whispered as she joined Jimmy on the bench. "I was sitting in the café with Dad the day Souza pulled a gun on him." Jimmy pulled her close, his mouth nibbling playfully on her ear lobe.

"Pretend you're my girlfriend," he said. "Keep your face hidden." *Why does it have to be pretend?* Emma wanted to ask as she offered her lips for a *cachaça*-flavored kiss. Jimmy obliged, gently pushing open her lips. She absorbed the taste of him as fully as if he had entered her bloodstream. For Emma, the crowd around them melted momentarily away. Then the bedlam reasserted itself, slicing through her desire. Behind them, Souza shouted once more. Jimmy drew his mouth away and placed his cheek on Emma's. Emma now had a full view of the *garimpeiro* sitting at the bar. He continued to sip his drink and stare straight ahead. The door to the saloon opened, heralding the arrival of another customer. He was slight, with elastic features that seemed to have a hard time staying in one place.

Emma drew in her breath. "Jimmy," she whispered. "You won't believe who just walked in. Amoeba."

"What the hell's *he* doing here? Mike should have come here instead of interviewing the minister. This is clearly where the action is."

The *garimpeiro* might not recognize them, but the pilot definitely would. "We should leave," said Emma.

"Tell me when Amoeba's looking in the other direction, and we'll clear out." Emma heard the muffled sound of laughter coming from the direction of the billiards table. It wasn't a happy sound. It was more of a self-satisfied, mocking kind of laughter, the kind you sometimes hear on playgrounds when one group of kids bullies another.

"What's happening?" Emma asked Jimmy.

"Souza just won the game," Jimmy said.

"He's so drunk, I'm surprised he can see straight," said Emma.

"His luck is that the other guy is even more incapacitated," Jimmy said. "Oh shit."

"What?" Emma pulled away to see what was happening. She glanced over her shoulder and caught sight of a triumphant Souza throwing his cue on the table as his adversary, a large bearded man with buck teeth, frowned and teetered. Jimmy protectively pulled her head into the curve of his neck as the conversation between Souza and his adversary became audibly heated.

"Souza's won the bet, but the other guy won't pay up," Jimmy reported. "We should get out of here. Like now." Emma shifted position so that she could surreptitiously glimpse the action at the back of the bar. As she watched, Souza shoved at the bearded man's chest. When the man took a step back, Souza moved in. The bearded man wound his fist back, preparing to swing. In an instant, Souza had pulled out his gun. A split second later, the bearded man put a hand to his hip as blood spurted from his body. Emma's stomach turned.

Souza threw his head back, laughing as he shot the man two more times. Blood sprayed as the man fell back to the floor.

"Fuck!" Jimmy swore. His white T-shirt was now spattered with red. Emma put a hand to her own hair and felt the hot drops of moisture. She felt sick. Jimmy grabbed the back of Emma's head once more and pulled her in as Souza stepped toward them. Out of the corner of her eye, Emma saw him pull off his black T-shirt and grab a bottle of *cachaça* from behind the bar. He screwed off the cap and poured the entire contents of the bottle over the material, soaking it through as the alcohol splashed onto the counter and dripped to the floor. The woman behind the bar wisely did not challenge him. Souza stepped back toward his victim and carelessly tossed the alcohol-seeped T-shirt onto his head. He reached into the pocket of his jeans, pulling out a small packet of matches. Souza struck a match and threw it onto the T-shirt, which immediately burst into flame.

The bar had been so noisy that, up to that point, most of the customers hadn't noticed the dead man in the back. Now, they turned to the flames rising from the victim, and the saloon erupted in chaos. Souza unloaded his pistol twice into the ceiling, clearing a path for himself as he headed for the door. The bleeding man was now completely engulfed in flames, and the putrid smell of barbecuing human flesh filled the air. Whether it was in desperation to leave the scene of the crime or simply to escape the fire, the crowd mobbed the exit door. The bartender, Emma noticed, was the lone exception, choosing to duck through a small opening in the space behind the bar. No one seemed to spare a thought for the murdered man as they fought their way out. Smoke filled the room as flames licked the billiards table. Jimmy grabbed Emma's hand and started to lead her toward the door.

"No!" Emma said. "We'll never make it out that way. Too many people. I saw the bartender head through here. There must be another exit in the back." Hand in hand, Jimmy and Emma passed the seat where the *garimpeiro* had been sitting just moments before. He was nowhere in sight. And he had left his briefcase behind. Without thinking, Emma reached out and grabbed it before pulling Jimmy with the other hand through the opening in the wall. The smoke was swiftly filling the bar, invading Emma's lungs. Breathing was painful. Jimmy started to cough. Behind them, people were shouting, screaming in their desperation to funnel out the door. In the darkness at the back, Emma spotted a rectangle of light—a door, a way out of this hell. Relieved, she held Jimmy's hand tightly and pushed through to the late afternoon sun. Emma panted for breath. Jimmy was spattered with blood and sweat. The brightness of the sun was overwhelming after the dark of the bar.

"You're kidding me," Jimmy said, glancing down at the briefcase. "Why the hell did you take that?"

"The *garimpeiro* left it behind. I couldn't just leave it to burn up. It's evidence."

"Of what, our theft? Shit, Emma!" Jimmy glanced around. There was no one else on their side of the saloon. "Well it's too late now. Let's get out of here!" They ran around the side of the building toward the Fiat and scrambled inside. Emma placed the briefcase on her lap and flipped open the lock.

"What are you doing?" Jimmy asked as he turned the key in the ignition.

"I want to see if the gold bars are still inside," Emma said. "Maybe he handed them off to someone when we weren't looking." The car was unbearably hot, and Emma rolled down the window as Jimmy scraped the gears. From inside the bar came the sickening sound of men screaming. "People are dying in there!" Emma yelled. "Maybe we should do something!"

"There's nothing we can do about it! We were lucky to get out ourselves!" Jimmy was backing out, trying not to run over any of the men now fleeing the murder. As he paused to put the Fiat in gear, Emma felt the press of metal against the skin of her neck.

"Don't move," said a squeaky voice. "You have something that belongs to me, and I promise you I'm not holding a camera lens."

CHAPTER TWENTY

Mud

"TAKE IT EASY," SAID Jimmy. "You can have it."

"Keep you hands on the wheel," Amoeba warned. "We don't want anyone to get hurt."

"Emma," said Jimmy in a low voice. "Maybe you should give our pilot friend what he wants."

Emma slowly lifted the briefcase up, pushing it toward Amoeba through the open window. As he reached for the handle, Emma whispered, "Floor it!"

Jimmy did. The Fiat flung forward. Amoeba pulled the briefcase toward him. As they peeled away, Emma looked back and saw the briefcase open, its contents tumbling to the ground, Amoeba bending down to retrieve the gold bars. Jimmy swerved, narrowly avoiding a young man fleeing from the bar. The saloon was now fully on fire, and smoke was everywhere. Jimmy swung the Fiat onto the dirt road in the direction of town.

"Fuck!" he screamed. "Fuck, fuck, fuck!" His hands slammed down on the steering wheel with every curse he uttered. "You know he's coming after us, don't you?"

"We have a head start."

"Depending on what kind of car he's driving, it's doubtful we can beat him in a race all the way to Boa Vista."

"So turn off the road," Emma suggested, remembering how they had almost lost the *garimpeiro* on the way there. "There!" she shouted, spotting a break in the trees just ahead of them. Jimmy turned the car wheel sharply to the left onto another road—if it could be called a road. *More like a glorified path,* Emma thought. "Pull up in between those trees."

Jimmy did as she suggested. He braked and turned to confront Emma. "Why did you take that briefcase?"

"You were the one who said we could find out who murdered Milton Silva!" Emma shouted. "Did you think we could take on something like that without running any risks? Maybe you're the one who should just aim for a spot on television. The weather report might be right up your alley."

"Fuck you!" Jimmy slumped in the driver's seat, spent. He ran a hand through his hair, damp now with sweat and blood. A moment later, with the abruptness that only Amazonian weather can muster, a lightning bolt split the sky and released a downpour. They hurriedly rolled up the windows to avoid flooding the car. The windows steamed up quickly, limiting visibility to nothingness. For a moment it seemed they were floating in a bubble on their own, somewhere in the Amazon forest. The car was unbearably humid. Emma longed to open the window just a crack, but she knew that even the smallest opening would invite the deluge in. Their only connection to the world was the pounding of the rain on the roof. The noise was deafening. For fifteen minutes, the two of them sat in silence, avoiding each other's gaze. Emma didn't want to look in Jimmy's angry eyes or confront the blood on his shirt, the moistness in his hair. For once, she would have given anything to be far away from him.

She was startled from her dark reverie by the abrupt, jarring silence that signaled the end of the downpour. It was as if someone had just turned off a blaring television set. The steam lifted, and Emma and Jimmy rolled down their windows. Drops of warm water from the roof splashed inside the car. The sky was rapidly brightening, and within minutes, the windshield had defogged.

"Listen, I'm sorry about the weather remark," Emma said tentatively. "We'd better get back to the hotel. Dad might wonder where we are. I should probably send him a text, let him know we're on our way." She took her iPhone out of her pocket and pressed some buttons. "No service," she shrugged. "No biggie. We'll be back soon anyway."

"The humidity probably doesn't help cell phone reception," Jimmy responded.

The engine started reassuringly. Forcing the steering wheel to the right, the Fiat inched from its hiding spot. Jimmy tried to move the car back onto the main road, but it wouldn't obey. Instead, the discouraging sound of spinning tires drifted from the front. Frowning, Jimmy turned off the engine. He opened the door of the Fiat and got out, splashing into a puddle.

"Emma!" he called when he reached the back of the car. "Get in the driver's seat and turn on the engine!"

Emma got behind the steering wheel. "Turn the key and give it some gas!" Jimmy shouted. Emma put it in gear and felt the car move forward slightly, as Jimmy pushed from behind. But just as she thought they would lurch forward out of the mess, the car sank deeper into the ground. Jimmy swore fiercely. He moved toward her, and Emma stared at him in amazement. He looked like a participant in a mud-wrestling contest, caked from head to toe in wet red clay.

"I'm going to need help pushing the car," Jimmy said. Emma stepped out. The Fiat was so low to the ground now that the water was almost at the height of the door. She put her foot in what she expected to be a shallow puddle and immediately sank up to her knees. Her feet were pulled into the ooze at the bottom as if by the suction of a giant vacuum cleaner. She struggled to lift one foot, then another. Her flip-flops stayed behind. Swearing under her breath, she felt around for them in the brown mud. Nothing. She'd have to leave them there. Jimmy offered her a hand and pulled her around the back of the Fiat. "Watch out for snakes," Jimmy warned. "It's pretty hard to see them in this mud."

"What happens if I get bitten?"

"Don't ask," Jimmy sighed. "I don't have any anti-venom on me. Okay, let's just do this as quickly as possible." Jimmy positioned himself on the right side, Emma on the left.

"On the count of three? One, two… Emma lifted up and pushed at the Fiat with all her might. Beside her, she felt Jimmy straining. The car didn't budge. "One more time? Like our lives depend on it?"

"Which they may. Okay. *Um, dois, três…*" They lifted and pushed, but no amount of effort seemed to make a difference. "It's pointless. This thing is stuck, Emma. I'll call Carlos, see if he can send a truck." Jimmy took a cell phone out of his breast pocket and looked at it. His face fell. "I'm not getting a signal either," he said. "I don't know if it's the storm or if we're just too far out of town. We'll need a shovel and maybe another car to get this thing out of the mud. Come on, let's get up on higher ground. The snakes might like the look of this mud, but I don't." Jimmy sloshed a few steps through the puddle and reached out a filthy hand to Emma. Emma tried to take it, but as she attempted to climb out, she slipped and fell. She grabbed the side of the bank and pulled herself up, now dripping with wet red clay.

"You're barefoot," said Jimmy, staring down at Emma's feet.

"My flip-flops wanted to swim with the snakes."

"Here. Take mine." Jimmy pulled his sandals from the back pockets of his shorts and offered them to Emma. The black and white rubber flip-flops, which had probably cost no more than a few dollars, now seemed valuable beyond measure: protection against stinging ants and everything else the jungle could throw underfoot.

"You should use them," Emma said.

"Listen, I insist. Otherwise, you'll just slow us down. In case you haven't noticed, there's not much light left."

"Maybe we should just stay with the car."

"We'd be an easy target for anyone coming down the main road from Boa Vista. Robbers, kidnappers. Anyway, if we head toward the river, we're likely to find some houses. We'll just have to hope the residents are friendly. Let's get moving."

Emma reluctantly accepted the flip-flops and followed Jimmy up the red path. It was hard going. Monkeys screeched down from the treetops above. Even this short distance from Boa Vista, the forest seemed more like jungle. Emma felt a stinging sensation on her arm and looked down to see three mosquitoes feasting on her skin. Soon, she and Jimmy were slapping their skin in chorus. The sound mixed in with the howls of the monkeys and the squishing of their feet. She tried not to think about the darkening sky above them, focusing only on moving as quickly as possible down the road.

They came to a fork. It seemed pointless to strategize over which direction to take, since neither of them had any idea where the paths would lead. Jimmy moved to the left, and Emma followed. She was beginning to tire, although she tried not to show it. The mud made every step an effort. Jimmy's flip-flops, which would normally feel light on her feet, were heavy with caked clay. To make matters worse, the road was becoming increasingly narrow and wet. The mud slowed their progress to a crawl. Jimmy, a few steps ahead, looked back at Emma, his eyes staring at her brightly from beneath the red filth that covered his face and hair.

"It might be a good sign that it's wetter here," Jimmy said encouragingly. "Probably closer to the river."

Emma was the first to spot a light through the trees. She cried out excitedly to Jimmy, pointing in the direction of the house. "Look!" she cried hopefully.

"Let's hope they're open to visitors caked in mud," he said. It was almost pitch black by the time Emma and Jimmy covered the final yards and arrived at the house. Staring at the entrance, they exchanged glances and laughed.

"Someone is on our side today," Emma remarked. They were at Ronaldo's front door.

Relieved, Jimmy and Emma moved toward the steps. But just as Emma placed a foot on the first stair, the door opened and their smiles were wiped from their faces. They were staring into the barrel of a shotgun.

CHAPTER TWENTY-ONE

Party

"RONALDO!" JIMMY CALLED OUT. "*É a gente!*"

Ronaldo squinted through his glasses into the dim light barely illuminating Jimmy and Emma. He had obviously failed to place Jimmy's voice. Emma realized that with their faces caked with mud, it might be difficult to make out their identities. She heard the click of the gun as Ronaldo unlocked it. Fear shot through her.

"It's Jimmy and Emma!" she shouted.

"Ah!" Ronaldo said, lowering his gun. He forced a half smile. "I am sorry. Milton's murder has made me nervous. I have need to protect us." He took in their wild appearance. "But why?"

"We got stuck out on the road during the storm," said Emma.

"Is a hose over there," Ronaldo gestured to the side of the house. Emma and Jimmy stepped toward a spigot with a hose attached. Under the weak stream of lukewarm water, they attempted to wash off the worst of the mud.

"If we hadn't seen your house, we'd still be out in the jungle," Emma told Ronaldo as she let the water flow over her hair. Dripping wet, she passed the hose to Jimmy. He rinsed off what he could, then turned off the water.

"Wait!" Ronaldo said. "I get towels."

Several minutes later he reappeared with a stack of fluffy white towels. Emma grabbed two, wrapping one around her head, another around her torso. Jimmy patted himself down and threw a red-tinted towel over his shoulders. They stepped inside, shivering in the air-conditioning. Emma looked ruefully down at the mud they were dripping onto Ronaldo's wooden floor as their host struggled to collect himself.

"No, is okay!" he said. "I am happy you come here."

"*Quem está aquí, pai?*" Jimmy and Emma heard Rita call out from the other room. Within moments, she came into view. With the light from the living room illuminating her blond hair, she looked like a surprised angel.

"Sorry about the floor," Emma apologized.

"It's fine," Rita said. "The maid will clean it. But how did you end up here?"

Jimmy offered a truncated explanation about how they had been stuck in the mud and abandoned the car when they couldn't get a cell phone signal to call for help.

"Service is pretty spotty out here," Rita said. "Especially after a storm. Sometimes I wander through the house, trying to get a connection. Let me show you to the showers. I'll get you both some clean clothes. I can give you a ride into town later if you like," Rita continued as they walked through the living room and down the hall. "I'm going to a party."

"In this mess?" Jimmy asked.

"I'll be fine," Rita responded confidently. "My new pick-up can get through just about anything."

Rita opened a door off the corridor. "This is the guest room, Jimmy. The shower's through there. Emma can use the one in my room." Emma recalled that Brazilians' obsession with cleanliness meant the average middle-class Brazilian house had a lot more bathrooms than she was used to. Emma followed her hostess through another door. It looked like the room of a little girl, with a pink bedspread and a doll on the pillow. Suddenly, Emma realized that something was missing.

"Where's Charlotte?" she asked.

Rita frowned. "I had to let her go," she said softly. "Dad insisted. She was getting bigger and wilder every day. Milton always meant for me to release her into the forest, once she had grown up a little. My father and I took a boat fifteen miles downriver so that she wouldn't be able to find her way back.

"That must have been hard for you," Emma said.

"It's better for her," Rita said, opening the door to the en-suite bathroom and switching on the light. "My father and I left her playing with a family of monkeys. She'll live in the jungle now, like it was meant to be. Help yourself to shampoo, soap, whatever you need."

Emma stepped under the stream of water, grateful for the warm temperature of the electric shower. As she scrubbed off the wet red clay, the events of the past few hours came flooding back. She recalled the bearded man, shot through, bleeding on the floor of the bar. She could still hear the screams of the men trapped in the burning building. She felt the metal of Amoeba's gun on her neck. The flood of emotion she had been holding back suddenly overwhelmed her. She shrank down to the basin of the shower, the water streaming over her, tears racing down her cheeks. She had no idea how long she sat there. A knock came on the door.

"Emma?" It was Rita. "Are you alright? You've been in there a long time."

Emma struggled to speak. "Yeah," she called out. "I'll be out in a minute."

She opened the door, physically clean, but mentally still sullied. Rita stood frowning at her. "I left a dress and some panties on the bed for you," she said. "Here's a pair of *Havaiana* sandals. What should I do with your old clothes?"

"Burn them."

"Probably best. The dress and bikini are pretty wrecked. I'll let you get dressed. There's some fresh bread, salami, and cheese on the table for you. Come to the dining room when you're ready."

Fighting to bring her emotions under control, Emma put on the simple black dress that Rita had spread out on the bed for her. The somber color suited her mood. The underwear was Brazilian style—semi-thong, and more abbreviated than Emma's American underclothes. After passing a brush through her hair, she took a deep breath and opened the bedroom door. To her surprise, Jimmy was waiting for her in the hallway.

"Are you alright?" Jimmy asked, placing a hand under her chin and lifting her face. "Your eyes look puffy."

Emma avoided his gaze. "I keep thinking about that dead guy," she said. "And all those people who got caught in the fire."

"Classic survivor's guilt," Jimmy said, brushing a finger tenderly along her jaw. "Learned about it in med school. Thing is, doesn't do the victims any good. Or the survivors. Focus on the future. People need you. Remember, Soraia's counting on us to take her sister to the hospital."

Emma took a deep breath and lifted her eyes. The intense concern in Jimmy's expression threw her off for a moment. "I know. Don't worry. I'll pull it together. Still mad about the briefcase?"

The corners of Jimmy's mouth turned up, revealing his nearly perfect teeth. "It was risky," he said, "but we have something to go on now. We know the *garimpeiro* and Amoeba are in on something together. We just have to find out what it is."

"Well, we can't do any more sleuthing right now," Emma said. "Let's go eat."

Minutes later, she lowered herself onto a chair in the dining room and eagerly eyed the heaping plates of food the silver-haired maid was placing on the table. She suddenly realized how hungry she was. All she'd eaten that day had been the appetizers at Fernando's poolside party.

"My cell phone is working," Jimmy announced as he bit enthusiastically into a slice of bread and cheese. "I managed to send a text to Mike. So at least he won't worry."

"Emma, you and Jimmy are guests with me tonight," Ronaldo said kindly. "The road is too bad." Emma was relieved at the invitation and accepted immediately. She didn't fancy heading out in the dark. But their hostess did not share Emma's qualms.

"The roads are fine!" Rita said sharply, eyes flashing with determination.

"Rita just got her driver's license," Ronaldo explained, clearly embarrassed by his daughter's reaction. "She is always wanting to go out. But tonight, there's too much mud. Too much danger. Too much."

"It's too much mud," Rita said slowly, as if she were talking to a child and not her father, "if you drive a small car. But I have the pick-up now. My father doesn't want to let me out of his sight," she said, appealing to Emma and Jimmy. "It's just that I was supposed to meet some friends at a birthday party. They'll be *so* disappointed if I don't go."

"No," Ronaldo responded firmly. "You must stay home."

"I'm going!" Rita shouted, unable to hold her anger in check.

"Maybe your dad's right," said Emma. "We wouldn't want to get stuck in the mud again."

"Thanks, Emma," Rita responded sarcastically.

"How's your research going, Ronaldo?" Jimmy diplomatically changed the subject.

"Is too good!" Ronaldo responded. Emma had been in the country long enough to understand the odd phrasing. Brazilians often confused *very* and *too* when they were learning English. "I do research for nutritive elements," Ronaldo explained to Emma, grateful to pursue another line of conversation. "A university in Texas called with offer to fund my research. They have heard of Milton's death, and it made them too sad." He launched into a lengthy description of his research, which lasted until the maid began to clear away the dishes from the table.

"I'll finish getting ready for the party," Rita said as they stood up from the table. Emma was surprised that she was being so insistent. This time, Ronaldo exploded. His face screwed up with anger as he shouted at his daughter, who responded with equal fury. Emma and Jimmy watched helplessly from the sidelines. When Rita mentioned the name of Milton, Ronaldo lifted his hand as if to strike her. She drew back, her eyes filled with fear. Ashamed, Ronaldo looked at his hand as if it didn't belong to him before lowering it to his side. Rita burst into tears and ran off as her father, visibly distraught, apologized for the commotion.

"Why don't we watch some television?" he suggested as they entered the living room. "Rita will calm down soon." Still frowning, he lowered himself into a chair and reached for the remote. Emma sank onto the sofa, grateful to avoid conversation after the ugliness of the father-daughter spat. Jimmy sat down beside her, his hand brushing casually against her arm as a *novela* flashed on the screen. *Novelas,* Mike had once explained to Emma, were like soap operas in the US, except that they only lasted for a few months and usually aired at night.

Emma was fascinated by images of a beautiful young woman turning into a jaguar, then back into a woman. As the characters skinny-dipped and rode horses, she stole a glance at Jimmy, who was clearly more captivated by the action on the screen than she was. Jimmy's borrowed clothes strained across his muscular body, adding to his appeal. On television, a group of cowboys was caught in tense conversation. Emma was having a hard time keeping her eyes open. Her thoughts were becoming jumbled. She fought to keep awake, but it was a losing battle. Slowly, against her will, she drifted to sleep.

Emma woke up a few hours later. It took a moment to orient herself. She was lying in the darkness, still on the sofa in Ronaldo's living room. A pillow was beneath her head, and a thin blanket covered her. She wondered who had put them there. Jimmy? She wished she could have him next to her. She was all too aware that he was presumably sleeping just down the hall. Would anyone notice if she just crept down the corridor and into his bed? Would Jimmy want her there?

With a start, Emma realized that someone was sobbing. It was Rita. Her hostess spoke in urgent tones from the dining room, and from the one-sided conversation, it was clear that she was on the phone. She wondered why Rita had come to this part of the house to make the call. Was she looking for a better cell signal or moving out of her father's earshot? And who could be causing her such anguish?

"*Te amo!*" Rita whispered. Emma knew what that meant. The phrase was repeated often enough on the *novelas*. *I love you.* So Rita had a lover. Emma wondered why Rita had never mentioned him. Maybe it was a new love interest. Emma guessed the birthday party tonight might have been for her boyfriend, which would help explain why she was so upset. There was a faint beep, like someone clicking off a cell phone, signaling the end of the conversation. Then Emma heard Rita padding slowly away, through the living room and down the hallway. *Maybe,* she thought, *Ronaldo doesn't like Rita's choice of boyfriend.*

CHAPTER TWENTY-TWO

Viper

THE SMOKE ROSE DARKLY from the forest below. Even at this height, seated in the front of Fernando's plane, Emma could smell the burnt wood.

"What's the point of destroying all those trees?" she asked.

"Fastest way to clear the land for planting or ranching," said Carlos from the back seat. "The Yanomami do it too. But we just clear a small area and move on after a couple of years. Those guys ruin the soil completely."

They had boarded Fernando's seaplane from a dock near the center of town. Although the craft had bobbed up and down precariously when they entered, the takeoff from the river in Boa Vista had been smooth. From her plush leather seat, Emma now had a clear view of the jungle below. Soraia Yanomami, transformed into a cheerful young girl by the prospect of returning home, occupied the seat behind her. Carlos, who had come along to interpret, had taken the other, Jimmy squeezed on the floor between them.

"You like the plane?" Fernando shouted over the roar of the engine. "Cessna. Planes are my hobby." Sporting aviator sunglasses, he looked reassuringly in charge of the high-tech pilot controls. Despite his friendliness, Emma sensed that she barely registered on his sexual radar. She remembered how standoffish he'd been with the girls at his party and wondered for a moment if he was gay.

"An improvement over Amoeba Airlines," Emma said.

"Speak for yourself!" Jimmy objected from his cramped position.

"You're okay," Emma teased, reaching back to pat Jimmy on the head. In the privacy of their hotel rooms, she might have taken a chance on a hook-up. But to her chagrin, Jimmy was still keeping his distance.

The terrain below was changing. Emma had grown accustomed to the relative flatness of the jungle near Boa Vista. Now they were flying over hills, and up ahead loomed even taller mountains. The drone of the engine made it easy to avoid conversation and just enjoy the scenery. After almost an hour of steady flying, Fernando moved a lever and the plane swerved slowly to the right.

"What are you looking for?" Emma asked.

"The Mujari River."

"Hard to know if we're in Brazil or Venezuela," Jimmy said, peering out from behind Fernando's seat.

"I'm pretty sure we're still in Brazil," Carlos asserted. "But Soraia's *shabono* is just over the border." *Shabono*, Emma knew, described the single thatch building that constituted an Yanomami village. "I'd like to come up this way to do some mapping," he continued, "after I finish the area near Boa Vista."

"Is against the law to enter Venezuela from here," Fernando said.

"Something tells me no one's going to check our passports," Jimmy replied.

The mountains below were an impressive height. Ahead was a snaking waterway. Fernando lowered the plane, pointing the airplane's nose at the narrow Mujari. As they lost altitude, the trees came into better view, towering like skyscrapers above them as the tiny plane moved in for a landing on the liquid airstrip. Fernando's brow wrinkled as he split his focus between the controls and his target. Remembering the flight with Amoeba, Emma briefly closed her eyes. But the plane touched down gently, floating runners skimming the water. When Emma opened her eyes again, Fernando was smiling broadly, and the Cessna was moving as smoothly as a motorboat on the water. Soraia shouted out in glee from the back, no longer able to contain her excitement. Dressed in the oversized T-shirt that had been a present from Dr. Herzog, she seemed small and vulnerable. If she were with her tribe, Carlos explained, she would probably just run around naked. But she was eager to show off her new Western clothing, complete with the incongruous *Beatles Fab Four* image lasered on the front.

"She recognizes the area," Carlos said.

"FUNAI, agency for Indian relations, keeps a dock here in dry season," Fernando explained. He no longer had to shout over the sound of the engine. "But now is under water. Back there is a boat." He brought the plane to a floating stop. "Jimmy, Carlos, help me throw out the anchor."

Fernando pushed open the door on his side of the airplane, allowing the warm, moist air of the jungle to rush in. The humidity here was even more oppressive than in town. To protect against mosquitoes and other creatures, Emma was wearing a lightweight long-sleeved shirt and long pants, and she now wondered if that had been a bad choice. Fernando enlisted Carlos and Jimmy to help him inflate the dinghy that would take them to shore. Emma eyed the contraption doubtfully. It didn't look very solid, and she wondered how it would hold all five of them. Fernando threw the boat into the water and slid a handgun from under his seat to a holster around his waist. Emma shot him a questioning look.

"In case we run into *garimpeiros*," he said, jumping into the dinghy. The others handed down supplies: boat paddles, backpacks with sandwiches and water for the trip, plus a metal and canvas stretcher that they could use to transport Soraia's sister to the seaplane. They had left Boa Vista as early as possible in order to make it to the Yanomami village and back in one day. Fernando warned them that he wouldn't be able to pilot the plane at night, and they wouldn't want to be stuck in the jungle in the dark, nursing a young Yanomami girl with malaria.

"I don't like the look of that water," Jimmy said, peering down from the plane. "Piranhas. Alligators."

"No problem in rainy season," Fernando said. "Only if you have a cut, they come for your blood."

"I'd be more concerned about the candiru," said Carlos. "Also known as the vampire fish."

"What's that?" Emma asked.

"Almost invisible," said Jimmy. "It swims into any hole it can find—your nose, ears or—well, you use your imagination. Once inside, it opens up its spines like an umbrella. Takes serious surgery to remove it."

Jimmy jumped down from the plane, followed by Carlos, who reached up a hand to help Soraia. But the Yanomami girl took one look at the inflatable dinghy, so different from the dugout canoes of her tribe, and took a fearful step back. Emma realized that she was probably more used to airplanes than rubber boats.

"Soraia," Emma called to her as reassuringly as possible. "It will be okay." She grabbed the girl's hand and gently pulled her to the edge. The Yanomami girl still balked, screaming as she attempted to retreat back into the plane. Emma steeled herself and took a flailing Soraia in her arms, handing her down to Carlos. As Soraia struggled, the dinghy sloshed back and forth. Not wanting to prolong the girl's misery, Emma immediately stretched out her foot to join them. Losing her balance, she almost toppled over the side but managed to throw herself to the bottom of the boat before she went overboard. Fernando stood up to shut the door of the plane. The boat twisted precariously, water splashing in the sides.

"Alright, Emma?" Carlos asked, furrowing his brow.

"Yeah." Channeling her summer camp days, Emma grabbed a paddle and, with Fernando's assistance, maneuvered the boat to what passed for a shore. Thankfully, Soraia calmed down once they started moving. There was no sandy beach, or even a definitive edge to the river—just a place where the water stopped and solid land began. The trees near land were partly submerged.

"Rainy season," Fernando explained. "Later, some trees go completely under water. The fish eat the fruits and poop the seeds out. Like this the tree spreads its seeds." A splash caught their attention. Emma just caught sight of a huge, long fish falling back in the water. "Is a monkey fish," Fernando said. "He jumps out to get a frog or spider. Once I saw one at more than one meter—as tall as me. Got a small monkey baby."

"How do you know all this?" Emma asked.

"I know not much about fish," said Fernando. "But I spend much time in the forest doing research. I want to study botany when I go to university."

"Botany?"

"Yes, last year I did an internship that gave me passion. It was with a famous botanist around here. I think you know him. His name is Ronaldo Nascimento."

It was not much cooler in the forest than it had been on the water. After an hour of uphill hiking, the humidity was getting to Emma. It felt as if she were walking through a tunnel of heat. Her backpack weighed heavily on her shoulders. Soraia led the way, followed by Jimmy, who kept his camera at the ready in his hands. Occasionally, Carlos would turn and offer Emma a hand to get over a rough patch. Emma was satisfied to see what she thought was jealousy spark across Jimmy's face each time she accepted Carlos's help. Every now and then, they stopped to drink water, Soraia jumping up and down, impatient to start moving again.

"We need to make better time," Carlos warned when they stopped for their third water break. The deep jungle was not what Emma had expected. For one thing, she was surprised by the noise. Birds chattered away in the branches. Mosquitoes buzzed in Emma's ears, not exactly in swarms, but enough to make her grateful that she had plastered herself with bug spray. A chant accompanied them as they walked, a three-note scale of "*do, re, mi*". Carlos identified it as a seringueiro bird. The song became so constant that Jimmy began to absentmindedly imitate it, whistling "*do, re, mi*" as they trudged along.

"It's so dark," Emma commented, gazing up. The long branches at the upper level of the tree canopy blocked the sun. Plants here were engaged in a botanical battle for the rare beams that broke through to the forest floor, and vegetation at the ground level was sparse. They walked on a bed of decaying leaves, some the size dinner platters.

"When scientists from other places come here," Fernando said, "they are too amazed at what they find. In other countries, a botanist probably does not discover in his life a new species. But I have already discovered one. It's not hard. Look!" he said, flipping over a rotting log in their path. The five of them watched as a flurry of ants and other insects scurried away. "There is probably new kind of species of beetle right here! Over there is a strangler fig," Fernando continued, indicating a nearby tree that looked as if it had been covered with a thick wooden net. "It begins as a tiny plant that grows on other tree. Later, his branches feel up to the skies and his roots feel down. Now, the strangler has lots of food for himself. If we come back in a few years to this same place, is like a hollow column, the other tree all eaten. The tree inside is a victim of the strangler. Is dead."

Amidst the references to death, Emma's thoughts turned to Milton's funeral and Fernando's relationship with Ronaldo. *So they did know each other. But from Fernando's description, they sound like friends, not enemies. What happened? Did they fight over who discovered a certain species of tree?* She wanted to press Fernando on the topic, but she had to first find a way to diplomatically formulate the question. *'Why does your ex-mentor hate you?'* was probably not a good lead-in.

Suddenly, Fernando cried out in pain as the top of his head was hit by a seedpod. From above, they heard the chattering of the monkeys that had dropped it. Soraia laughed as the small tan creatures swung away through the branches above. Emma took advantage of the break to take another swig from the water bottle. She turned to hand it to the others. Then, she froze. Fernando had removed his handgun from the holster and was aiming it right at her.

"Don't move!" he growled.

CHAPTER TWENTY-THREE

Shabono

FERNANDO PULLED THE TRIGGER. A blast rang through the jungle, and Emma jumped as if her body had been electrified. Soraia screamed. Emma stared down at her limbs and torso, expecting to see blood. None. He had missed her. But he was already taking aim again. With a determined expression, Fernando advanced. Emma knees wobbled. He kept coming. Emma glanced at Jimmy and Carlos, but they both stared past her.

Eyes focused on the ground, Fernando shot again as he stepped by Emma, who continued to shake even as the fear ebbed. Placing his gun back in its holster, Fernando reached down and picked up something from the top of a fallen tree trunk. It was light brown with dark brown markings. Fernando held it up as if it were a trophy and walked back with the head. The corpse of the snake stretched out to what Emma estimated was eight feet.

"Bushmaster pit viper," Carlos identified the monstrous serpent. "A bite from one that size would be deadly."

"Thanks," she murmured as Fernando dropped the snake back on the ground.

"No problem," he said, grinning at her.

"Nice entertainment break," Jimmy said. "But we'd better get moving."

"Not so fast," Carlos said. "We've got company. I advise you to take your hand off the holster, Fernando. Death by poison arrow is not a pleasant experience."

Emma followed Carlos's gaze and was shocked to see that they were surrounded. Three men, faces decorated with black and red war paint, glared at them with threatening black eyes. Their bows were stretched, arrows pointed. Alone in her boldness, Soraia cried out and ran toward one, talking quickly as she went. She tugged on his arm, and he lowered his bow. The other two did the same. Carlos exchanged some words with the men in Yanomami. One of the men placed his arm protectively on Soraia's shoulder. As Carlos and Soraia spoke, the mood rapidly shifted.

"Meet Soraia's uncle and friends," Carlos introduced the men. The warriors' fierce expressions melted away, and all three grinned at the visitors.

"They've been following us for some time," Carlos explained, dropping his pack and tearing off his T-shirt, which he offered to one of the men. Jimmy immediately did the same. Fernando hesitated.

"C'mon, man," Jimmy urged. "We're showing our good will. There are three of them, in case you hadn't noticed."

"And I'm not giving up *my* shirt," Emma said.

"I'll give you some of my bug spray," Jimmy added. "Fair trade."

"Is All Saints," Fernando protested. A second look at the Indians' bows and arrows seemed to convince him, though. He took his shirt off and folded it meticulously as if he were a salesman in a shop before handing it to the Yanomami. "If I'd known, I would have worn Hering."

"The village is there through the trees," Carlos said, laughing.

———

The sun's strong rays broke through. Soraia's village *shabono* sat in a clearing just ahead. As soon as she spotted it, the young girl sprinted in front and into an open entrance of the large structure, its thatched roof supported by wooden poles made from the trunks of trees. The three warriors strode in a dignified manner toward the opening. The others followed. Just outside the *shabono,* a low screen of leaves and branches had been set up. From inside came a long, loud moan.

"What's in there?" Emma asked Carlos.

"A menstruating girl," he answered. "Yanomami believe the blood from menstruation is poisonous. She has to be separated from the rest of the tribe and squat over a hole to let the blood drip in. When her period is over, they will cover the hole up, and she can rejoin her tribe."

"That's horrific!" Emma said, recalling the super-sized tampon she had inserted into her own vagina that morning.

"The good news is that Yanomami women don't menstruate very often. After their first bleeding, they get a husband. They are usually pregnant after that." Carlos greeted a woman standing just outside the menstruation tent. As they spoke, she placed a piece of *mandioca* on a sharpened stick and pushed it inside. "The girl is not allowed to touch food, and no one is allowed to touch her," Carlos continued. "She eats from the stick."

The warriors beckoned, and Emma followed, not sorry to leave the menstruation tent behind. A small group had already gathered immediately inside the village entrance, curious to see the visitors. Jimmy's camera clicked away. A woman ran up to Emma and reached under her shirt, fingering first her bra, then her breast. With the other hand, she pulled Emma's shirt out to inspect her cleavage.

"What the hell is she doing?" Emma asked.

"She wants to see what a white woman's breasts are like," Carlos said, grinning.

"Call her off!" Emma pleaded. Carlos said a few words to the woman, who immediately released Emma and stepped back. Pulling the backpack off her shoulders, Emma took out a pad and pencil to take notes. "Can I leave this here for a while?" she asked Carlos, gesturing toward the pack.

"You can if you never want to see it again. The Yanomami don't own anything. Those T-shirts we handed out will eventually make the rounds of the entire tribe. It's all communal property here, so they'll consider your backpack up for grabs. I'll carry it for you if you want."

"I can take it," Jimmy volunteered, stepping forward.

"Don't you need both hands on your camera?" Carlos asked, irritated.

"I'll take it," Fernando suggested, stepping forward to pick up the pack.

The warriors led them through the *shabono*. The structure was built in the form of a doughnut, surrounding a large open area in the center. A group of indigenous people—about one hundred of them, Emma guessed—were dispersed in smaller family groups throughout the village. Hammocks, drying fruit, and other items hung haphazardly from the poles. The thatch on the roof was brown except where it had been recently repaired with fresh green palm leaves. The structure rose from about four feet at its lowest point to approximately ten feet at its highest. Yanomami eyed them from their hammocks as they passed. A group of twenty noisy, naked children, ranging in age from about three to ten, formed around them. From the open area at the center came the strong smell of meat cooking. The large carcass of a pig-like creature was suspended on poles over a fire.

"The Yanomami up here are luckier than the ones near Boa Vista," Carlos commented. "Fewer miners means more wild game. Someone made a killing. Looks like there's going to be quite a celebration tonight. Hallucinogens and everything. For the boys. Not for you, Emma."

"Yes, too bad we can't stay so that I can see the rest of you get high," Emma said. "Anyway, right now we need to find Soraia's sister."

At that moment, a cry of unbearable anguish rang through the *shabono*. Emma dropped her pencil and pad and rushed toward the sound. She was shocked to see Soraia standing by a small fire, screaming in rage. Emma instinctively took a step towards her, but Carlos grabbed her arm and pulled her back.

"Leave her!" he said, his face blanching. "She has to let her anger out. In her mind this is the work of an evil *shaman* from another tribe."

"No!" Emma cried, turning away from the harsh truth etched in Carlos's face. She didn't need translation. They were too late. Soraia's sister was dead.

CHAPTER TWENTY-FOUR

Witch Doctor

"WE CAME FOR NOTHING!" Emma moaned, tears streaking her face.

"That's not true," Carlos said, wiping the moisture away as he pulled Emma to his bare chest. "We brought Soraia back. That's worth something."

"Just so she could find out her sister was dead."

"She's with her family now, Emma. They need each other."

Jimmy and Fernando had caught up, and it was clear from their expressions that they immediately understood what was going on. Soraia's cries of pain were torturous. A young woman with short sticks in her lip reached down to lift her up and carry the grieving girl to a hammock. Placing her on the woven cloth, she began to rock the child back and forth as if she were a baby. Emma turned away, unable to watch any longer.

"We might as well get back to the plane," Emma said quietly, pulling away from Carlos and trying to catch her breath. "There's nothing more we can do here." She reached out to take her backpack from Fernando. The pad and pencil she dropped by now had become communal Yanomami property, which was fine with her. She was no longer in the mood to take notes.

As they turned to leave, a young girl of about five, hair covered with white feathers and black beads around her neck tugged on Carlos's arm. Carlos bent down and exchanged words with her. "Wait," Carlos said, straightening up. "This little girl wants us to see her mother before we head off. She wants us to take her away to the land where people are cured and bring her back. Just like Soraia."

"But we must leave," Fernando warned. "I can't fly at night."

The girl looked up at Emma, innocent and full of hope. Emma knew she couldn't refuse. "This won't take long," she said, as she wiped the wetness from her cheeks and allowed the child to take her hand and lead her away. The others followed behind. They passed through the clearing where a dozen Yanomami squatted near the roasting wild boar. On the other side of the *shabono*, the young girl's mother lay in a hammock. Her eyes barely registered the strangers' presence. The young girl passed a worried hand over her mother's forehead. Her concern was understandable. As they watched, the woman's skeleton-thin body doubled over in a coughing fit that threatened to steal her last breath. Hovering over the hammock was an elderly man, red feathers tied onto bands around his upper arms, a black ladder painted across his bare chest. Unlike the other Yanomami in the village, this one wore Nike gym shorts instead of a loincloth. In his hand was a scraped down stick, which he passed over the woman's body as he chanted a repetitive tune, his short legs stomping an accompanying rhythm on the dirt floor. He appeared not to notice the visitors as they approached. But when he finished his song, he stepped back and allowed them to take a look at the sick woman.

"He's a *shaman*," Carlos said. "The Yanomami's version of a witch doctor."

Jimmy approached the hammock and gazed down at the woman in sympathy. "Classic clubbing on the hands." He gently lifted her wrist, examining her fingers. "See how they are swollen at the tips?"

"Malaria?" Emma asked.

"No," Jimmy frowned. "This is an advanced case of tuberculosis."

Emma drew in her breath. The last thing this village needed was another epidemic. "How bad?" she asked softly. "Will she survive?"

"Unless she gets the right treatment, I'd give her a five percent chance. Maybe less," said Jimmy.

"We have to take her back with us," Emma pressed. "Dr. Herzog might be able to cure her. We can do it. We have the stretcher, and we've got room on the plane."

Jimmy held a hand to the patient's forehead and shook his head. "Too risky," he said. "She's burning up with fever. It's cooler here in the shade of the *shabono* than it is in the jungle. Out in that humidity, her temperature could spike. I can't guarantee she'd survive the trip."

"So we leave her here to die?" Emma asked, incredulous.

"Do no harm," Jimmy said. "The physician's creed. Here she'll pass away peacefully, with her family around her." The woman writhed in the hammock and began to cough again.

"She doesn't look peaceful to me!" Emma said. "Jimmy, we have to try!"

"Emma's right," Carlos said, placing a hand on Emma's shoulder. "If we take her back, she stands a fighting chance."

Jimmy sighed. "Alright, you win."

"Wait," Fernando said, taking a step back. "Tuberculosis is, how do you say—*contagioso*."

"If you haven't got your shots, you can take a course of isoniazid when we get back to Boa Vista," Jimmy said. "Basic TB prevention. If this woman's going to make it to the plane alive, though, I'll have to bring her temperature down." Stashing his camera in the bag, he pulled out a small bottle of aspirin. "I brought these just in case. Let me see if I can get her to take a couple."

"Call her Ana," Emma suggested, suddenly understanding Dr. Herzog's need to give her patients an identity. "It feels funny not to know her name."

"Ana it is," said Jimmy, placing two tablets inside the woman's mouth as Carlos spoke to her in a soothing tone. Ana screwed up her face, but she kept her mouth closed as the pills dissolved. "Her fever should start to come down within the half hour," Jimmy predicted.

"In the meantime," said Carlos, "we should eat our sandwiches so that we'll have energy for the trip back. Then we'll need to leave. Fernando's right. We can't afford to stick around much longer if we're going to make it back to the plane before the sun sets."

Emma turned away and was surprised to find her path blocked by the *shaman*. The old man stood in front of her, studying her intently. The way he looked at her made Emma's skin prickle at the back of her neck.

Without physically touching her, he passed his stick over her body, just as he had done with Ana. Once again, he began to chant, as if he were casting a spell. The witch doctor locked his eyes with hers as he stomped the ground. The dust rose up like smoke, and Emma felt dizzy. The *shaman* kept singing. When he finally stopped, he spoke in a voice that seemed detached from his body, so deep it seemed to come from the earth itself.

"He says he knows the answer to your question," Carlos translated.

"But I didn't ask him anything." The *shaman's* black eyes opened wide, and he gestured wildly, pulling his hands through the air and pointing towards the sky.

"He wants you to know about the monster. He says things are not as they appear. The monster walks backwards in the forest to throw you off the trail. If you follow it the wrong way, you will lose yourself, never find your way back home."

No one said a word. The silence grew, holding Emma more and more tightly in its grasp. She looked into the old man's eyes, feeling she would be able to see her future if she stared long enough. She was losing control. She thought that if she continued to stand there, she would drown in the big, dark pools of his eyes. Then Jimmy put a hand on her shoulder, and she was pulled instantly back to the moment.

"Emma," he said, frowning. She felt utterly drained. Her head throbbed. "What's happening to you? He's just a witch doctor."

"I need water," Emma said. Jimmy handed her the bottle, which she consumed in greedy gulps.

"The way he looked at me—" said Emma. "I can't describe it. It was like he could see into my soul." From above the *shabono*, lightning split the sky. Indians scrambled to remove the wild boar from the fire and get it under cover. Then the thunder rolled, and the rain came down.

⁓

Torsos glistening with sweat, muscles rippling, Jimmy and Carlos carried Ana Yanomami in the stretcher between them. The way back had been much tougher than the trip to the *shabono*. This time, Fernando did not bother to explain the botany of the forest. They trudged along in silence, every bit of energy channeled to moving forward. Emma lifted a hand to her forehead, which was drenched in sweat. The ground was wet from the afternoon storm, and Emma slipped as she climbed the hill, falling twice to her hands and knees. At the top of the hill, Jimmy and Carlos placed the stretcher on the ground and fought to catch their breath.

"*Puta!*" Jimmy swore, running a hand through his damp hair. Emma glanced down at Ana. The aspirin had taken effect, and the Yanomami woman appeared more aware of her surroundings than she had been two hours earlier. Unfortunately, that meant she also looked more frightened than ever. Emma bent over her, gently lifting her head and raising the water bottle to her lips.

"Fernando and I can take over for a while," she suggested. "It's downhill from here." Jimmy and Carlos were too spent to protest. When they had all managed to steel themselves for the final push, Fernando lifted up the front end of the stretcher. Emma took the back. Above them, the birds and monkeys screeched. Emma stepped cautiously, but the wet ground was slippery. She lost her footing and came down hard. With massive willpower, she managed to keep the stretcher elevated above the ground as she fell. Panting, she struggled to her feet. Jimmy walked ahead and Carlos brought up the rear as they battled their way down the steep slope. A third of the way down, Fernando came to an abrupt stop.

"What's wrong?" Emma asked.

"That tree," Fernando said, nodding toward a large palm nearby. "I don't like it."

Emma could see nothing wrong with the tree, except that it was tilted at an angle to the slope.

"Move to the side!" Carlos said urgently. "Now!"

Carlos and Jimmy moved parallel to the side of the mountain, and Emma sashayed after them. Her hands gripped the stretcher. "What's wrong with a tilted tree?" she asked. "It's not like it was going to fall on us."

"Tilted trees are a warning sign," Carlos said, breathing hard.

"Warning of what?" Emma asked as Fernando slipped on the mud and fell down. This time, the stretcher was brought to the ground with a thud, and Ana moaned from the impact. Emma swore under her breath.

"That the earth underneath it is unstable," Carlos explained.

Fernando scrambled back to his feet. Emma took another step to the side. Then, suddenly, the ground gave way beneath her feet. One moment she had been standing on solid earth. The next, she was sinking in a sea of mud. She was thrown back, falling, desperately trying to hold onto the stretcher. It was no use. The force of the impact wrested the handles from her grasp. In a panic, she reached out, trying to grab hold of something, anything, to halt her descent. But she was helpless. Something reached for her. Ana Yanomami. Her heart in her throat, Emma put her arms around the sick woman and held on. Clinging to each other, they plunged down the hill on a wave of mud. Branches and other debris clawed at their bodies as they plummeted down the slope. Emma held her breath, wondering when it would end.

They slowed to a stop like children reaching the flat of a sledding hill. Emma held Ana Yanomami tightly in her arms as if she were the only person left in the world. She uttered a silent prayer of thanks. At least she hadn't lost her. She looked down. Her own clothes were in muddy tatters and every inch of her body felt bruised. But they had made it. Emma desperately scraped away the mud from Ana's body, horrified to see that her smooth, brown skin was covered in dozens of cuts. Ten feet away from them, Fernando stood up in zombie-like fashion, dazed and covered in red clay.

"Help us!" Emma called. But Fernando didn't reply.

"Emma!" She turned to see Jimmy and Carlos scrambling down the hill, just beyond the area hit by the mudslide. "It's okay, Ana," she murmured to the woman in her arms. "We made it. We're alright." She gazed into Ana's face, cradling her weak body. Ana lay still. Frighteningly still. It seemed as if time had come to an abrupt stop. Then, Ana's white eyes rolled upwards in their sockets, and Emma's stomach dropped.

She placed her ear by Ana's face, terrified. "She's not breathing!" Emma screamed. Carlos put a hand on her shoulder. Jimmy panted by her side.

"Cardiac arrest," he said softly.

"Do something!" Emma pleaded.

"No." Jimmy's eyes glazed over as he stepped back. "I'm not a doctor."

Emma's eyes filled with tears as she looked up at him, wordlessly begging for help.

"I can't help her!" Jimmy protested, holding up his hand.

"You have to try!" Emma shouted. "We're responsible for her, don't you see? Ana!" In desperation she placed Ana's small body on the ground, grasping at memories of a CPR class she had taken years before. Meshing her fingers together, she stretched out her arms, pressing on Ana's chest. She pumped ten times, then leaned in to place her lips on the Yanomami woman's mouth, expelling her breath rhythmically. Emma pulled up, looking down in the hope of seeing a sign of life. Still, Ana didn't move. "She's dying!" Emma cried. "Jimmy!" She reached for him. "Please."

Jimmy took another step back.

"Help me save her, Jimmy! She's fading away. You're the only one who can do it." Jimmy looked into Emma's eyes.

"*Puta!*" he swore. As if a spark had electrified his body, he threw off his backpack and bent down beside Ana. Entwining his fingers, he pushed against her chest, more vigorously than Emma had. Pausing, he placed his lips on hers. Then he used his hands to pump once more at her heart. "No, no, no!" he said over and over as he thumped with his fist at her frail body. Ana's body lay limp as life drained away.

"Jimmy!" said Carlos, his eyes filled with fear. "Let her go! It's over! You did what you could!"

"It's not over!" Jimmy replied fiercely, continuing to press at Ana's frail body. Jimmy's frantic attempts to save her were now more frightening than his inaction had been.

"Jimmy!" Emma said, tears streaming down her face. "Jimmy!"

Suddenly, Jimmy stopped. He stood up, screaming. "I killed her! Are you satisfied? I told you I'm not a doctor!"

Emma stared down at Ana. Her eyes widened. Miraculously, the Yanomami's body was showing signs of movement. Gently, Emma reached out and lifted Ana's head. "Look! She's breathing! She's breathing!" Emma sobbed with relief as she saw the Yanomami woman appear to come back to life in her arms. Ana blinked as her eyes regained focus.

"The boat!" From a few hundred feet away came the sound of Fernando's voice. He walked toward them, looking like an animated clay Greek god. "The boat," he repeated as he drew near. "My boat. Is there!"

Emma stood up, holding Ana in her arms.

"I guess we were closer than we thought," said Carlos. Taking Ana from Emma, he turned in the direction of the Mujari. Jimmy put his own backpack on his back and grabbed Carlos's bag. The stretcher was gone, probably buried under a thick layer of mud. Emma's backpack was nowhere in sight, but with Fernando's plane so close, they wouldn't miss the remaining food and water supplies inside.

"Come on!" Fernando urged.

Emma became vaguely aware of a new sound rising above the noise of the forest birds and monkeys. It was the noise of wood cracking. Carlos froze. "Listen," he said.

"What's that?" Jimmy asked.

"We have to get out of here," Carlos screamed. "Now!"

From the top of the hill came a rumbling. Emma glanced up at the hill in shock. A mass of mud, much larger than the last, was crashing down the slope in their direction.

CHAPTER TWENTY-FIVE

Flight

EMMA STOOD TRANSFIXED. SOMEONE grabbed her hand. It was Jimmy, pulling her forward. Then, suddenly, the only thought in her mind was escape. She ran. From above came the sound of collapsing earth. Emma didn't dare look back. She focused only on moving her legs, keeping pace with Jimmy as he ran beside her. The ground beneath them was dark. It was moving, and Emma thought for a moment that the earth was giving way under their feet. With a sense of revulsion, she realized that thousands of ants had emerged from the ground and were fleeing the onslaught of mud. She was sprinting over a black, slimy carpet. The roar of the mud slide rang in her ears.

Ahead, Emma glimpsed hope. The river. They were almost there, almost at the boat. Fernando jumped first. Carlos was next, Ana still in his arms. Then, hand-in-hand, Jimmy and Emma leapt together from the edge of the forest into the dinghy. As Fernando pushed off with a paddle, she turned back to the jungle, awed by the sudden devastation behind them. The first mudslide had been a non-event compared to this one. The forest they had run through minutes before had been reduced to a pile of broken trees and mud. But there was no time now to contemplate the magnitude of what had just happened.

"We're taking on water!" Jimmy warned. The dinghy must have lost some of its air since they had used it that morning. A layer of dark water had accumulated in the bottom of the rubber boat, placing them dangerously low in the river. At any moment, the dinghy might sink.

"Where's the other paddle?" Emma asked.

"I don't know," Fernando said. "I only found one."

"A monkey could have taken it," Jimmy said. "Look, we're moving too far downstream! We're going to miss the plane!" It was true. The Cessna, which had been straight in front of them, was now off to the right.

"Emma, take Ana," Carlos ordered, transferring the Indian woman from his own arms to Emma's. "Fernando, give me the paddle."

Ana looked up at Emma with terrified eyes. Carlos grabbed the small oar and pushed hard against the current. His superior skill, probably culled from his time as a tribesman, put them back on course for the airplane. But the sides of the rubber boat were lower than those of the Yanomami's dugout canoes, and Carlos's more vigorous movements also made the boat shift back and forth. Despite his efforts, they were taking on more water.

"After all that, I'm not losing these photos," said Jimmy. Emma noticed for the first time that he was the only one still sporting a backpack. He must have dropped Carlos's on the path when they ran for the boat. Now, Jimmy took his bag off his shoulders and held it up out of the water.

"We're almost at the plane!" Emma called.

"We're going under," Jimmy warned as water streamed in. The boat was sinking, and they slipped fast into the murky waters of the Mujari.

"Hold on, Ana!" Emma said as she maneuvered the Indian woman onto her back. She could no longer feel the rubber of the boat beneath her feet. She fought to hold her head above the river. They would have to swim for it. With a growing sense of dread, she remembered Fernando's comment about the piranhas. They only come if they smell blood, he had said. The four of them struggled through the water. Carlos got to the runner of the plane first, pulling himself out of the water and reaching for the door of the airplane. Fernando was the next to reach safety. Even Jimmy, slowed by his efforts to keep his backpack with the camera out of the water, was almost there. With the extra weight of Ana on her back, only Emma lagged behind. Fear ran through her as she realized that she was not making progress against the current. She needed to swim faster. But she was so tired. No matter how she strained toward the plane, it seemed only to get further away. She felt something brush against her legs, and her stomach turned over with dread. She wasn't going to make it.

"Jimmy!" she called. Jimmy had just reached the Cessna, holding his bag aloft. He looked back, and Emma realized that in order to help her, he would have to let the camera bag fall into the water. He hesitated only a moment. Just as he released the bag, Carlos grabbed it. Jimmy let go of the plane's runner. In seconds, the stream carried him to Emma. Aligning himself beside her, he shifted Ana partially onto his back.

"Swim like hell!" he urged her.

"I can't," Emma said. Her legs were as immovable as jelly.

"Swim, dammit!"

Emma drew every remaining ounce of strength remaining inside her. Kicking, she propelled herself through the water, sharing the weight of Ana with Jimmy. Slowly, they inched closer to the Cessna. Finally, they were almost there. Emma reached out to grab the aluminum runner as Fernando grabbed Ana from the water. Then Emma felt Carlos's strong hands under her armpits, pulling her up to safety.

CHAPTER TWENTY-SIX

Pets

"HELLO?"

"I want to speak with *Papagaio*," Jimmy said, using the password Carlos had given them. Emma breathed in Jimmy's body wash smell as she pressed her ear to his, listening in on the conversation. Carlos had lent them a brand new cell phone just for the call. Anonymous was the way to go, he had insisted. Better if they couldn't be traced. A pause on the other end of the line made Emma wonder if they had somehow already blown it. Maybe the password had changed.

After what seemed like an eternity, the man spoke. "Who is this?"

"I'm a consultant for an American pet store owner," Jimmy said. "A friend said you could help me."

"Which pet store?"

They hadn't expected this question. Emma pushed the cell phone away and whispered in Jimmy's ear, "Exotic Pets of Miami." *Let's hope they don't check that out,* she thought.

"Exotic Pets of Miami," Jimmy repeated into the phone.

"What do you want?" The heavily accented voice growled.

"I was told you have special pets for one of my top clients," Jimmy said.

Another pause. "How much money?"

"One hundred thousand. Maybe two."

"Dollars?"

"Dollars."

"Call back in one hour."

Emma eyed the kiosk from the safety of the truck's cabin. It looked just like any other newsstand in Boa Vista, selling an eclectic assortment of soft drinks, snacks, newspapers, and magazines.

"Are you sure that's the one?" she asked.

Jimmy double-checked the address he had jotted down. "Looks like it."

"Pretty nondescript. I guess that's the point." Emma's cell phone pinged and she glanced down. "Dr. Herzog says Ana's responding well to treatment."

"Glad to hear I didn't kill her." Jimmy exhaled, running a hand through his hair. The dark smudges beneath his eyes bore testament to the stress of the last few days.

"One tragedy averted," Emma agreed. "Your parents weren't mad about the Fiat?" Jimmy's parents had generously agreed to foot the bill for the ruined car, which Carlos obligingly replaced with a rugged black truck.

"They don't get mad about money."

"Must be nice."

"If you're into money." Jimmy pivoted in the driver's seat to look Emma in the eyes. "Listen, I heard back from *National Geographic* this morning. They liked the photos, but they need a story to go with it. You're the one to tell it."

"Amazing those photos didn't end up as alligator food on the bottom of the Mujari." Emma deliberately avoided Jimmy's invitation. *National Geographic* was based in DC, not far from New York. Definitely within Horowitz's sphere of influence. Once the editors at the magazine heard her name, she was fairly certain they'd lose interest. Maybe she could write under a pseudonym. It wouldn't do her own career any good, but at least it would help Jimmy's. "*National Geographic*," she repeated. "Eight million readers."

"If we found out who killed Milton Silva, we'd have a bigger audience than that."

"Slow down. I'll settle for just breaking open a smuggling ring."

"I'm working on it. So here's the deal. They move around to a different airstrip every few weeks to avoid detection. One abandoned by miners." Jimmy took an envelope from the pocket of his shorts and handed it to her. "That's the good faith payment for you to hand to the newspaper vendor. Five thousand dollars."

Emma drew in her breath. "It's a lot of money, Jimmy."

"Took out every cent in my bank account. Listen, are you sure you're up to this? Why don't you let me do it?"

Emma shook her head. "I prefer that you man the getaway car—or truck."

"Once you've handed over the cash, he'll give you the magazine. Walk two blocks up, take a right, and walk one block back down. That will give us a chance to make sure no one's on your tail. If the smugglers suspect anything, they won't hesitate to pay off a hit man. I'll be waiting for you." Jimmy reached out and placed a hand on her knee. Emma wished she could grab it and hold on, or better yet, pull it a little further up her thigh. But she had a job to do.

"Wish me luck!" she forced a smile and opened the door.

"I wish you more than that."

Emma hadn't carried a purse since her arrival in Brazil—too tempting for muggers in the city, and impractical for hikes through the rain forest. She rummaged in the pocket of her dress for the envelope. She had never had this much money on her at once, and it heightened her sense of vulnerability. The downtown shopping area in Boa Vista was busy. No one paid attention as she approached the stand with what she hoped was a casual air. Emma pretended to consider the magazines on offer while the elderly man behind the counter handed a pack of Derby cigarettes to the customer in front of her in line. Taking hold of his smokes, the man let out a long, low whistle at Emma. She pointedly turned her back and the customer gave up, walking away with his purchase. Emma gathered her courage. She had rehearsed the Portuguese phrases.

"*Tem Monica GB?*" she asked. She held her breath. According to the script, the man would ask her exactly which publication she was after.

He did. "*Qual?*" His smile was almost a sneer.

"*Monica na Amazonia.*" He said nothing for a moment, and she wondered if she had come to the wrong kiosk. Then the old man leaned toward her. Emma smelled his sour smoker breath as his face came disconcertingly close to hers. "*Cinco mil,*" he whispered. Five thousand dollars. He straightened up and looked down his wart-spattered nose at her.

At least she knew she was in the right place. A lump forming in her throat, Emma pulled the envelope out of her pocket and placed it on the counter. He grinned slyly as he snatched it away. She heard the tearing, then the rustling of paper from beneath the counter on the other side. He was counting the money. The clang of metal rang out as he stashed the payment in a cash box. He could simply choose to keep the money, Emma realized, and there would be nothing she could do about it. She couldn't exactly call the police. Another customer approached the stand, heightening her discomfort. Slowly, obviously enjoying the situation, the old man fetched a comic strip featuring the black-haired, bucktoothed *Monica*. He dangled it in front of Emma as if he were promising meat to a dog. Emma snatched it angrily from his hand and turned away, clutching the comic strip to her chest.

She had to make sure no one was following her, not an easy task. The street was bustling with shoppers, and in Emma's eyes everyone was suddenly suspicious. *Two blocks up.* She glanced behind. A man with a mustache followed, too closely for her taste. She couldn't tell if he was on her tail or just out for an afternoon stroll. A young woman clutching a shopping bag brushed past her on the right, while a boy jostled her on the left. Any of them could be onto her. Emma's breath became shallow. On the side of the street was an open door. Emma ducked inside. She stood at the glass window, gasping for oxygen as she looked out at the pedestrian scene. From this vantage point, nothing appeared threatening. The crowd kept moving on as usual.

A man called to her from the counter as he stood up unsteadily, empty beer glass in front of him. Time to leave. Emma stepped back into the street, more confident this time, turning right before backtracking a block. Arriving at the corner, she glanced furtively around. No black pick-up. Where was Jimmy? She wondered how long she could stand at the corner without attracting attention. An SUV turned the corner and pulled up to the curb just in front of her. The driver, a miner-type with gold chains under an open linen shirt, emerged. He looked right at her, just feet away. It would be easy for him to grab her and stuff her inside the vehicle. Who in this crowd would notice or care? The man's hand strayed to his waist. *A gun*, Emma thought. *Shit.*

CHAPTER TWENTY-SEVEN

Lost

THE MINER LIFTED THE edge of his shirt. Emma instinctively sashayed to the side to throw off his aim. The man's fingers reached up, fingering the hair under his belly button. He leered at Emma as he scratched his ample stomach. No gun. *I'm losing it,* Emma thought. She tightened her grip on the comic strip and almost cried with relief when Jimmy pulled up.

"Sorry, I had to go around the block once more because you weren't here the first time," Jimmy apologized as she got in. "What took you so long?"

"I stopped at a bar to make sure no one was following me," she said breathlessly.

"You okay?" Jimmy's voice was tinged with concern.

"As long as I didn't just hand over five thousand dollars for a comic strip worth fifty cents." Emma regarded the cheap-looking comic strip. Hands trembling, Emma turned the first page, inadvertently tearing the ultra-thin paper. She stared down. Scribbled in pencil at the bottom of the first page, just above an image of *Monica* holding a suitcase, was a series of numbers. She read them out. "Latitude 2, 50, 10 North. Longitude 60, 39, 23 West."

Jimmy grinned. "Carlos will map that, no problem. As long as the truck can get through, we're there!"

"Wish we could just fly. A quick in and out."

"Fernando's still cleaning out the mud and blood from our last trip," Jimmy said.

"Is he still angry?"

"He calmed down a little after I gave him some isoniazid. But we don't need Fernando. We can always get a lift back from the jungle with Amoeba."

"Not funny, Jimmy." Emma remembered the feel of the pilot's gun on the nape of her neck.

"If he's involved, we'll get a reaction when we mention his name."

"And then we'll have connected him to the smuggling ring. The only thing I don't understand is the flow of cash. The *garimpeiro* launders the money he's received from government officials by buying gold. Then he delivers the briefcase to Amoeba. But why would Braga be paying *him*? If the poachers are bribing the government to look the other way, wouldn't the money be going in the other direction?"

"Don't assume Braga's involved. Could be any corrupt government official. To me the payment's obvious. Hit man money. For Milton's murder."

"Maybe."

"We'll find out more when we get to the poachers' camp." Jimmy cast her a sideways glance. "Depending on how far it is from Boa Vista, we might have to spend the night in the rain forest. You okay with that?"

Emma *wanted* to spend the night with Jimmy, but not in the jungle. Still, there was too much at stake to back out now. "Whatever it takes. This is our last chance, Jimmy. Dad's booked our flight back to Rio for Tuesday."

"I know. He told me Raquel's flying in tonight to spend the last few days with him before you head off."

"At least she'll keep him busy. He's not going to notice if we're gone for a couple days."

"If I get back to Rio before you leave for New York, maybe we can go out for a drink."

And that will be it, Emma thought.

CHAPTER TWENTY-EIGHT

Semi-Automatic

"I THINK WE LOST the road," Jimmy said, downshifting gears.

"We've been following a road?" Emma asked. "You could have fooled me."

"Let's look at Carlos's map." Jimmy braked to a stop.

The printout was as detailed as a map of the jungle could get. It depicted areas most likely to be flooded in wet season, essential information if they wanted to avoid getting stuck in mud again. Carlos had taught them to use a compass and the truck's speedometer to calculate their latitude and longitude down to the second. But to Emma and Jimmy's untrained eyes, the trees all looked the same. At least it hadn't rained that afternoon, and the truck, unlike the Fiat, was air-conditioned. Even so, navigating the forest was proving a bigger challenge than either of them had anticipated. The dim light of the forest didn't help, and it would only get darker.

"Looks like we should head back a few kilometers, near where we saw the abandoned shack," Emma said. Jimmy maneuvered the truck around.

"Check the compass to make sure we don't veer too far north," Jimmy said.

"We're too far to the left," said Emma. Jimmy adjusted his direction, and they seemed to return to some kind of path. The sun had lowered in the sky. It was getting more and more difficult to see what lie ahead.

"We should probably stop for the night," Jimmy suggested. "It's getting dark."

"According to the map, we're almost there anyway," Emma agreed. "If we get an early start, we should easily be able to make it by ten tomorrow morning." Which was when they were supposed to meet with the wildlife smugglers.

Jimmy turned off the engine. "Sandwich?"

Emma shook her head. She was about to spend the night in the jungle with Jimmy, and her insides were in a tumult. She wasn't sure she could hold down any food.

"Better eat now while the truck's still cool," Jimmy urged. "And inside here we're safe from the ants." Remembering the carpet of ants by the Mujari, Emma shuddered. She reached into the cooler stored at her feet, pulling out hard rolls stuffed with ham and cheese, and two fresh water bottles, slightly warm from the trip.

"So let's go over the plan again," she suggested, handing a sandwich to Jimmy. "You introduce me as your client. We tell them which animals we're looking for and negotiate a price."

Jimmy nodded. "I'll turn on the hidden camera in my watch to record the whole thing." The Dominus was another purchase facilitated by Carlos and Jimmy's parents' seemingly unlimited funds. It would provide crucial footage—proof of the smugglers' operation. "I'll drop Amoeba's name into the conversation. We'll see how they react. It could all tie into Milton's murder."

"If it does, we should talk to Iara before we break the story to see if she wants to make an announcement herself. Anyway, as soon as we get what we need in Poacherland, we get the hell out of there."

"We're *this* close, Emma."

Emma peered out into the jungle. "I keep thinking about what the *shaman* told me, about the creature who walks backwards through the forest and how I'm on the wrong track."

"I've heard that story before, from other tribes. The *Curupira* is a popular folktale. He's an elf that protects the forest. If a hunter takes just enough meat to feed his family and friends, the *Curupira* leaves him alone. But if the hunter gets too greedy, the *Curupira* will try to trick him. He disguises himself, sometimes as a beautiful woman, sometimes as a wild boar or deer, and the men chase after him. But the *Curupira's* feet are on his legs backwards. So when the hunters follow the footprints, they're actually going in the wrong direction. They end up hopelessly lost. A good story to tell your wife if you come home from a hunt without any meat. Just blame the *Curupira!*"

"When he told me the story, though, it felt like he was speaking specifically to me."

"A good *shaman* makes you feel like that. Listen, we'd better set up camp. First order of business is repellent. The mosquitoes are fierce."

Jimmy pulled a bottle of citronella oil out from under the driver's seat. After pouring a small pool of it into his palm, he reached for Emma's left calf, spreading the oil on her lower leg with rhythmic circular motions. He was taking his time. A different wetness appeared between Emma's legs as his fingers moved gently but insistently past her knee to the edge of her shorts. When he paused to tip more oil onto his hand the absence of his touch felt like torture. He reached for her other leg. The odor of the citronella blended with the smell of Jimmy's shampoo as his head brushed against her chest. Once again, his hand moved slowly up her leg until his fingers caressed the inside of her thigh. Emma opened her legs, inviting him to explore further.

Jimmy pulled back. "You might want to put some on your arms and neck," he said hoarsely, handing her the bottle of citronella. "I'll get the mosquito net set up over the back of the truck." He opened the door, and the humidity of the forest flooded in. From outside came a cacophony of howls, squeaks, and chattering. Emma descended from the truck's cabin.

"Let's get the sheets on that mattress," Jimmy said, as they both climbed into the open back of the truck. Emma eyed the narrowness of the makeshift bed. "Close quarters," Jimmy commented with a wink, causing the blood to rush to Emma's abdomen. He took one end of a white sheet and handed Emma the other. Together they fit the material over the mattress. Another white cotton sheet would serve as their blanket. Jimmy reached into the duffel bag once again, drawing out a black metal object. Emma drew in her breath. He was holding a handgun.

"Is that necessary?" Emma asked.

"Everyone else seems to have one. We're at a disadvantage if we don't."

"I hope you know how to handle that thing."

"It's easy," Jimmy said, jumping to the ground and reaching his left hand to help Emma down. "Semi-automatic. Favorite of criminals from São Paulo to Chicago. Any moron can shoot it. And many do."

"Another purchase facilitated by Carlos?"

"Carlos is anti-gun for some reason. This one I had to get on my own. Not difficult on the black market. The first thing is to unlock it. Look. Just slide." Jimmy clicked the locking device into place on the upper part of the gun and handed it to Emma, covering her hand with his. "Relax," he said as they raised the pistol together. "Keep your shoulders square to the target. Imagine that tree over there is the one person in the world you wouldn't mind taking a shot at." Emma pictured Professor Horowitz standing in front of her. "If you stretch out your arms, you'll have more control. Use your left hand as a support. Like that. Now all you have to do is press the trigger."

The force of the bullet issuing from the gun made Emma jump back. She smelled burned wood, and the target tree bore a black mark. Jimmy was right. It was easy.

"One more time," Jimmy whispered. Emma squeezed the trigger again. Another black smudge marked the tree.

"It's getting dark," Emma said, disconcerted by her success. She had just shot a gun for the first time in her life, and the ease of the act frightened her. "Let's lock that thing up. I'm going to brush my teeth." Jimmy slid the lock back into place and laid the gun on the mattress.

"You'll find some night vision goggles in the bag," Jimmy said. "Those *do* come courtesy of Carlos."

Emma scrambled into the back of the truck and fished in the duffel bag. "Do these really work?" she asked as she fished out the goggles, which resembled a pair of high-tech binoculars.

"Try them. I'll pull the mosquito net around so the bugs don't eat us alive," Jimmy said as she scrambled into the back of the truck. A screech rang through the forest, as if a young woman was crying out in terror.

"Tell me that was just an owl," said Emma.

"That was just an owl. I think."

Emma put the goggles to her eyes, and the world took on a greenish tint. They would be more effective once it got dark. Jimmy pulled off his T-shirt, revealing his smooth, masculine chest. "I feel stiff from driving the truck all day. I'm going to do some *capoeira*. Helps me relax."

"What's *capoeira*?"

"Sort of like Kung Fu, except it's not for self-defense. It's a dance. Pretend fighting." Jimmy walked back twenty feet from the truck and sat on his haunches. For a few minutes, he didn't move a muscle. He could have been a statue adorning an exotic garden. Jimmy balanced, perfectly still, staring at the forest floor as if he had gone into a trance. Then, slowly, he stood up to his full height. Muscles undulating, he swung his legs up and over. Reaching gracefully down, he placed his hand on the ground and threw his body around in a half-cartwheel. The moves were part martial arts, part ballet. To Emma, Jimmy had never looked more beautiful than he did at this moment. His fluid movements gave him an animal-like quality. The jungle formed a lush backdrop to his fluid dance. Emma was hypnotized.

Blackness was moving in. Emma squinted into the forest, but it was getting difficult to distinguish Jimmy from the shadows surrounding him. She held the night vision goggles to her eyes and rummaged in the duffel bag for a flashlight. Her hands closed, gratified, around a hard metal tube. She turned back to Jimmy, observing his green-tinted dance. A movement by the tree caught her eye, and she refocused the goggles. Emma froze. Just feet from Jimmy, an animal crouched, half hidden by the tree trunk, absolutely still. Its position reminded her of a hunting house cat studying a squirrel. Except this was not a house cat. It was a jaguar, and Jimmy was the prey.

CHAPTER TWENTY-NINE

Jaguar

"JIMMY, DON'T MOVE!" EMMA said. The cat looked in her direction at the sound of her voice, momentarily confused as to which human would make easier prey. Jimmy stood motionless. The jaguar bared its teeth, pivoting to the closer target. Emma imagined the sharp ends of those fangs ripping open Jimmy's skin. And hers. She had to think fast. Emma turned on the flashlight, shining the beam directly into the cat's eyes. Temporarily blinded, the creature growled and clawed at the air. The respite lasted mere moments. When its eyes adjusted to the light, the jaguar resumed its hunting position. Emma had to do something. But her options were limited. In desperation, she hurled the flashlight at the creature. It landed, impotent, at the cat's feet, throwing a beam off a nearby tree. The jaguar let out a low, threatening rumble. In a matter of seconds, it would all be over. Instinct took over. Through the goggles, Emma spotted a black spot on the mattress. The gun. She grabbed it, and casting the goggles momentarily aside, felt for the lock. It clicked into place. Trembling, Emma raised the pistol with her right hand, her left holding the night vision goggles to her eyes. The pistol was heavy. She struggled to hold it up.

"Run!" she screamed at Jimmy. The jaguar leaped. She pulled the trigger. Once. Twice. The jaguar roared in pain, a terrible sound that sliced through the jungle. Then, there was silence. Emma's heart pounded. She used the goggles to search for the jaguar, scanning the sea of trees before her. At last she spotted him. The once vibrant animal now lay lifeless on the ground in a pool of blood. Emma stared at it in horror. Someone was tugging at the gun and the goggles. Jimmy. He locked the pistol and laid it with the goggles at the edge of the truck. Then he pulled her into his arms, speaking softly in Portuguese. Emma didn't know what the words meant, but she didn't care. Jimmy was alive. And he was holding her in his arms.

Her mouth sought his. She eagerly pushed it open with her tongue. This time, nothing would hold her back. Her desire mounted. She entered that throbbing zone between exquisite pleasure and pain. Her body called out for his touch. She wanted his skin on every inch of her being. When he pulled back, she cried out from the physical deprivation. Slowly, taking his time, he undid each button of her shirt until it hung open on her body. Gently, he eased it off her shoulders and reached behind her to unhook her bra. Her breasts were naked and eager for his touch.

His tongue lapped at her nipples, and Emma pushed her hand down the front of his pants, seeking the hardness she knew she would find beneath it. Impatient now, they quickly removed the rest of their clothing. Jimmy groaned with desire as she lay back on the mattress, his for the taking.

"*Meu amor*," he murmured, his tongue grazing her toes, then her ankles and legs. When he reached her thighs, Emma couldn't bear it any longer. His tongue felt like silk, exploring, finding crevices she hardly knew existed. But she wanted more. Her body was an open vessel that needed to be filled. He entered her, and she guided him in a samba of pleasure. Emma pulled him toward her, straining, wanting to absorb every inch of his being into her own. Every touch, every kiss pushed her toward the brink of ecstasy, and when she fell over the edge, Jimmy caught her soul in his arms.

They clung to each other for a long time afterward, unwilling to separate. From above came the screeches of birds and monkeys. But Emma wasn't afraid. She felt as if she had just made love, really made love for the first time. What had happened with Jimmy had nothing in common with the sexual encounters she had experienced in the past. She felt as if they had become melded together.

Jimmy rolled onto his back and pulled Emma on top of him, burying his face in her hair. "I thought this would never happen," he said.

"You didn't try very hard."

"Every time I made a move, you pulled away. Come on, I wasn't imagining it, was I? You were the most standoffish girl I've ever come across."

"It's because—there's more to it than just us." Emma pulled herself off Jimmy, stretching beside him on the mattress.

"What? A suicidal boyfriend back in New York? " Jimmy threw a bare leg over hers.

I might as well tell him, Emma thought. *It's part of who I am.* She told him everything, how Horowitz had almost raped her, how she had pounded him with her cell phone, and how she was now looking into the abyss of a court case and a prematurely failed career.

"I hope I never meet that guy," Jimmy said. "I'd probably end up in jail for first-degree murder. Can't you fight back? In the courts, I mean?"

"I'm trying. Allie, a friend of mine, told me she had heard about other women who had trouble with Horowitz. I put out feelers, but just one of them got back to me. And she's traveling in Malaysia. Everyone's scared."

"Of what?"

"That Horowitz will ruin their lives, just like he's trying to ruin mine. As of now, I might not even be able to finish up my degree at NYU. Jay, my lawyer, told me I wouldn't stand a chance in court unless he could paint me as a virgin saint. No compromising shots of me with other boys."

"So that explains the fit you had over Rita's photo."

"It wouldn't look good, would it? Loose woman. Gives credibility to his claim that I offered to sleep with him for a higher grade."

"So why did you finally decide to take a chance with me?"

"Hopefully, no one's stalking us in the jungle with a camera. I *know* Horowitz must have a history. I'm not the only one he's hit on. If just one other woman came forward, I think others would too. Safety in numbers."

Jimmy bent over her, brushing his lips against her temple and stroking the hollow of her belly with his fingertips. "I feel so close to you," he murmured. "I want to stay like this forever."

"Forever's a long time."

"Not long enough."

"But you're the one who's still holding back."

"What are you talking about?"

"You're a really good photographer, Jimmy, but I saw how you were in the hospital with those patients. Why did you give up medicine?"

Jimmy withdrew his hand. His body stiffened. "I told you I don't want to talk about it."

"You see?" Emma said. "You want to know everything about me, but you still keep secrets. I want *all* of you, not just part of you."

When Jimmy spoke again, it was in a strained voice. "She was mixed race, with long straight hair and skin the color of burnt cinnamon," Jimmy said. "Way too beautiful for Rocinha, biggest shithole *favela* in Rio. I was interning at the clinic there. She came in complaining of a headache. I took her temperature—slight fever, but nothing out of this world. She was flirtatious, and I joked that she could come back to see me any time. I figured she had a cold virus, gave her some Tylenol. A week later, she returned. I could see immediately that she had gone downhill. Her fever had spiked. When she said her neck was stiff, I knew immediately that she had meningitis. I took some spinal fluid and hooked her up to IV antibiotics. I ignored all the other patients to take care of her. I stood by her hospital bed, watching as she grew weaker. It was torture. She was fading fast. I increased the dosage. A few hours later, she looked at me with her big eyes, drew her last breath, and passed away."

Jimmy's own breaths had become heavy and laborious. He was clearly suffering from the memory of his failure. Emma was sorry she had forced him to relive those painful moments. But she was glad for the knowledge. She reached out and pulled him toward her. A tear ran down his cheek, wetting her own. She kissed it away.

"Doctors aren't gods," said Emma. "They make mistakes."

"If it weren't for me, she might be alive."

"If it weren't for you, Ana Yanomami would be dead."

"I went to that girl's funeral. Paid for the coffin myself because the family didn't have money for one. Her mother actually thanked me for my help. Said her daughter's death was fate."

"Maybe it was, Jimmy. Who are you to say?"

Jimmy trembled, and she pulled him closer until, arms and legs wrapped around her own, he succumbed to the blissful amnesia of sleep.

CHAPTER THIRTY

Poached

"GOOD MORNING AMERICA!" THE voice dripped with oil. Emma opened her eyes. A monstrously large man loomed over her, running his eyes frankly over her nudity. Emma scrambled to sit up, pulling the loose white sheet over her bare breasts and nudging the still slumbering Jimmy with her toe. Jimmy's eyelids fluttered as he instinctively reached out for Emma.

"We have company," Emma alerted him. Jimmy sat up, naked and startled, his hand groping at the bottom edge of the mattress.

"Looking for something?" the man asked, brandishing the black semi-automatic before tucking it into the back of his elastic-waisted gym shorts. "I'll take care of it for you. Papagaio doesn't like to speak with people carrying guns."

Papagaio. Emma thought the word, which meant "parrot" in Portuguese, was just a password, not the name of a real person. So the man standing over them was a poacher.

"Papagaio is looking forward to meeting Exotic Pets of Miami," the man continued, smirking lasciviously. "Clothing optional. The boss would enjoy the show." He called instructions out to two squat men who were loading the bloody carcass of a jaguar onto the luggage rack of a Land Rover, parked just beside their truck. "Thank you for the cat. More profitable alive, but skin and penises always have some value." He laughed a greasy, humorless laugh. Emma wondered, as the bile rose in her throat, just how long he had been observing them. The fat man stepped down from the truck. "When you're ready," he said, heaving his weight onto the ground and into the passenger seat of the Land Rover.

Emma fumbled frantically around the bed of the truck for her clothing, discarded in haste the evening before. Jimmy had already pulled on his shorts and a T-shirt.

"You don't think they were watching—"

"Don't let your mind go there, Emma," Jimmy murmured, jewels of perspiration forming on his forehead. "Our cover still works. They don't give a shit if I slept with my client. They'd be more surprised if I didn't. As far as they're concerned, everything's still legit. Let's just go with it."

Dressed, Emma jumped down from the truck as the fat man rolled down the window of the Rover's passenger seat. "Follow me!" he ordered. He was clearly not prepared to wait around while they donned more suitable attire. Jimmy and Emma climbed into the cab of their own black truck.

"They must have heard the shots," said Emma, hastily running a brush through her hair as Jimmy turned the key in the ignition.

"And now we have the privilege of a personal escort by Big Guy." They were moving.

"Did he hear us say anything?" Emma wondered aloud.

"Doubt it. We were speaking pretty softly. And as far as I remember, we didn't say anything incriminating."

Emma glanced at Carlos's map. According to the printout, they should be at the camp by now. Through the trees, a cluster of rough stick huts became visible, seeming like a metropolis in the remoteness of the forest. The Rover pulled to a stop. They had arrived at Smuggling Central. Jimmy turned off the truck and squeezed her thigh.

"Ready?" he asked.

"As ready as I'll ever be."

"Then let's get this over with." Jimmy put his cell phone in the pocket of his shorts and switched on the Dominus watch camera. Emma stuffed her phone in the outer pocket of her backpack and put it over her arm. Opening the door of the truck, they were greeted by a cacophony of grunting and screaming. It was difficult to tell how much of the noise was coming from the jungle around them and how much from the camp itself.

"*Vem!*" Big Guy beckoned them down a short path carved out between the shacks. The camp was a beehive of activity. At least a dozen men wandered around, some of them staggering under the weight of heavy sacks. The few who looked up from their tasks to register their arrival peered out from bowed heads with inscrutable eyes. Big Guy motioned Jimmy and Emma into a hut where a dark-skinned woman with a large, ugly bruise around one eye stood hunched over a wood-burning stove. As she stirred an enormous pot, sweat trickled from her neck to the top of her substantial breasts, disappearing into the opening of her cleavage.

"Zilda!" Big Guy called out to her. "*Água!*" An unsmiling Zilda fetched a gallon of water from a mud-spattered white refrigerator. She slammed the bottle down with a thud on the white plastic table in the center of the hut. "Wait here," said Big Guy. "I will see if Papagaio is ready to see you."

Zilda carelessly splashed some liquid into two dusty, chipped mugs.

"*Obrigada,*" Emma murmured as the woman returned to her pot, maintaining a furtive eye on the visitors. Emma raised the cup to her lips and pretended to take a sip. She once again reminded herself of their cover. She owned a pet shop in Florida, Exotic Pets of Miami. Some of her customers had unusual requests, and they wanted to set up an account for shipment. Jimmy, as the agent, had arranged the meeting and would handle the details.

"Papagaio will see you now," Big Guy called to them from the door of the hut. The squeals of trapped animals rang in Emma's ears as she and Jimmy followed Big Guy to a squat metal trailer a short distance away. A makeshift set of wooden steps marked the entrance. Big Guy opened the door with a flourish, and together Jimmy and Emma stepped into the coolness of Papagaio's air-conditioned lair.

"Welcome." The raspy voice was accented, but not Brazilian. Emma's eyes took a moment to adjust to the dim light of the trailer. Once they did, she saw a tall, blond man with a broad forehead enthroned behind an enormous mahogany desk. The set-up would have been better suited to an executive suite in London than the middle of the Amazon jungle. Four long, deep scars that could have been the mark of a wildcat tracked down Papagaio's left cheek. He wore a snakeskin vest beneath a leather jacket. Draped over his shoulder was a beautiful woman, skin the color of charcoal, hair elaborately braided and pinned into a bun. Around her neck hung a heavy gold necklace embedded with brilliant jewels. She was bizarrely dressed in a bikini fashioned out of jaguar fur.

"Sit down," Papagaio urged them. "Feel free to take a look at my collection. No extra charge."

An air-conditioner droned in the background as Jimmy and Emma lowered themselves into the stiffly upholstered armchairs facing the desk. Dozens of glass eyes peered at them from the taxidermal creatures scattered around the trailer. On the wall above Papagaio's desk was an enormous stuffed python. An aquarium gurgled in the corner, filled with fanged grey fish Emma recognized as piranhas. They were feasting on what looked like the remains of a rat. Her eyes were drawn to a head hanging from a nail on the wall, displayed like a moose head at a hunting lodge. Emma flinched. It was the shrunken head of an Yanomami woman. Papagaio and his companion laughed at her reaction.

"Useless in life, worthless in death," Papagaio said. "A dead frog is more valuable than a dead Indian. Only better prize would have been the head of Milton Silva."

Jimmy positioned his wrist to get a clear shot of the gangster. "At least that Indian lover is fucking dead now!" he said, chuckling.

"Got what he deserved," Papagaio said, as he ran his eyes over Emma. "I hear *you* have an appetite. And not for food. I have an appetite too. They say the penis of the jaguar does wonders for a man's performance, and I promise you it's true. I enjoy threesomes, and I have enough stamina to spread around. We could arrange some alternative entertainment for your—agent."

"I have urgent business back in Miami," Emma said firmly, trying to sound professional in spite of the circumstances and hoping no one would notice that her heart had moved to her throat. "Let's get to the point. I'd like to set up an account."

"Straight to business," said Papagaio, as the woman in the jaguar bikini ran her tongue over his ear lobe. "No small talk. Well, suit yourself. As you can see, I am not desperate for female company. What can I do for you?"

"I have some exacting clients," Emma said. "They have very specific ideas about what kind of pets they want."

"I understand," said Papagaio, smiling. "I also have very specific ideas about what kind of pets I want as well." The woman behind him giggled and began to massage his crotch.

"We pay half upfront, the other half when my client receives the animals," Jimmy bargained.

"Unfortunately, we only accept complete payment upfront," said Papagaio. "It prevents misunderstandings."

"What happens if I don't receive the animals?" Emma asked. She had to act as if she cared about the money, even though she knew the bank transfer would never occur. "Or if they arrive dead? My customers are pet owners. They are only interested in live animals."

"If there is a mishap along the way, we will arrange for a refund of course," Papagaio responded in a prickly tone. "But we will take precautions to see that nothing happens to the creatures. We fly the most expensive ones to the port of Belem in the north. Any animals worth less than five hundred dollars are sent up river by ship. From there, they go by boat to Florida."

"What happens at customs?" Jimmy asked.

"Before arrival, the animals are drugged. No need to worry about noise when they are unloaded. You pick the crates up at the port. For all the customs officials know, they are soybeans or coffee. By the time the animals wake up, you have them in a cage in your pet store."

"And if a customs official asks questions?" Emma pressed.

"We have the means to distract curious officials," said Papagaio. "When a bribe doesn't work, we have other methods. What kind of animals do you want?"

"Tamarins," Emma responded. "Golden lion if you have them. If not, black. And a jaguar."

"I have only one jaguar, and it already has a buyer," said Papagaio. "They are getting harder to come by. I thank you for the one you shot for us last night. I will put you on a waiting list for a live cat as soon as one becomes available." The woman in the bikini slipped her hand underneath Papagaio's pants, and he shifted in his chair to accommodate her. Emma would have given almost anything at that moment just to get out of there.

"We need to ensure that the animals are in the best physical condition when they arrive," said Jimmy, his voice surprisingly steady. "The greatest health risk is when they are being flown out, of course—temperature and altitude changes."

"Our pilots are trained in such matters," said Papagaio. *Yeah, right,* Emma thought.

"My contact in Boa Vista told me we should ask for Amoeba," said Jimmy. "Said he's the best." Emma held her breath. Papagaio pushed his girlfriend's hand out of his pants and leaned back in his chair.

"I'll make sure Amoeba handles your order," he said. *So it was true,* Emma thought. Amoeba *was* in on the smuggling ring.

"My client will pay fifty thousand for a golden lion tamarin," Jimmy continued smoothly. "Ten thousand for a black one."

"You will pay seventy thousand for the golden lion, twenty for the black tamarin," said Papagaio. "I am not a Moroccan carpet seller. I do not negotiate."

Emma pretended to consider his proposal for a moment before nodding her head. "Agreed," she said, coolly.

"Delivery within two months," Jimmy pressed. Papagaio nodded his ascent. Emma stood up to leave. *The faster we get out of here the better,* she thought.

"*Senta.* Sit down," Papagaio said, his voice taking on a musical cadence. "I never conclude a business negotiation without a drink. Bad luck."

"Whisky, not *cachaça,*" said his companion. "Papagaio has class." It was the first time she had spoken, and her accent gave her away as Brazilian. She leaned down and opened a cabinet of the enormous desk, pulling out a bottle and four shot glasses. Emma tried not to think about where her hand had just been as she served the alcohol.

"To a long and profitable business relationship," said Papagaio, lifting his glass.

"Cheers," Emma said, downing her whisky in a single gulp. It burned her throat as she swallowed it. When the others had emptied their glasses, she placed her hand in Papagaio's sweaty palm for a shake.

"I will ask my man to show you the animals before you leave," said Papagaio, disentangling himself from his girlfriend's embrace. He stood up, and for the first time Emma realized that he was almost seven feet tall. He walked them to the door. Emma grabbed her pack from the floor and followed, feeling whoozy from the alcohol on an empty stomach. Big Guy stood just outside. As guard, Emma realized.

"I will attend to some overdue *business* here," chuckled Papagaio, as his woman blew him a kiss from behind the desk. "We will fulfill your order as soon as you transfer money into our account. Enjoy yourselves. Better than a trip to the zoo."

Emma and Jimmy stepped out of the air conditioning and into a wall of heat and humidity. Big Guy, who had been waiting outside the trailer, gestured for Emma and Jimmy to follow him. The animal sounds grew louder as they strode down the path. At the edge of the camp was an area with dozens of cages, some haphazardly stacked on top of each other. The pungent odor of animal excrement was overwhelming. More workers milled about, some carrying buckets of food, others pushing wheelbarrows. Emma and Jimmy stopped at the first pen, where a small black-faced monkey eyed them forlornly from the bottom of a filthy basin. Its water dish was blackened with dozens of drowned ants.

"Titi," said Big Man, identifying the species. Emma stared at the creature's almost human face. He looked sadly up at her as if pleading for help. With difficulty, she tore herself away, steeling herself not to show emotion. The next cage hosted three different types of parrots, which moved listlessly back and forth on their cramped perches. Emma heard the next animal before she saw it. The jaguar's roar made her spine tingle. But her eyes fell on a very different sight than the one that had unnerved her the previous evening. These cats ruled the rainforest at night, but the kingdom of this particular animal had been reduced to a miniscule cage. The jaguar had just enough room to pace three steps in either direction before it was forced to turn around and go the other way. Every now and then, it paused to bite and claw ineffectively at the bars of the cage. Its fur rippled impatiently; its eyes were filled with agony.

"Reminds you of some special moments?" Big Guy leered at them. Emma resisted the urge to tell him to mind his own business. They passed cages of anteaters and tapirs. At the end of the row were two small glass enclosures that housed an assortment of bugs and frogs.

"Pets?" Emma asked. Big Guy shrugged his shoulders.

"People think they have magic powers," he said. "Some will go into aquariums, but most will be turned into powders and ointments. What do you think of our collection?"

"Impressive," Jimmy said. A droning sound from above was getting louder.

"*Entrega!*" a worker called out.

"A plane is arriving to pick up a delivery of parrots," said Big Guy. "Come! You will see how we do it." He called out orders to one of the men. Emma looked up to see the glint of metal as the craft came in for a landing.

"Time to make our exit," Emma whispered to Jimmy. "Might be Amoeba. Let's make our excuses."

"Amoeba flies a different model of plane," Jimmy reassured her, placing a hand on her elbow. Big Guy was already walking up the path. "But I can't wait to get out of this hell hole. We've got enough material. I'll just ask Big Guy for my gun back, and we can say our polite goodbyes."

Emma and Jimmy followed Big Guy past the huts to the runway, if you could call it that. It was barely wider than the path they had just walked down and seemed much too short for a plane to land. But the craft touched down expertly, braking to a halt just before it hit a crop of trees at the other end. Propellers created a wind that whipped at their hair as they walked toward the plane. A pilot, thankfully not Amoeba, lowered himself down from the cockpit. Big Guy wrapped him in a generous bear hug and spread his hands in a gesture toward Emma and Jimmy, introducing them as his clients. The pilot displayed a crooked grin as he shook their hands. Emma was grateful that the poachers didn't go in for Brazilian-style kisses.

"Thanks for your hospitality, but my client and I need to get back to Boa Vista," said Jimmy in a casual tone. "We've got a long drive back."

"Yes, of course," said Big Guy.

"The gun?"

"Oh yes," Big Guy said in mock surprise as he reached into his pocket and pulled out the semi-automatic. "I hope you have plenty of ammunition," he said as he handed it to Jimmy. "The forest is a dangerous place. Too bad you didn't take Papagaio up on his offer to spend the night. I'm sure you would have had an interesting evening."

"Another time," said Emma. As they turned to go, she spotted a man emerging from a hut at the end of the runway. He was small with dark hair. Emma knew she had seen him before but couldn't place him. She detected a mutual flicker of recognition in the worker's eyes. Then, as quickly as an Amazon rainstorm, the man's identity came to her. It couldn't be, but it was. Emma's stomach twisted.

"José," she whispered to Jimmy as they started up the path towards the truck. "Amoeba's mechanic." She turned for another look. This time, he was staring straight at her. José had obviously, in that instant, figured out the connection as well. He quickened his pace, calling out to Big Guy. Their cover had been blown.

"*Puta!*" Jimmy swore.

"Let's get the hell out of here!" Emma said. They broke into a run. The few moments it took for Big Guy to figure out what was happening—that they were journalists, not clients—gave Jimmy and Emma a valuable head start. It didn't last long.

"*Pega os filhos da puta!*" shouted Big Guy to the others. *Get those sons of bitches.*

Jimmy unlocked the gun as they sprinted away, turning briefly to fire a warning shot at their pursuers. Emma raced ahead, backpack in tow. By now, the entire camp had been alerted. From all sides, workers were closing in. A pair of muscular arms grabbed at Emma. She twisted away, eluding their grasp. More workers were heading in their direction. She needed to cover more ground, and quickly. A hand had got hold of her hair. She pivoted. José. In desperation, Emma heaved her backpack at the mechanic's head. She pulled away, ignoring the pain in her scalp as a few strands of hair stayed behind. The black truck came into view. She was almost there.

But the path was blocked. Papagaio. Emma was trapped between him and the workers behind. She didn't have time to think. With a swift movement, she smashed her foot into Papagaio's balls. His eyes bugged out in surprise. Howling in pain, he shriveled to the path. From behind, Jimmy pulled the trigger of his handgun. Blood spurted from Papagaio's leg as Emma ran past. She glanced back, panting, as a barrage of bullets splattered around her. The poachers had an arsenal of weapons. Even Jimmy's semi-automatic would not hold off their firepower. Just a few more steps to go. Emma lengthened her stride. A gunshot rang out, bouncing off the black truck. Her heart raced as her hand reached for the door handle. She climbed into the driver's seat and turned the key in the ignition. Finally thinking she had made it to safety, a gun cracked and the windshield splintered.

CHAPTER THIRTY-ONE

Logs

SHARDS OF GLASS RAINED down on Emma as she gripped the gears. In the rearview mirror, she caught sight of Jimmy. *Thank God.* He wouldn't make it to the cab, but he might make it to the back. Yes! Jimmy leapt into the truck bed. But he wasn't alone. Right behind him, José stepped on the truck's fender, lip curling as he aimed his pistol at Jimmy's sprawling figure. Emma floored it. José fell back, hitting the ground with a thud. A symphony of metal hitting metal rang out as fresh gunfire sprayed the pick-up. Just behind them, the Land Rover backed out, riding up over the bump of the fallen mechanic. The poachers were on their tail, one man hanging out of the passenger seat with a well-aimed rifle. Emma flew down the narrow jungle path. Branches clawed at the truck as it bounced over the uneven ground.

Jimmy pointed his gun at their pursuers, unleashing a fresh series of shots. From the Rover came a horrific shriek as blood spattered the side of the car. Emma glanced in the mirror again. Jimmy had put a bullet through the shooter's arm. As it dangled from the side of the car, a branch hit with such a force that it severed the man's limb, leaving a bloody stump behind. The armless man screamed in agony. Taking over the hunt, the driver trained his gun out the side and fired. The rear window behind Emma exploded, and she felt a stinging pain in her neck. Emma kept her foot to the floor, taking advantage of her pursuer's troubles to gain a few yards of distance. She was definitely driving too fast. The jungle darkened as it closed in more tightly. She had to keep it together. She had to focus or she would lose control. The Rover was closing the gap. In the mirror, Emma saw Jimmy grab the duffel bag and sling it at the windshield of the car behind. The bag found its target, blocking the driver's view before it bounced into the jungle. The Rover swerved.

All at once brilliant sunshine flooded in from overhead. A road. Emma turned the steering wheel sharply to the left to avoid plowing into a tree. A thud issued from the back of the truck as Jimmy was thrown against the side. Emma looked in the mirror to see if he was okay. Her stomach rose to her throat. An eighteen-wheeler, heavily laden with logs, was headed straight toward them. The deep tone of a horn pierced the air.

Another honk sounded, longer this time, followed by the low-pitched strain of brakes. Then came the sickening sound of metal crashing as the eighteen-wheeler smashed into the Rover. A blast pealed as the car burst into flames. Jimmy let out a whoop of joy as they fled the destruction, but Emma couldn't celebrate. Not yet. There could be others behind her. For a long time, she thought of nothing but keeping her foot glued to the pedal.

Without the protection of the windshield, dust flew in her face and hair. She had no idea where she was going. But the road must lead somewhere, Emma reasoned, and anywhere was better than the place they had left behind. She pressed on, fear ebbing from her body with every mile the pick-up conquered. Yet despite her pressure on the gas pedal, the truck began to lose speed. Emma pressed harder, but it was no use. Soon, the truck was just coasting. She leaned forward as if she could accelerate by sheer force of will. It was no good. Slowly but surely, they came to a complete stop.

"Shit!" Emma swore.

They both jumped down from the truck.

"Woohoo!" Jimmy shouted as he wrapped her in an enthusiastic hug. His mouth found hers. He tasted like salt and dust. "*Meu deus!*" he said when he pulled back and took in her appearance. "You look like a clay Venus."

"Nice to meet you, Apollo." Jimmy was also caked in red. Emma reached to the back of her neck. Her hand, when she took it away, was dark red.

"You're bleeding."

"One of the shards from the windshield must have cut me. I don't think it's serious."

"Let me take a look." Jimmy lifted her hair and inspected the wound. "Doesn't look too deep. I'll get you some antibiotics when we get to Boa Vista. Listen, I know we're pretty far from the camp, but they could send someone after us. We should get moving."

Emma didn't want to tell him. But she had to. "I wish we could," Emma said. "But the fact is, we've run out of gas."

CHAPTER THIRTY-TWO

Ashes

"WE COULD WALK IT," Emma suggested.

"No way," Jimmy said, suddenly deflated. "Might take days to get back to Boa Vista. We don't have nearly enough food and water." He pulled his cell phone out of the pocket of his shorts, pressing a button. "No signal. What a surprise."

"Mine was in the backpack I slammed in the face of one of the poachers."

Jimmy stirred up a cloud of dust as he ran a hand through his hair. "Listen, maybe things aren't so bad. This road is obviously used for logging, and I think it goes in the direction of Boa Vista. Someone's bound to come along."

There were all sorts of things wrong with Jimmy's statement. It was far from certain, for one thing, that any driver coming along this road would be disposed to come to their aid. The next people to pass by could very well be from the smuggling camp they had just escaped.

"At least we still have the gun," Emma said, trying to sound upbeat.

Jimmy took the semi-automatic out of his pocket and inspected it. "As useful as the truck right now. Out of ammunition."

"Could be used in a pinch, as a scare tactic, couldn't it?"

Jimmy didn't answer as he pocketed the gun. Emma squinted as the sun bore down. A trickle of sweat ran down her back. "Right now we need to move into the shade before we pass out from the heat," said Jimmy. "Better get what's left of our food and water supplies from the truck before they roast."

Emma fished the remaining backpack from the cab and rummaged through it. "A bruised banana, some crackers, and a water bottle."

"Veritable feast."

"How do the indigenous tribes manage?" Emma asked. "Must be some food in the forest. Nuts and berries.'

"They plant crops and hunt," Jimmy reminded her. "And even then, they barely survive. The Amazon is one of the biggest food deserts on the planet. Unless we want to go in for slug sandwiches, which may not be a bad idea, depending on how desperate we get."

"No use saving the banana," Emma pointed out as they lowered themselves to the ground at the side of the road. "It will rot in a few hours." She pulled down the bruised peel, broke off the top half and handed it to Jimmy.

Jimmy took a swig of water and offered the bottle to Emma. "We'll have to be careful with the water," he pointed out. "We don't know how long we'll be here." It took a force of will for Emma to refrain from guzzling down the entire contents of the bottle.

"Did you get it all on film?" she asked, anxious to move the conversation away from their flimsy provisions, which were already occupying way too much of her brain space.

"Think so. May not be the best quality, but we can always enhance it. When we get back to Boa Vista." Emma sensed that Jimmy had avoided the word *if* for her benefit.

"I would so love to see those guys in jail."

"You have more faith in the Brazilian justice system than I do."

"So why didn't you just shoot Papagaio dead while you had the chance? You deliberately aimed at his leg."

Jimmy stared at the ground. "Leftover from medical training, maybe. The sanctity of life."

"They'll be a public outcry, once people see the film. The feds will have to act."

"They need to catch the poachers first. You can bet that those guys will not be sticking around that location."

"The story has to be put out in the right way. I wonder if it was Papagaio or Amoeba who warned the journalists away from Milton's funeral."

"Could have been either." A parade of tiny red ants paraded toward them. "Fire ants," Jimmy said. "Their sting is painful." They shifted position a few yards further up. The heat was unbearable, and the shade at the side of the road was little help.

"I'm having these fantasies about sitting at a café with an ice cold bottle of *Guaraná* in front of me," said Emma.

"Don't do that to yourself. Try to think of something else."

"How about an ice-cold bottle of Coke?"

"Right now, I'd settle for a warm beer."

A low rumbling interrupted their fantasies. *Thunder*, Emma thought. But the sky was still clear.

"Someone's coming!" said Jimmy. Seconds later, a glint of metal became visible in the distance.

"What if it's someone from the camp?" Emma's voice was tinged with fear. "Maybe we shouldn't risk it."

"Listen to me, Emma," Jimmy said fiercely, grabbing her by the shoulders. "We'll die out here on our own. We have barely any food or water, and no way to defend ourselves. We have to take a chance."

"But if it's a poacher—"

"It's not a poacher. It's a logging truck. Look." A logging truck. Emma could have cried with relief. The truck, reassuringly loaded down with lumber, was coming nearer. Jimmy and Emma planted themselves in the middle of the road, signaling to the driver to stop. The truck strained to a halt, and the driver, a thin, moth-eaten type, leaned over to push open the passenger door. He grinned, revealing two uneven rows of gray teeth, a single gold one glinting in the corner of his mouth.

"I don't like his looks," Emma whispered, holding back.

It's not a beauty contest. Let's see if he'll give us some gas." Jimmy stepped forward to talk to the driver.

"*A gente pode emprestar gasolina?*"

The man shook his head and mumbled something that ended with the words *Boa Vista*.

"He can't spare any gas, but he's offered us a ride to Boa Vista," Jimmy murmured to Emma.

"Do we have a choice?" she whispered back.

"No." Jimmy was right. This was their best chance of making it back to town alive, and they had to take it. Jimmy climbed in first, placing himself between the driver and Emma. Emma hoisted herself up to the high cab after him and shut the door. The driver pressed the gas pedal, and the black pick-up faded from sight in the side-view mirror.

"*Magrão*," the driver stated. "Big Skinny", Jimmy whispered. "It must be a nickname." A morose man with a few days' stubble on his chin, he was not prone to small talk, and Emma was grateful. She was nervous to utter a word for fear of giving herself away as a foreigner. She didn't imagine that Americans were popular with the loggers around here. With her skin caked in mud, undulating dark hair her most striking feature, she figured she could pass for Brazilian. She pulled the water out of her backpack. Now that they were headed to town, there was no need to ration their supplies. After offering some to the driver, they downed the rest of the bottle. The liquid felt heavenly on Emma's parched tongue. They drove on, every mile of forest looking the same as the one they had left behind. Every now and then, Jimmy touched her hand for reassurance. *We'll be in Boa Vista soon*, Emma thought. She began to fantasize again about what she would order at the restaurant when they got back to town.

"*Estamos parando?*" Jimmy asked. They were slowing down. Magrão didn't respond. He stared straight ahead, his lip curling in a smile, gold tooth glinting. The truck turned, laboriously, onto a path that was far too narrow for the eighteen-wheeler. Branches grabbed menacingly at the metal sides. Emma took in Jimmy's tense expression. A knot formed in her stomach.

Suddenly, the path they were driving down ended, and they found themselves at the edge of a black sea. Gone was the soothing monotony of the jungle. The jagged remains of hundreds of tree stumps lifted their scorched wooden fingers to the sky as if in supplication. For miles around, there was nothing but charred wood and ashes. The stench of burnt earth permeated the enclosed truck. The silence of the place, devoid of bird song and animal chatter, was as ominous as a jaguar's roar.

Emma tried to silence the voice inside her head that told her something was very wrong and strove for optimism. Magrão was probably just stopping for some gas or provisions. This could be the Amazon version of a roadside café. Maybe there would be a table heaped with rice, beans, and chicken waiting for them. Emma's stomach growled. In the midst of the blackness, a tower rose up. *A cell phone tower,* Emma thought. *Jimmy can check his signal.* Beside the tower stood a house, if you could call it a house, that is. It was more like a shack. And just beyond that ran a milk-toned river. The driver strained to a halt in front of the hut, out of which emerged a short, stout man who walked with a limp. Without explanation, Magrão descended from the truck and approached the limping man. They spoke in low tones, glancing every now and then back at Jimmy and Emma who had stayed behind in the cab. The limping man gave a twisted smile.

"I don't like the look of this," said Jimmy.

"Neither do I. What about the gun? It might scare them off."

"Too risky without bullets. We'd be better off making a run for it."

"Let's do it." But as Emma reached for the handle passenger seat, the limping man pulled a pistol from the back of his trousers and trained it on them.

"Too late," she said. Magrao yanked open the passenger door and motioned them out. Jimmy held up his hands to signal that he posed no threat, and Emma did the same. Slowly, they emerged from the truck. There was no point in giving the gunman a reason to pull the trigger. The limping man indicated with the pistol that they should move toward the shack. *It's useless to run now,* Emma thought. *They'd shoot us on the spot.* Magrão pushed open the rotting wooden door, and they stepped in.

Emma's eyes struggled to adjust to the dim light. She turned to look at Jimmy, expecting to see her own fear mirrored in his face. To her surprise, Jimmy winked. Emma was unprepared for what happened next. Abruptly, as if he were performing a *capoeira* dance move, Jimmy leaned down and swung his legs around, his feet propelling the gun out of the short man's wrist. A shot fired. Jimmy seized the moment to rush forward, knocking the short man to the ground. As Magrão lunged at the fallen gun, Emma lobbed her foot into his scrawny waist. He fell to the ground. Swiftly, Emma grabbed the pistol from the floor and pointed it at the driver. With a petrified look in his eyes, Magrão turned and fled.

Jimmy was on top of the short man, fists pounding his face. Emma lifted the gun and took aim. She could take him out. She knew it. But just as she was about to pull the trigger, the short man managed to push Jimmy off, and they tumbled through the shack like a human ball. Emma aimed again, but this time, she couldn't get a clear shot. She could scare him at least. Emma trained the gun at the walls of the shack and shot twice. The limping man froze, and Jimmy stood up. Then a door slammed behind Emma. One look at Jimmy told her something was wrong.

"Watch out!" he called. Emma turned. Magrão was back, this time gripping a large metal rod.

Emma trained the gun on him, pulling the trigger. The gun popped, but no bullet came out. Magrão smiled, his gold tooth shining in the light that filtered through the boards of the shack. Emma suddenly realized what she had done when she unloaded the bullets into the wall of the shed. She had destroyed their only chance of escape. Magrão had counted the shots. He knew there were no more bullets. The driver grinned sadistically as he raised the metal bar and aimed it at her skull.

CHAPTER THIRTY-THREE

Trapped

LUKEWARM WATER POURED OVER Emma, rousing her from unconsciousness. She heard the laugh before she opened her eyes. She would recognize that sound anywhere. Souza.

She opened her eyes. He stood before her, Magrão at his side holding an empty bucket of water. From a bench at a flimsy card table in the corner, the limping man pointed and smiled. Emma realized in horror that they were admiring the way her wet clothes now clung to her body, outlining the pertness of her breasts all too clearly. Daylight seeped through cracks in the wooden planks of the hut. Emma recognized it as the weak light of day's end. *How long have I been knocked out?* Her head ached. She tried to raise her hand but couldn't. Her hands were bound together behind her, and her feet were tied with a rough rope that was tethered in turn to a post of the hut.

Emma glanced to her right. Leaning against the wall next to her was Jimmy, similarly helpless. His hands tied behind him, minus the watch with the hidden camera. Their kidnappers must have taken it. Even if the Dominus' hidden camera escaped them, they must have figured it was worth something. Jimmy's eyes were trapped fire. It was horrible to see him like that. But he was alive. Souza knelt in front of her and caressed her breast, a sick smile on his face. Emma tried to twist away from his touch but had no way to escape. She was a caged animal at the mercy of her abductors. Jimmy writhed helplessly by her side as Souza put a dirty hand under her chin and raised it up. Emma stared back, filled with loathing at the sight of his oily mustache and expensive cowboy paraphernalia. Memories of Horowitz flooded back.

"*Bonita.*" Souza grunted and laughed again. Pretty. Emma didn't take it as a compliment. He leaned toward her, his lips aimed at hers. Filled with disgust, Emma gathered saliva and spat in his face. Souza pulled back, licking her saliva from his lips. His eyes burned bright with rage as he drew back his fist. Emma recoiled, but had little wiggle room. Souza's punch caught her on the edge of the chin. The pain was searing. Next to her, Jimmy struggled to free his hands. *He would kill Souza right now if he got the chance,* Emma thought. She expected Souza to hit her again, but instead he stood up and began to unfasten his belt. The meaning was not lost on Emma. She felt dizzy with nausea. Jimmy struggled next to her, kicking his feet futilely in Souza's direction. His helplessness made Souza laugh again as he unbuttoned and unzipped his pants.

The sound of a ringing telephone cut through the air. It was coming from Souza's front pocket. He seemed irritated at the interruption, but closed his fly and pulled out his cell phone, pressing a button and putting the device to his ear. Whatever the person on the other end of the telephone said, Souza was not pleased. He screamed curses, venting his anger for a minute or two before disconnecting the cell and placing it back in his pocket.

"*Vou lidar com ela depois,*" he said to the other two men. I'll deal with her later. He shot a venomous look at Emma and Jimmy. Then he strode out the door, his two accomplices like pet dogs at his heel. Emma heard the sound of a truck driving away. She and Jimmy were alone. Emma felt tears of relief streaming down her cheeks.

"I'll kill that fucker!" Jimmy exploded.

"Don't think about that now. Let's focus on getting out of here," Emma said. "Can you slip out of the ropes?"

"I can barely move."

"Me too," Emma said, chafing at the rope. "What's Souza doing here?"

"Apparently the truck driver smelled the odor of a lucrative kidnapping when he picked us up." Jimmy spat out the words. "He moonlights for Souza and brought his boss here to see the goodies he had caught. I guess Carlos was right when he said Souza doesn't make his money from farming alone. When Souza recognized you, he couldn't have been happier. Their next move will be to contact Mike and ask for a ransom."

"How much?"

"A million *reais*."

Emma gasped. Five hundred thousand dollars. Her dad didn't have that kind of money. "You must be joking! And what about you? Will they contact your parents too?"

"I gave them a fake name, but they'll catch on eventually, and then they'll raise their ransom demand. I've been listening to their conversation. Apparently Souza's an old hand in the kidnapping business, when he's not burning down trees for his plantations. This is officially Yanomami territory, but he bribed a local official to issue him a deed."

"Why did he leave?"

"From what I could understand, some environmental protestors have set up camp on another piece of land he was about to set the match to. He's gone to ask the local police to evict them. Fortunately, it's the kind of problem that will take some time to resolve. Shit! It's no use, Emma. I can't get out of these ropes."

"I'm not getting anywhere either," Emma said.

They were trapped. Emma understood all too well what that meant. While Souza was waiting for the ransom money to come through, he wouldn't hesitate to use her for his own pleasure. Emma felt the bile rise in her throat at the thought. She opened her mouth. She wanted to tell Jimmy that no matter what happened, it wasn't his fault. Her thoughts were interrupted by the incongruous ring tone of an electric guitar.

"My cell!" Jimmy said. "Magrão left it behind!" Emma spotted the cell phone lying tantalizingly near the edge of the card table.

"I might be able to get it," Emma said. "I've got a longer tether than you." She crawled toward it, straining at the tether that bound her feet to the pole. With difficulty, she managed to raise herself on her knees. Lifting her hands off her back, Emma reached for the phone. It lay just out of reach. In desperation, Emma pushed with her head at the legs of the card table. The sudden movement sent Jimmy's cell flying to the dirt floor. She looked down at the caller ID and drew in her breath. Emma maneuvered her bound hands and managed to press her thumb on the answer button behind her, putting the cell on speaker.

"Hello?" Carlos murmured through the static.

"Carlos!" Emma shouted.

The phone went dead.

"He'll call back," said Jimmy.

"I don't think so," Emma responded. "The phone just ran out of batteries."

CHAPTER THIRTY-FOUR

Ransom

"They're in trouble."

"Who *is* this?" Mike frowned into the phone.

"Carlos."

Mike sucked in oxygen. "What do you know about it?"

"I tracked Jimmy's cell phone before it went dead. They're well into the forest—at least half a day's drive from here. I know that part of the jungle. It's controlled by Souza's gang. He drove my tribe out of there when he burned their hunting grounds."

"What the hell were they doing out in the jungle by themselves?"

"Working on a story. Infiltrating a smuggling ring. Thought it might be connected to Milton Silva's murder."

"How do you know all this? Were you involved?"

Carlos hesitated. "I gave them the contact number," he admitted. "And the truck."

"If anything happens to my daughter, asshole, I'll make sure you rot in hell."

"Listen, I want them back too. Do you want my help or don't you?"

"Help? What kind of help could you possibly provide?"

"I know the location. We can organize a rescue."

"A *rescue*? Listen, Superman, I've been kidnapped myself. Do you know what it's like? You're watched over day and night by a bunch of trigger-happy thugs who think they're doing you a big favor if they let you use the bathroom by yourself. Don't talk to me about a rescue. We have no way of knowing what we'd be walking into."

"So what's your plan?"

"Pay the ransom, as soon as I can come up with the money."

"Even if you do, there's no guarantee they'll be released alive."

"Thanks for the vote of confidence. Now, if you'll fuck off, I need to make some phone calls."

CHAPTER THIRTY-FIVE

Cards

THE MOMENTS WHEN THEY were too tired to talk were hardest. At those times, Emma knew exactly how the jaguar at the smuggling camp must feel. A quiet desperation could sneak up on you when your mind wasn't occupied. It was their second day of captivity, and Emma felt she would soon go mad. At least the jaguar could pace the cage. With her hands and feet bound, Emma couldn't even move. She tried to separate her mind from her body. It had been days since either of them had eaten a regular meal, and their churning stomachs were audibly crying out for food. Mosquitoes crawled through cracks in the walls of the shack. Emma felt that every inch of her body must have been bitten at some point. Her arms and legs were covered with red welts.

But the greatest torture was the lack of water. It had rained the evening before. The sound of the water falling outside had driven Emma crazy. When some drops escaped through the roof to trickle down the wall behind them, they had licked the moisture off the boards with their tongues, dirt and all. They hadn't gotten much, but it helped, at least until morning, when they were once again overcome by thirst. Their captors seemed to have forgotten them. *They've left us here to die,* she thought.

The dim light that seeped through the cracks of the hut was beginning to weaken again when Emma heard the sound of a truck arriving. Her stomach turned as she expected to see Souza walk through the door at any moment. *If we're lucky, he'll just shoot us and get it over with,* Emma thought. The door opened, and Magrão and the limping man entered the hut. Souza wasn't with them, and Emma hoped that that was a good sign. Maybe he had picked up the ransom money and sent his two workers to set them free. Magrão, holding a rifle, stepped toward them, a sick smile revealing his gold tooth. He lifted his foot and kicked Jimmy in the stomach, chuckling when his victim doubled over in pain. His cohort was carrying a half-empty bottle of vodka in one hand, a deck of cards in the other. Both of them were drunk, Emma realized, and seemed intent on getting drunker. Propping his rifle on the sidewall of the hut, Magrão said something in Portuguese to Jimmy, who reddened with anger. The kidnappers laughed as they settled down at the card table, bottle of vodka between them. The man with the limp shuffled and dealt the cards.

"What did he say?" Emma asked, although a part of her didn't want to know.

Jimmy just shook his head, his expression contorted with pain.

"Tell me," Emma said. "Just tell me. I know we're probably going to die. I want to prepare myself mentally for exactly how they're planning to do it."

"They said—they're making a bet. That's all. For who wins the game of poker."

"Does the bet involve me?"

Jimmy didn't answer. Emma knew what he refused to put into words. She was the prize. She felt the air bubble of disgust rise from the pit of her stomach to her throat, but as hard as she gagged, there was nothing in her stomach to throw up. The light was fading quickly. Magrão fetched some flashlights from a shelf in the corner, turning them on and setting them upside down on the card table. Insects cast occult shadows on the ceiling. Every time the two men finished a round, they would each take a swig of the vodka. For Emma, time seemed to pass so slowly it was as if the earth had forgotten to spin on its axis. After a few hands, the man with the limp started to slur his speech. *Maybe they'll get so drunk that they pass out,* she thought hopefully. The minutes dragged by, the men saying little, but speaking in louder and louder voices when they did. After a while it was clear that the man with the limp was losing. Magrão leered at Emma and directed some words in their direction. Jimmy's face darkened. This time, Emma didn't ask him to translate.

The trucker stood up, reached for the vodka bottle, and emptied the last drops of liquid into his mouth. He walked toward Emma, smiling sickly. He had won his bet and would collect his reward. He pulled down his pants, revealing a fat, erect, hairy penis. Outside the hut, a bird wailed out its night song.

CHAPTER THIRTY-SIX

Quiver

CARLOS PLACED HIS FOOT in the mud at the side of the river bank. One good thing about rainy season was that it muffled any sounds. Another good thing was that the rain had swollen the water enough that they could pull up close to the hut. Without a sound, ten men stepped out of the two canoes. Two would stay behind in the boats, their paddles ready for a quick getaway.

The tribe knew this spot all too well. It was sacred: the site of the river of tears they had cried when Souza's men had blackened the earth. They could still smell the acrid odor of the trees' ashes. Those trees could have given them much. Now, they were gone. Tonight, the Indians would exact their revenge. Under the cloak of night, the twelve warriors had slid down the river from their village. Face decorated with red and black streaks, Carlos was indistinguishable from the others.

Silence was their weapon of choice. Every step was taken with care as the moon lit their way. The warriors did not speak, even in a whisper. They didn't need to. The goal was clear. The plan had been carefully laid out. Carlos led the group, moving stealthily with the others close behind. The lack of trees here meant that the full moon shone down, lighting their path. They didn't have far to walk before they spotted the ramshackle shack that Souza's men had thrown up after they burned the land. Slowly, the ten painted men encircled the hut, assuming their designated spots. Four Yanomami stood by the shuttered window; the others, including Carlos, moved to the entrance.

Carlos eyed the rotting wood of the door and allowed himself just one moment of doubt. He was putting multiple lives in danger: not just Jimmy's and Emma's, but those of his Yanomami brothers. What if it all went wrong? But he couldn't allow himself to think that way. His mother would not have approved. Remembering her, Carlos reached into his soul, calling on the warrior inside.

A raid by miners the week before had deprived the Yanomami of their rifles. They would have to make do with their longbows and dart guns, which should be sufficient. In bamboo quivers on their backs they carried arrows and darts tainted with frog venom. Once a poisoned dart pierced the skin, its victim was not long for this world. Carlos looked around, making sure the men were ready. The arranged signal was the cry of the potoo bird. Carlos hooted a convincing imitation. A warrior friend hooted a response. It was time to make their move. Casting any remaining qualms aside, Carlos threw himself against the door, the other Yanomami following his lead. The door collapsed under their collective weight. At the same moment, to the side of the house, warriors split open the shutters of the only window and clambered through. Magrão was caught by surprise with his pants around his legs, his rapidly deflating penis hanging out from the black bush of his abdomen.

The limping kidnapper, fully clothed, reached for a rifle that had been propped up against the side of the hut. As he did so, the men standing behind Carlos loaded their bows, pulling back on the string with all their might. They let their arrows fly. Three arrows hit the short man. He fell on top of the card table, which collapsed beneath him. The playing cards scattered. Magrão had managed to pull up his pants and was lunging for the rifle that his companion had failed to get a hold of. His hands closed on the gun, and he lifted it up, aiming it at Carlos. Carlos put the dart gun to his mouth, took aim, and blew as hard as he could. The dart, balanced delicately at the edge of the wooden pipe, flew through the air and found its target, just above the kidnapper's heart. Magrão fell back with a great thud. Carlos reached for his knife and looked around the hut.

CHAPTER THIRTY-SEVEN

Blade

THE FLOOR OF THE shack was now littered with blood-spattered aces, jacks, queens, and kings. Emma recoiled as an Yanomami warrior leaned toward her, knife glinting in the beams of the overturned flashlights.

"Emma!" Emma looked into a pair of familiar almond eyes and was hit by a wave of relief.

"Carlos!"

Carlos pulled a knife from the pocket of his shorts and cut through Emma's ropes. She rubbed her wrists. A few trickles of blood escaped from the area where the rope had cut into her skin. She placed her wrist in her mouth. It tasted like freedom. She reached for the knife.

"Let me do Jimmy's," she said, moving the blade back and forth like a saw at the cords holding Jimmy's hands behind his back. On the last slice, the rope fell away. Emma and Jimmy began to hack at the cords tethering their feet. Their two abductors were sprawled on the dirt floor, unmoving. With a cry of triumph, Emma sliced through the last strands of rope holding her captive.

"Let's go!" Jimmy cried. "Who knows when Souza will get here and what kind of reinforcements he'll bring with him."

The hut was in chaos. The limping man was lying facedown in a pool of his own blood. Magrão was sprawled on his back, still as a crypt, eyes shut. A wave of disgust overcame Emma as she looked at them. The Yanomami hooted a war cry of victory. Emma stood up shakily as Jimmy beckoned her toward the door. Emma could feel the night breeze wafting into the shack and longed to embrace the freedom of the open air. She turned to run. Then, she heard the shot. Pain seared her thigh. Emma wanted to move, but her leg wouldn't obey. She glanced behind her. Unbelievably, Magrão was on his feet, aiming his rifle at Emma's heart. But she wouldn't let him kill her. Not now. Not after what she'd been through. The rage that erupted in Emma gave her a burst of energy. Knife still in her hand, she lunged at her would-be rapist. She felt the resistance as the blade met the man's skin, but she didn't pull back. She thrust it forward. As the knife entered his body, the man's eyes bulged out in an expression of stupid surprise. Emma felt the wetness around her hand as the man fell on top of her.

"Get him off me!" she screamed.

Mercifully, the weight lifted. Emma looked up into the shocked faces of Carlos and Jimmy. Jimmy offered her his right arm to pull her up. Together, the three friends stared down at the dead man, who was spread out faceup on the floor of the shack. Blood oozed from his chest. His body gave a last spasm, and the kidnapper's eyes rolled back in his head as he stared with grotesque blankness at the world. There was no doubt this time that he was really dead. Carlos extracted the rifle from the trucker's lifeless hands and motioned Emma towards the door.

"Come on!" Carlos urged them. The pain in Emma's leg was unbearable. She tried to take a step but failed. Then, she felt Jimmy's arms enfolding her, lifting her up.

"It's okay," he whispered as he carried her over the threshold of the shack. Emma felt a wet warmth on her leg where Jimmy was holding her. The Yanomami were already in the waiting canoes when Carlos, Jimmy, and Emma made their way down the bank. The river's water lapped reassuringly at the boats. Emma felt herself being lowered into the safety of a hollowed-out tree; then the world became blackness.

CHAPTER THIRTY-EIGHT

Water

EMMA AWOKE TO THE sensation of water spilling over her feet. Was she at the river? No. She opened her eyes and saw sunshine filtered through slats in the walls. Her stomach lurched. For a terrible moment, she thought she was back at the shack. Then, with relief, she noticed the pretty young woman by her side. Her eyes sparkled under her dark, smooth bangs, and she smiled broadly. Emma knew at once that she was Yanomami.

Emma felt the woven mat underneath her. Her thigh shot with pain, despite the Indian's gentleness as she dressed the gunshot wound. The woman carefully wound cloth strips around the open sore. Emma lifted her hand to her hair. To her surprise, it felt smooth and clean. A large *I Love NY* T-shirt hung loosely on her torso over a pair of lime green gym shorts. Emma could smell the fragrant flowers that must have been used to bathe her. As the woman finished bandaging her leg, the pain lessened to a more bearable level. Emma smiled gratefully at her caregiver, who called out to the others in the hut. Within minutes, Jimmy was at her side.

"You're awake!" he said euphorically. "I was so scared after you fainted. There—was a lot of blood. Here … drink this." He pressed a bottle of water to her lips, and she drank long and deep.

"Where are we?" she asked when she finished drinking her fill.

"Carlos's village. Brand new *shabono*. Notice the green." Emma looked up at the freshly built thatch of the roof. The structure, much smaller than the one they had visited to the north, smelled of freshly

cut palms. Objects were scattered haphazardly around, as if the Yanomami were just settling in. Emma noticed for the first time that Jimmy
was sporting a bandage on his arm. She caressed it lightly.

"What's this?"

"The bullet that hit you grazed my arm," he explained. "Not a big
deal."

"You carried me even though you'd been shot?"

"I wanted to take care of you, Emma. If you hadn't stabbed that
guy—" his voice trailed off as he decided not to finish the thought.
"Anyway, you're okay now."

"I killed someone," Emma said flatly.

"In self-defense. He would have died soon anyway from the dart
poison. Not that it matters. I don't think anyone's going to be reporting his demise. Souza will probably dump both bodies in the river.
Something tells me neither of those two guys will be missed very
much."

Emma chewed her bottom lip. "Did Dad know about the rescue?"

"He warned Carlos not to risk it. Thought it was too dangerous.
He was planning to pay the ransom. But Carlos worried that Souza
would take the money and kill us anyway, which he probably would
have. Mike will forgive Carlos once he sees you're safe. Which will be
soon. In a couple of hours, we'll be back in Boa Vista."

"In a couple of hours? How's that possible? Aren't we in the middle of the jungle?"

"Carlos asked Fernando for one more favor." Emma didn't need
to ask what the favor was. In the distance, she heard the drone of a
motor.

"Could I speak to Carlos?" Emma asked softly.

Jimmy's ebullience slackened, and he hesitated a moment before
letting out a whistle. Moments later, Carlos came into view. His almond eyes squinted in concern as he knelt by her side.

"I'll go see about the plane," Jimmy said softly, stepping away and
leaving Carlos alone with Emma.

"Are you in pain, Emma?" Carlos asked, taking her hand in his.

"Nothing unbearable. Listen, I just wanted to say—"

Carlos cut her off. "Don't. I was feeling guilty about giving you guys the number for the poachers. And my tribe grabbed at the chance to get even with Souza. The only disappointment was that he wasn't there at the hut so that we could finish him off for good." The smell of cooking food wafted toward them. "Listen, I'm not going back to Boa Vista with you. There's going to be a massive party here tonight. I'm staying behind to celebrate. I've been meaning to spend some time with my family, and now's as good a time as any. Fernando will get you and Jimmy to the hospital in Boa Vista."

Jimmy was walking back toward them. "Fernando's waiting for us on the river," he said softly. "We should probably get going."

Carlos leaned down and gently took Emma in his arms. As the three friends walked through the village, dozens of Yanomami clustered around them, chattering in excited voices. They had already started to get ready for the party. Many of them sported fresh paint on their faces and new feathers in their hair. As a group, they paraded down the short stretch to the water's edge, the Yanomami chanting and singing as they went. At the edge of the water, a canoe stood waiting. It would take Jimmy and Emma out to Fernando's plane, which now rested like an alien space ship in the middle of the river.

"So this is it," said Carlos, lowering Emma into the canoe.

"Just saying 'thank you' doesn't seem like enough," said Emma.

"Then don't say it," Carlos grinned. Jimmy gave his friend a half embrace before joining Emma in the canoe. Several Yanomami men stepped forward to push the boat off from the shore. Emma and Jimmy waved as they floated on the water. In the middle of the river, Fernando was lifting the metal hatch of the hydroplane.

CHAPTER THIRTY-NINE

Iara

A PALE MIKE TOOK a tentative step into the bleach-infused hospital room, where Emma was hooked up to an intravenous feed. He carried a small duffel bag, which he dropped at the foot of the bed.

"I brought you some fresh clothes," Mike said softly. He trained his gaze on the floor, struggling to find the right words. The next moment, he covered the remaining distance between himself and his daughter. He took Emma gingerly in his arms, taking care not to disturb her intravenous needle, his crippled hand sliding helplessly between her shoulder blades. Mike's body convulsed with sobs. "Emma, Emma!" he said over and over. Emma had never seen him like this. She hugged him with her free arm, and they sat like that for a few minutes. When Mike regained his composure, he pulled away.

"Have you had anything to eat?" he asked.

"A smoothie," Emma responded, nodding to the empty cup sitting on the standard-issue wooden nightstand. "They said I should take it easy on food for the first few days. Apparently my body was moving into starvation mode."

Mike shook his head in disbelief. "I still can't believe the danger you were in. You could have—"

"But I'm okay. You aren't mad?"

Mike looked at her in amazement and let out a guffaw. "The question is whether you're angry with *me*. I blame myself, partially, for everything that happened. I should have been paying more attention to what you were up to."

"You were focusing on your work. So was I." Emma gestured to a chair, and her father sank into it. Emma didn't know how to cope with an emotional Mike. Thankfully, a gray-haired doctor chose that moment to come into the room and introduced himself. With the professional air of someone in charge, he took Emma's leg carefully in his hands and unwrapped the bandages. Mike grimaced at the sight of her wound. The physician studied the information a nurse had posted on a clipboard. Satisfied, he tenderly re-bandaged the injury, speaking for a few moments with Mike before nodding politely out of the room.

"They removed the bullet," Mike explained. "You're dehydrated and you need antibiotics to stave off infection, but the IV feed should take care of that. Better than we could have expected."

"How's Jimmy?" She knew he was being taken care of in another part of the hospital.

"He'll be fine. His biggest problem now is dealing with me. I know he put you up to that trip out to the jungle."

"No, no, Dad, he didn't. It was my idea as much as it was his. And you would have done the same thing, in our position. Don't you remember how it was when you first got started as a journalist? How hungry you were?"

Emma could see from Mike's expression that she had hit a nerve. "You know," he said, "I would have come up with the money for your ransom. Would have borrowed it from Jimmy's dad if I had to."

"I know. But you didn't have to. And something good came out of this."

"What?"

"You'll never be able to tell me again that I'm only worth a few hundred dollars."

Mike laughed. "No, you're worth at least half a million, which is quite a bargain if you ask me. Your mother's going to kill me when she finds out. I haven't told her yet about the kidnapping. She left a voicemail an hour ago, demanding to know why we never respond to her texts."

"I'll call her later," Emma responded. "Although I'm not sure how long I can keep her in the dark. Once the poacher story breaks, she can read about it in the papers." They had lost Jimmy's film, but Emma still had a story to tell. "Could make front page."

"You have a lot more courage than I gave you credit for," Mike said. "Make a damn good journalist. We're done here in Boa Vista, though. As soon as you're feeling strong enough, we can head back to Rio."

On one hand, Emma couldn't wait to get away from this city and its gun-toting crazies. But then—"I'm sure Raquel will be glad to have you back."

Mike cleared his throat. "Actually, Raquel has moved out."

"Oh, Dad, I'm so sorry! What happened?" Although Emma didn't like Raquel, she *was* sorry to hear that her father was alone again. He needed someone to take care of him.

"When she came up to visit, she gave me an ultimatum—either make our relationship a priority or call it quits. She couldn't get used to the fact that I have deadlines and—family obligations."

A sharp knock came at the door. When Mike opened it, Emma was startled to see a perfectly groomed Iara framed in the doorway, her solemn black clothes especially striking against the white walls of the hospital. She was carrying a small box wrapped with a golden ribbon, which she placed on the nightstand. "*Chocolate,*" she said, using the Portuguese pronunciation. She pressed a hand to Emma's forehead as if checking for fever and murmured condolences.

"Iara was in town for a funeral when she heard you and Jimmy were in the hospital," Mike translated. "She decided to pay you a visit."

"Another funeral? I hope it wasn't anyone we know."

"Actually, it was. I heard this morning myself. The funeral was for Amoeba, you know that crazy pilot. After what he did to us, though, I didn't feel it was necessary to attend."

Emma sucked in her breath. Iara observed her reaction with interest before stepping away from the bed to gaze out the large window of the air-conditioned room. The sun's rays lit her up as if she were standing in a heavenly spotlight. Her back half-turned to the room as she gazed down at the park below, she began to speak in a steady, deliberate tone.

"She wants you to know about Amoeba," Mike said. "How he got killed." Iara spoke again, and Mike translated. "Milton Silva was the one who had the idea to recruit the crazy pilot as a spy for the government. In the months before his death, Milton was increasingly concerned about a poaching ring encroaching on Yanomami territory. The smugglers were culling the tribe's hunting grounds, terrorizing their villages. I guess Jimmy was right about the blue feather he found in Amoeba's plane. Have to admit, I thought it was pretty far-fetched at the time."

"What kind of spying did Amoeba do?" A knot was forming in Emma's stomach.

Iara spoke, and Mike interpreted. "They were trying to crack a notorious wildlife smuggling ring headed by an insane man who goes by the name Papagaio. The feds paid Amoeba for information on their actions and whereabouts. He was an expensive informant, but apparently worth the money. He helped the feds build a watertight case against the smugglers. This week they moved in for a raid. But when they got there, the camp was deserted. Someone had tipped them off. I wonder if it had anything to do with the poaching operation you and Jimmy were trying to flush out."

Emma looked into Mike's eyes. He knew. The fantasy world she had built up around her, the one in which she and Jimmy were star journalists taking necessary risks to get to an important news story, had just come tumbling down. "How did Amoeba die?" she whispered.

"Single gunshot to the head, execution style. Body was dumped outside the house of the feds' courier, Alfredo."

"Courier?" It just got worse.

"The feds had a go-between man on their payroll, Alfredo. He funneled funds to Amoeba and retrieved information to pass on to Braga. Helped Amoeba maintain his cover. Incredible story. Would have made great copy. I'm sorry Amoeba's dead. Wasn't the most reliable pilot, but he didn't deserve to die like that. Do you think the poachers were onto him when we took that ride? I didn't trust that mechanic, what was his name?"

"José," Emma said flatly.

"José, right. Good memory. He could easily have tampered with the engine. Killing three journalists would only have been an added benefit for that gang."

Emma was almost afraid to ask the next question. But she had to know. "What did Alfredo look like?"

Iara described him. "Typical *garimpeiro* type," Mike interpreted. "Short and chubby with lots of gold chains. Lucky thing he was away from town when Amoeba got killed, or he probably would have suffered the same fate as the pilot. Braga's now got Alfredo's whole family under protection in Brasilia."

Emma's private humiliation was complete. She finally understood what the *shaman* had been trying to tell her. Nothing had been as it seemed. She, the huntress, had followed the tracks of false prey, lured by the backward footsteps of the *Curupira*. And now, she was as empty-handed as an Yanomami after a failed hunt.

CHAPTER FORTY

Beamer

"FLIGHT'S TOMORROW," JIMMY SAID, as Emma leaned over to turn the key in the ignition for him. The spanking new Volkswagen Beetle, rented from a local car agency, was automatic shift out of necessity. Jimmy was driving one-handed, and Emma, with her wounded leg, couldn't drive at all. They had left the hospital early that morning, heading back to the *Itamaraty* briefly with Mike. "I already checked out of my room by the way," Jimmy continued as he pressed on the gas, casting Emma a mischievous look.

"Oh you did?" Emma replied in a teasing voice. "Where were you planning on spending the night?"

"I know this nice Jewish girl," Jimmy said in a teasing voice. "You know, we could have just called Rita and Ronaldo. It's not necessary to go all the way out to their house."

"They saved our asses that night after Souza set fire to the jungle bar," Emma said. "I want to say goodbye in person."

"No one's following?"

Emma pivoted and took in the cars behind them with newly expert eyes. "I don't think so. But you might want to take a couple extra turns just to make sure."

"So what should we do about the smuggling piece?" Jimmy asked as he took a right.

Emma sighed. "Not happening. Unless we want to expose ourselves as the people who ruined a major federal investigation." She told Jimmy all that Iara had divulged. It crushed her to see how the information deflated him. "Mike thinks they were already on to Amoeba when we took that plane ride, that José tampered with the engine. I don't know. I can't shake the feeling that we got an innocent person killed."

"Don't do that to yourself. Mike's probably right. If Amoeba hadn't coasted back to the airport, he would have crashed into the jungle, and we would have all been meat for the jaguars."

"He had a parachute."

"Not very useful when you're flying over a jungle. Unless you prefer to get skewered by a palm tree."

"After everything we went through, we still don't know who murdered Milton Silva."

"Souza has always been the most likely suspect. He had the motive and the means. He had issued death threats to Milton. Maybe the identity of Milton's killer has been under our noses all along."

Jimmy turned the steering wheel onto Ronaldo's driveway, but two vehicles blocked their way. One was a BMW sedan; the other Emma immediately recognized as the red pick-up Rita had purchased from Carlos. Leaning against the car was Rita, locked in a passionate embrace, her shirt hanging open to reveal her high, round breasts. And the guy with his tongue in her mouth, one greedy hand on her nipple, the other up her skirt, was Fernando.

The couple was so hypnotized by their amorous embrace that they only noticed Jimmy and Emma when they heard the doors of the Volkswagen slam shut.

"Oh, sorry," Rita murmured as Fernando pulled away, although Emma detected more pride than embarrassment as she buttoned her shirt. "I didn't hear anyone drive up. Well, no need for introductions. You know 'Nando. He told me all about your jungle adventures." At that moment, a chattering monkey jumped from the bed of the pick-up onto Rita's shoulder, tugging on her golden hair. "Oh alright," she said indulgently, pulling a treat out of her pocket and handing it to the monkey. "As you can see, Charlotte's just as spoiled as ever."

"I thought you had released her into the wild," Emma said, limping toward them.

"She managed to find her way back," Rita shrugged. "Some creatures just value love more than freedom, I guess. What are you two doing here?"

"We came to say goodbye to you and your dad," Emma responded. "We're leaving tomorrow for Rio."

"It wasn't necessary for you to come all this way," said Rita. "You should have just called."

"We wanted to say thank you in person for everything you did for us."

"You must come back some day," said Fernando in his stilted English. "Not for work. For tourism." He leaned towards Rita for a lingering kiss, then touched a finger to the tip of her angelic nose. "I must leave. *Ciao, linda.*"

"*Ciao!*" Rita responded, caressing the side of Fernando's cheek. "*Te amo.*" A memory came back to Emma—the last time she had heard Rita say those words. That time she had been sobbing over the phone. This time, Rita flashed a brilliant smile as Fernando clambered into his BMW. He blew her a kiss as he started the engine.

"Listen, I'd appreciate it if you didn't mention Fernando to my dad," she said in a confidential tone as Fernando pulled away. "He thinks I spent the night with a girlfriend."

"No problem," Jimmy murmured. *So Ronaldo doesn't approve,* Emma thought, as they retreated to their respective cars to drive the remaining distance to Rita's house.

"Fernando and Rita," Jimmy mused as he sat behind the steering wheel. "Now those are two people I never would have put together. I thought Fernando was hitting on *you*."

"You think everyone's hitting on me."

"Aren't they?"

Emma's mind was in overdrive. "This is not a new romance, Jimmy."

"Why do you say that?"

"I'm certain that Rita was planning to see him that night we got stuck in the mud. Remember how her dad wouldn't let her go into town? I suspected she had a boyfriend. Later on, I heard her on the phone talking to him. I just didn't know until now that her lover was Fernando."

"Interesting."

"You know, this explains so much. Remember how Fernando told us Ronaldo had been his mentor? We never found out why they had a falling out. Now, it makes sense. Over-protective father. Ronaldo can't stand Fernando because he's making love to his daughter. And Fernando used to be a smoker, right?"

"So?"

"That pile of cigarettes by the woods next to Ronaldo's place. What if it was left there by Fernando?"

Jimmy frowned. "You may be onto something there."

"Fernando could easily have been hanging around the night of Milton's murder. Maybe he saw Souza's man shoot Milton, but he's scared to go to the police."

"You're jumping ahead too quickly. It would be an incredible coincidence if Fernando just happened to be there the night Milton was killed. And if he's scared to tell the police, what makes you think he'd be willing to share the information with us?"

"Still—I'm going to ask him," Emma said. "We're leaving tomorrow, and we've got nothing to lose."

Her cell pinged and she glanced down. *BK IN NY*, it read. *CALL ME.*

CHAPTER FORTY-ONE

White

FERNANDO WAS NOT ALONE when he showed up at the *Itamaraty*. On his arm was Rita, glowing in a simple white dress. Fernando himself wore a pressed shirt and khakis. This time, Rita had left Charlotte at home.

"Thanks for coming by," Emma said.

"You said it was important," Fernanado murmured.

"It is," Jimmy responded.

"Better be," Rita said. "You interrupted an important celebration."

The two couples dragged white plastic chairs up to a patio table at the hotel's open air bar. The air smelled like fresh rain, but the extreme heat had faded with the sun, and it was comfortable to be outside.

"Antarctica," Jimmy ordered when the waiter approached.

"No," Fernando said. "I insist on champagne. Moët & Chandon, *por favor*."

"*Sim, senhor*," the waiter nodded.

"What are we celebrating?" Emma asked.

Rita smiled broadly. "Our marriage," she said.

Jimmy's jaw slackened. Emma was as shocked as if the couple had just dropped a bomb. This was not what she had been expecting. She knew they were in love, but they seemed way to young to be getting married. Emma recovered first.

"Congratulations!" she said, summoning as much enthusiasm as possible.

"Great news!" Jimmy said, forcing a smile. "It's a little sudden, though, isn't it?"

"Yes and no," Rita said as she fished in her purse. She pulled out a box. Derby. Emma had never seen her smoke before. Fernando flicked his lighter and held the flame to her cigarette. She took a drag and continued. "We were actually supposed to get married a couple of weeks ago, the night you got stuck in the mud and had to spend the night at my place. Had a big party planned. Well, you know how that ended. We were going to reorganize, but then when you guys saw us together today, I just thought how stupid it was to continue to keep our love a secret. I thought, what I really want is just to be with 'Nando. I don't give a crap about a wedding reception. So this afternoon we went to the priest and just did it." Rita held out her left hand, which was now decorated with a diamond-studded wedding band.

"No more hiding," Fernando smiled, placing his arm around his bride. She beamed up at him, and he leaned in for a kiss.

"But what about your dad, Rita?" Emma asked.

"He doesn't know yet," Rita conceded, as she took another puff of her cigarette. "I'll send him a text later on." A text didn't seem to Emma the best way to announce something like a marriage, but it wasn't her place to say so.

"Wouldn't he have wanted to attend the wedding?" Jimmy asked.

"In this case, it was better to present him with a *fait accompli*," said Rita. The waiter returned with the bottle of champagne, which he ceremoniously uncorked with a loud pop. He poured the transparent liquid into four tall glasses and set the bottle in a bucket of ice beside the table.

"*Outra coisa?*" he asked. Fernando shook his head.

"What happens now?" Emma asked. "Honeymoon? Where will you live?"

"The honeymoon will wait," Fernando answered. "Now, is enough to be together. My father bought for me an apartment in town. We will live there."

"Well here's to a long and happy marriage," said Jimmy, holding up a glass of champagne for a toast.

"So what is so important?" Fernando asked.

Emma set down her glass. "I just had to ask you something before I left Boa Vista, Fernando. It's this: What does your father-in-law have against you? I mean, he was your mentor. You seem to have a lot in common. But he seems to hate you now."

"Ronaldo is lonely man," said Fernando, smile fading from his face. "He has lost his wife. Now he has lost his best friend. He hates me because he thinks I will take Rita away from him."

"Which you did," Jimmy answered with a touch of irony.

"Is okay now," Fernando said with bravado. "Now I am family. He must accept me."

Emma was surprised by his confidence. "I hope you're right," she said. "Listen, Fernando, there's one more thing I need to know. That pile of cigarettes we found by the house—"

"I know what you are thinking," said Fernando. "That they are from Rita. But the cigarettes were mine. I am a man in love, and I am patient. Rita and I often waited until Ronaldo went to bed; then she would sneak out and we would go into town."

"Until I got my license," Rita added. "Then I could drive in myself."

"So the cigarettes didn't have anything to do with Milton's murder after all," said Jimmy. He seemed happy to put the incident behind. Fernando shook his head, but something in his expression told Emma he was not telling the entire truth.

"Fernando," Emma said. "You were spending so much time hanging around Rita's place. Did you see anything at all on the night Milton Silva was murdered?"

"Of course he didn't!" Rita said sharply, stubbing her cigarette out in the ashtray.

Fernando looked down at the rising bubbles in his glass as if weighing a heavy decision. "Yes," he said, finally. "I saw it all. I saw the murder of Milton Silva."

CHAPTER FORTY-TWO

Revelation

"No!" Rita looked at Fernando with pleading eyes. "We agreed not to say anything!"

"They must know, Rita," Fernando said, grabbing her hand and bringing it to his heart. "People will keep asking questions. I want to start life with you with nothing to hide."

Rita covered her eyes with her hands and began to shake.

"Rita," Emma spoke in what she hoped was a comforting tone.

"What?" Rita turned on her. "What do you want? You come to Boa Vista to snoop around. What does anything that happens here have to do with you?"

"Milton Silva belonged to the world, not just to Boa Vista," Jimmy answered sharply, putting a protective arm around Emma.

"I don't give a fuck about the world," Rita spat.

"Don't say such things, my love," Fernando said, as disturbed as if an angel had suddenly misplaced her halo. "Milton was your father's friend!"

"He should have stayed home that night, like everyone had warned him to do."

"But he decided to go to your house to play a game of cards with your dad," said Emma.

"Rita," Fernando said, caressing his bride's cheek with his thumb. "They will guess it. You can tell them. They are not police."

"Journalists," Rita said. "Almost as bad."

"Tell them," Fernando urged. She looked into his eyes until something she saw there made her lower her own. When she spoke again, it was in a firmer voice.

"Only for you 'Nando." She took a deep breath. "My father was never the same after my mother died," she began. "He seemed lost. The only two things he cared about any more were his work and me. He forbade me to go out with any boys. And for a long time, I wasn't interested. Until 'Nando came along. He started spending a lot of time at the house as an intern to my father. Ronaldo loved him. Said 'Nando was like the son he never had. But 'Nando and I didn't feel like brother and sister. We didn't want it to happen, but it did. We fell in love.

"My father was furious. Accused 'Nando of betraying him. Wouldn't listen to reason. Told me I could never see 'Nando again. I couldn't let that happen. We love each other. The night of Milton's murder, I planned to sneak away into town with 'Nando. From my window, I could see the light of 'Nando's cigarette through the trees. I knew he was waiting. I tiptoed to the door. My father was waiting for me. He waved the stub of a cigarette in my face. Said he'd found it earlier in the woods and that he knew what 'Nando and I were up to. Then we heard the pebbles hitting the window. My father grabbed a rifle. I couldn't believe it. He was planning to shoot 'Nando. He opened the door. I ran toward it as he fired the gun. It felt as if he had shot *me*. I screamed and ran outside, thinking I would see my 'Nando on the ground. Then my father started wailing too. Because it was not 'Nando who lay there in a pool of blood. It was Milton Silva."

Emma exhaled. After all this time, they had discovered the truth. And yet, the truth gave her no satisfaction.

"What you don't know is how much my father has suffered," Rita continued. "He was ready to turn himself in on the day of the funeral. Took all my power to convince him not to. He cries out in his sleep every night for his friend. But Milton is dead. Nothing can bring him back."

"Have you thought about going to Braga?" Jimmy asked. "It was an accident, not premeditated murder. They might go easy on Ronaldo."

"You saw the journalists here for his funeral!" Rita said sharply. "Right now, newspapers around the world are publishing articles about the Amazon. It's exactly what Milton wanted! He wouldn't want my father to tell the world he was killed by mistake. That's why Ronaldo has not gone to the police. He lives in a hell, but he knows that nothing he can do will make it better."

Fernando turned his widened eyes towards Jimmy and Emma. "What can we do?" he asked philosophically.

Emma couldn't let it go so easily. "Doesn't Milton deserve some justice?" Emma asked softly.

"Justice for Milton is not to put his friends in jail and watch the world ridicule his movement," said Rita. She turned and placed a manicured hand on Fernando's chest. "Let's go, 'Nando," she murmured. "We're done here." Fernando pulled out a wallet and threw a generous sum of cash on the table.

"Rita," Emma said as Fernando put his arm around his bride and they stood up to leave. "That text that I got in Rio, was that—"

"Nothing personal," Rita smirked. "I knew chances were that one of you journalists would eventually stumble across the truth if you hung around here long enough. The wonder is that it took you so long."

"And you were the one who mentioned Amoeba to Carlos—"

"But that part was true! I heard Milton and my father talking about him. I didn't mean for you and Jimmy to—" Rita didn't finish the sentence. She reached for her purse and turned away.

CHAPTER FORTY-THREE

Widow

"I HANDED IN THE keys," said Jimmy, stepping into the room of the *Itamaraty*. "All packed?"

A sharp knock came on the door. "Ready when you are!" Mike called out.

"We'll be right there!" Emma responded. Mike walked away, and Emma turned to get her suitcase.

"Just a sec," said Jimmy. "I have something for you."

For the first time, Emma noticed that Jimmy was carrying a small envelope.

"What's that?"

"Someone left it for you at reception. Go ahead and open it. Mike will wait a couple of minutes."

Emma tore open the envelope and looked at the handwritten script. "It's in Portuguese," she said, handing the letter to Jimmy, who translated as he read.

Dear Jimmy and Emma,

I want to thank you for everything you've done. Milton always said our success is not measured by results alone, but by what we learn in trying. I think of him as I write these words, because it was he who taught me to read and write. I have learned of Fernando's marriage to Rita. Ronaldo is devastated, but I feel that he may eventually reconcile himself to the idea. I hope so, for his own sake.

Yesterday, I ran into Souza while I was in town. It angers me to know that he is still walking around free, after his role in your kidnapping. Yes, I know it's no good to go to the police. They earn more salary from Souza each month than from their regular jobs. Looking at that man, I was reminded of how much he hated my husband, and how he had vowed to kill him. He would have done so, I am sure, if fate had not intervened.

And now, I must ask myself how my husband will be honored. Will people remember him as the victim of a terrible accident? Or will they remember him as a martyr to a cause that is so much bigger than any of us? The Amazon has been here for thousands of years. It is our purpose to make sure it does not die now.

I have been asked to give a speech about my husband's work in New York City at the United Nations. I have accepted. I will be taking a plane out of Boa Vista next week, flying over the ocean to a different country. Me! I nearly refused; it seems almost too much. But I know it's what Milton would have wanted—for me to spread the word. For us to talk about the Amazon, about the importance of saving it, to anyone who will listen.

And so I ask both of you to remember that this is my husband's legacy. When you think of him, when you speak of him, do not think of a single night in the forest, when everything human went wrong. Think of his work, and be brave enough to remain silent about the rest.

Yours,

Iara

Jimmy carefully folded up the paper and put it back in the envelope.

"So she knows," Emma said.

"I would say so," Jimmy responded.

"And she wants us to keep it to ourselves."

"Can we? Should we?"

"It's what Milton would have wanted."

CHAPTER FORTY-FOUR

Rays

EMMA EMERGED FROM THE swimming pool and wrapped herself in a big towel with a sun and water design. Jimmy, standing by the pool and dressed in abbreviated swimming trunks, smiled and offered her a sip of his *caipirinha* drink. Emma had acquired a taste for the Brazilian cocktail. Mike was at an event, and Maria had the evening off, so the two of them were left deliciously alone. Emma leaned in for a kiss, but was interrupted by the buzz of the cell phone she had left on the patio table. She reluctantly broke away from Jimmy and picked it up. *Desconhecido*, it said. Unknown caller—probably international.

"Hello?" she murmured.

"Slugger! Glad I caught you!" Emma immediately recognized the strong Brooklyn accent. "Well, all I can say is pack your bags!"

"What do you mean?"

"They came through. Mary gave a written statement yesterday, and some of the other girls on your list say they'll testify too. Safety in numbers, just like you said. Gotta hand it to you, I didn't think any of them would speak up against a guy like Horowitz. Now I'd be surprised, when all this is over, if he even keeps his job at NYU. May end up in jail. The administration has agreed to drop any charges against you and let you return in September for your final year."

"So—it's over?" Emma had a hard time digesting the news she had been waiting so long to hear.

"It is. Enjoy your last few days of vacation! You'll be hitting the books in a couple weeks."

Emma was silent.

"Emma? Are you still there?"

"Yeah, I'm still here. Um—thanks, Jay. Just—thanks. You came through in the end."

"My pleasure. Happy to nail the creep. Call me when you get back. I'll need you to sign some papers—release forms and stuff. See you at synagogue!"

Emma disconnected the cell phone and walked to the edge of the patio, looking over the railing to the beach and the Museum of Tomorrow. She had spent so little time in this city. She wasn't ready yet to leave. Jimmy kissed the back of her neck and wrapped his arms around her waist. Their wounds had healed. Emma turned and their lips met. "Who was on the phone?" Jimmy asked as he buried his head in her wet hair.

"Jay."

"The lawyer?"

"Yeah."

"Bad news?"

"Actually, no. He said I could finish my degree at NYU. I'll start classes in a couple of weeks. Better yet, Tony Horowitz is facing multiple charges of sexual harassment. I won't have to worry about him anymore. He's finished in New York."

Jimmy's expression showed he was fighting an epic battle of conflicting emotions. "So you're really going back?" he asked. Emma nodded. Jimmy took a step back and ran a hand through his hair. "I mean—I'm really happy for you. But why not take some time off school? Or a semester in Rio."

"I can't take a semester off my senior year. I need my degree, Jimmy. If I gave up now, I'd end up regretting it sooner or later."

"So it looks like I'll be stuck hugging a photograph."

"I'm sorry," Emma said. "No, that's not true. I'm glad. I want you to miss me desperately."

"I think you'll get your wish," Jimmy said. "When will you come back?"

"Next summer, definitely, whether Dad wants me to come or not. I'll be an independent girl with a college degree. Maybe some paper like the *Miami Herald* or the *LA Times* will offer me a job. In the meantime, we have the *National Geographic* piece to pull together. We can still be a team. Just long distance."

"Be warned that I may come after you."

"If you do, there's something I want you to bring me."

"Sure. Anything," Jimmy said, "as long as it's not some kind of exotic pet. What?"

"This." Emma took Jimmy's face in her hands and looked straight in his eyes. She then placed her lips on his and gave him a kiss. It was a kiss that erased the pain and eradicated the bad memories; a kiss that left nothing but joy and a promise for things to come.

ABOUT THE AUTHOR

VICTORIA GRIFFITH is the author of the award winning non-fiction picture book *The Fabulous Flying Machines of Alberto Santos-Dumont* (Abrams, 2011), which won numerous awards, including the prestigious Parents' Choice. The book was recently translated into Portuguese for the Brazilian market and was also released in audio book version. Before becoming a full-time author, Victoria spent twenty years as an in-  ternational journalist, fifteen of those years as foreign correspondent for the UK's *Financial Times*. During that time, she had fun writing on a wide range of topics, including Brazil's Yanomami, architecture, space exploration, the human genome, and the growth of the Internet. She even managed to fit in some book reviews. Her most terrifying assignment was preparing lunch for Julia Child, who praised the Brazilian fish stew but refused to touch the blackberry dessert. Victoria lives in Boston with her husband and three daughters.